A Higher Mission

A Higher Mission

The Careers of Alonzo and Althea Brown Edmiston in Central Africa

Kimberly D. Hill

K UNIVERSITY PRESS OF KENTUCKY

Copyright © 2020 by The University Press of Kentucky

Scholarly publisher for the Commonwealth,
serving Bellarmine University, Berea College,
Centre College of Kentucky, Eastern Kentucky University,
The Filson Historical Society, Georgetown College,
Kentucky Historical Society, Kentucky State University,
Morehead State University, Murray State University,
Northern Kentucky University, Transylvania University,
University of Kentucky, University of Louisville,
and Western Kentucky University.
All rights reserved.

Editorial and Sales Offices: The University Press of Kentucky
663 South Limestone, Lexington, Kentucky 40508-4008
www.kentuckypress.com

Cataloging in Publication data is available from the Library of Congress.

ISBN 978-0-8131-7981-0 (hardcover: alk. paper)
ISBN 978-0-8131-7983-4 (pdf)
ISBN 978-0-8131-7984-1 (epub)

This book is printed on acid-free paper meeting the requirements of the American
National Standard for Permanence in Paper for Printed Library Materials.

∞

Manufactured in the United States of America

Member of the Association
of University Presses

In memory of Dr. Sylvia Jacobs

In memory of Dr. Lamin Sanneh

Thank you for modeling ubuntu *in academia*

Contents

Chronology

1865	Founding of Fisk University
17 December 1874	Birth of Althea Brown in Russellville, Alabama
1876	Founding of Stillman Institute
19 July 1879	Birth of Alonzo Edmiston in Petersburg, Tennessee
1881	Founding of Tuskegee Institute
1884–1885	King Leopold II claims sole control of the Congo Free State during the Berlin Conference
1891	William Henry Sheppard and Samuel Lapsley found the American Presbyterian Congo Mission Congo Free State officials receive a decree to raise revenue from rubber and ivory as their foremost priority
1892	Althea Brown enters Fisk University
1895	The rubber harvesting industry starts to flourish in the Congo Free State
Ca. 1898	Alonzo Edmiston enters Stillman Institute
1898	The Presbyterian Church in the United States (PCUS) establishes a separate Afro-American Presbyterian Church William Henry Sheppard founds the Ibanche mission station
1899–1900	William Morrison and William Henry Sheppard start reporting evidence of human rights abuses in the Congo Free State
1901	Althea Brown graduates from Fisk University and attends the Chicago Training School for City and Foreign Missions
Ca. 1901–1902	Alonzo Edmiston graduates from the Stillman Institute seminary and enters Tuskegee Institute

1902	Althea Brown arrives at the American Presbyterian Congo Mission
1904	E. D. Morel founds the Congo Reform Association
	Alonzo Edmiston arrives at the Congo Mission
November 1904	The Ibanche station is destroyed during the Kuba revolt
8 July 1905	Althea Brown weds Alonzo Edmiston and they return to Ibanche
1905	Alonzo Edmiston starts directing the Ibanche Industrial School
26 May 1906	Birth of Sherman Kueta Edmiston
1908	Althea Brown departs on furlough; Alonzo Edmiston resigns from the Congo Mission under controversial circumstances
	Political transition from the Congo Free State to the Belgian Congo
1909	William Morrison and William Henry Sheppard testify against the *Compagnie du Kasai* rubber trade at a libel trial
1910	William Henry Sheppard and Lucy Gantt Sheppard depart from the Congo Mission
August 1910	The Secretary of the PCUS Executive Committee on Foreign Missions recommends unannounced restrictions on future appointments of African American missionaries
Ca. 1911	The Edmistons return to the Congo Mission at Ibanche
27 May 1913	Birth of Alonzo Leaucourt Bope Edmiston
1914–1916	The Edmistons relocate to Luebo; Alonzo Edmiston works on the Hillhouse cotton plantation
1916	Black southern Presbyterian congregations are reorganized from the Afro-American Presbyterian Church to the segregated Snedecor Memorial Synod
1917	Beginning of the state-mandated cotton planting industry in the Belgian Congo
1918–1919	Alonzo Edmiston manages the Agricultural College at Luebo

1921	Althea Brown Edmiston delivers the Fisk University commencement address
1922	Althea Brown Edmiston and Alonzo Edmiston are reassigned to the Mutoto mission station and Boys School
1922 and 1925	Publication of the Phelps-Stokes Fund reports regarding industrial education on the African continent
1926	The Belgian government commends Alonzo Edmiston for his agricultural service
1932	Publication of Althea Brown Edmiston's *Grammar and Dictionary of the Bushonga or Bukuba Language as Spoken by the Bushonga or Bukuba Tribe Who Dwell in the Upper Kasai District, Belgian Congo, Central Africa*
	The Congo Protestant Council recommends conformity to the Belgian Congo "State Educational Program," including agricultural training
1935–1936	Althea Brown and Alonzo Edmiston return to Selma, Alabama, during their final furlough and reside with the civil rights activists Samuel and Amelia Boynton
9 June 1937	Death of Althea Brown Edmiston at the Mutoto Station
1939–1940	Alonzo Edmiston retires and departs the Congo Mission
5 December 1954	Death of Alonzo Edmiston in Selma, Alabama
1960	Political transition from the Belgian Congo to the Democratic Republic of the Congo
1964	The PCUS Board of World Missions endorses a missionary petition against racial segregation in the United States
1965	Amelia Boynton Robinson and other Selma activists organize protest marches for voting rights

Introduction

In 1947 a Southern Presbyterian missionary named Julia Lake Kellersberger published a biography of one of her colleagues, Althea Brown Edmiston. Her book, *A Life for the Congo,* traces the inspirations and skills that enabled Brown to devote thirty-five years to overseas ministry until her death in 1937. Part of that storytelling process entailed describing how Brown met her future husband, Alonzo Edmiston, in the Congo Free State and how he shared her commitment to the American Presbyterian Congo Mission. Kellersberger argued that, because of the dedication that the Edmistons displayed at the mission stations over the decades, one had to conclude that their love for ministry superseded all other aspects of their lives. Even when they returned to the United States to enjoy visits with their family and friends, "furloughs were to them evils that had to be endured for health's sake and for work's sake. There was no doubt that their hearts were in Africa."[1] But what Kellersberger intended as a tribute to Althea Brown Edmiston's work ethic obscured the ways that Brown and Edmiston drew strength and motivation from their ties to historically black colleges and universities in the American South.

The careers of Althea Brown and Alonzo Edmiston represented the adaptation and merger of industrial education and classical studies for the benefit of African people surviving an oppressive colonial system. Because their academic training took place within institutions reliant on African American self-help ideology, the Edmistons were prepared to design their missions projects to promote community building, to value local resources, and to incorporate the perspectives of the African participants. Their marriage gave these missionaries an additional incentive to avoid academic dichotomies despite the growing popularity of industrial education programs in the early twentieth century. Althea Brown (a classics graduate of Fisk University) and Alonzo Edmiston (a graduate of Stillman Institute and a former Tuskegee Institute nursing student) came from institutions with divergent, well-publicized ideologies about black leadership. But these missionaries needed to combine their different academic paths into joint strategies in order to explain why they

1

should be permitted to continue working together overseas. The context of both colonial travel restrictions and racial segregation among Protestant missionary staff increasing after 1920 made this couple's educational work a rare example of African diasporic collaboration from 1902 through 1937.

To analyze their development of agricultural outreach, vocational programs, folklore, and translation study at the American Presbyterian Congo Mission (APCM), this book details the publications and journal records of Althea Brown and Alonzo Edmiston. Both missionaries published articles for an audience of potential donors in the United States, and they wrote books for anticipated classroom use. Edmiston wrote journal entries almost daily between 1914 and 1941 that contained his mission station business reports, pastoral updates, and personal observations. Correspondence, biographies, and official documents from their Presbyterian colleagues and from the Belgian government help explain contemporary conditions in the central Kasai region, where the APCM was based.

A hagiographic tone dominates existing biographies of Althea Brown, partly owing to her death on the mission field. Likewise, the articles and journals from Brown, Edmiston, and other Presbyterian ministers tend to highlight accomplishments and minimize setbacks to appease American supporters. This book offsets these factors by evaluating the contexts and relationships that motivated the missionaries to write and how their interpretations of certain events differed. Much of this context involved changes in the lifestyles of the African villagers and students who interacted with the Edmistons. Examples of African theology, ethnography of the Kuba kingdom, and studies of labor and folklore in the Belgian Congo provide insight into the perspectives of these groups. Early twentieth–century developments at historically black colleges and universities also provide an underexplored context for explaining why African American missionaries valued their work. This part of the argument is grounded in the comparative analysis of course catalogs and campus activities from the years when these missionaries were enrolled at Fisk, Stillman, or Tuskegee.

Their ongoing connections to three of the campuses most influential to the black missionary movement make the careers of Althea Brown and Alonzo Edmiston significant to the study of African American internationalism and its role in twentieth-century imperialism. The Bushoong dictionary and grammar book published by Althea Brown, as well as her translated hymns, are featured in studies of how some precolonial West African cultural traits were preserved through the twentieth century.[2] Studies of the

Congo Mission also sometimes feature Alonzo Edmiston in his supervisory role mediating disputes between African leaders and Belgian authorities.[3] His agricultural activities receive less scholarly attention, and in one case his first fourteen years of ministry were minimized as one more missionary attempt to teach farming skills that local Africans already understood better.[4] The advantage of this extended study of Edmiston and Brown is to show how they tailored their work over decades to contribute the artistic, nutritional, and spiritual benefits that villagers and students preferred in different circumstances. This adaptive strategy was undervalued by their employer (the Presbyterian Church in the United States, or PCUS) until the 1940s, when it proved advantageous for incorporating the mission schools into the Belgian colonial educational system.

The transnational approach of *A Higher Mission* helps recover the historical memory of historically black college and university (HBCU) alumni and students who contributed to the mission movement and helped shape colonial policy. Beyond comparisons with Tuskegee-style labor ideology, historical studies of individual African American missionaries up to 1950 tend to emphasize the affiliated Protestant denominations with less detail regarding the academic and geographic communities that supported these travelers.[5] This church policy–centered approach can miss a fuller account of how and why laity and students helped these ministers maintain transnational networks.[6] Suggestions of a broader perspective can be found in the scholarly works that compare mission school strategies with contemporary HBCU curricula or specify why black missionaries kept in contact with these academic institutions.[7] Andrew Zimmerman's *Alabama in Africa* offers a more comprehensive model by explaining the participation of Tuskegee students in the German Togo cotton venture as part of a campus-wide transition to promoting industrial education for the sake of controlling a designated labor force.[8] Likewise, analysis of how HBCU alumni from liberal arts–based universities served abroad can shed light on the increased signs of black self-determination at Fisk University and Stillman Institute by the 1930s.

Part of my objective in tracing the Edmistons' ministry strategies is to contribute to academic conversations regarding the distinctiveness of African American mission work. Sylvia Jacobs set a model with her publications analyzing several of these missionaries through their support letters and by identifying their academic affiliations. One of her final publications explains these connections to the United States as part of what helped the ministers keep identifying with American culture despite facing Jim Crow and feeling "a commonality with Africans" in the Congo Free State.[9] *A Higher Mission* traces a longer chronology to offer nuance regarding the American communities that inspired these missionaries to Congo, the African communities that interacted with them, and the white sending agency that set policies for the Presbyterian Congo Mission.

Intermittent changes in international and domestic politics through the 1930s challenged each group's viability and required its adaptation for survival. This book evaluates how African American missionaries altered their concepts of acculturation and racial consciousness in conversation with leaders from their college and university networks. Moreover, the book analyzes how these choices among African American communities led African and white American Christians to develop different leadership strategies. These strategies combined to help make the black missionaries' initiatives part of general Congo Mission policy and prepare African Presbyterians for a postcolonial future.

To address the theme of cultural affinity between people of African descent on the mission field, the book explores both the role of Africa in popular memory around 1900 and specific cultural and social priorities expressed by villagers in the Belgian Congo later in the century. These priorities were shaped by African traditional religion but with the goal of ameliorating crises specific to the expansion of colonial exploitation in the region. By learning the priorities and values that helped some of their neighbors survive during the colonial era, African American missionaries did not just learn about antiquity; they also learned to share the responsibility for envisioning improvements in African societies. The elements of African traditional religion explained in this work are presented through the perspectives of some of the African theologians who developed the discipline in its first three decades. By seeking a form of Christianity that responded directly to the matters of African nationalism and decolonization, the work of these theologians offers a relevant comparative model for understanding how African villagers influenced the Edmistons.

Analyzing historically black colleges as factors in African American missions also contributes to scholarship reevaluating the pedagogical feud between Booker T. Washington and W. E. B. Du Bois. This debate features in at least one popular textbook as a debate between allegiance to industrial education and allegiance to liberal arts education that escalated because of Washington's influence with wealthy philanthropists.[10] The seeming exclusivity of the two education strategies has been defused in part by studies that explain how they were often complementary in practice.[11] In particular, the high percentage of Fisk alumni teaching at African American industrial schools indicated that mechanical and agricultural training flourished when communicated by those who were prepared to address a variety of tasks.[12]

Both sides in the debate over African American education were linked through the leaders' interest in transnational applicability. The 1912 International Conference on the Negro that Booker T. Washington planned at Tuskegee Institute emphasized progress in missions and social conditions through strategies "to educate and uplift the Negro, either in Africa or America."[13] And W. E. B. Du Bois helped found the Pan-African Congress in 1919 to cultivate intellectual solidarity against colonial abuses. Though the latter conference promoted its political points more explicitly, both events embraced the premise that black education and its leaders remained relevant to global controversies. The legacy of the pedagogical feud involved not just the specific ways that black schools and colleges instilled education during the height of Washington's career but also the ongoing efforts of HBCU alumni to celebrate African Americans as both designers and recipients of higher education. After 1910 those efforts competed with the growing prominence of academic arguments that industrial education could solidify the categorization of certain ethnic groups.

Though industrial education was a popular topic among missionaries and corporate interests during the early twentieth century, the leaders who endorsed it rarely touted the students' goals as the primary objective. Supporters of mission outreach within and outside the United States often emphasized the civilizing potential of industrial education. The missiologist Brian Stanley's study of terminology at the 1910 Edinburgh World Missionary Conference provides some insight into the goals behind typical approaches to civilizing missions. A "civilizing mission" could encompass the field of industrial education within a long-term goal of altering the surroundings and habits of a specific group of people. The premise rested on confidence in the ability to demarcate groups as static and dissimilar in certain respects. Stanley noted that conference attendees often overlooked the originality within the work of the non-Western delegates because of the assumed dependency of "native Christians."[14] Industrial education could be prescribed as one of the means of acculturating certain groups to the standards of Western leaders. The standardization of industrial machinery was mimicked in the standardized methods dictated to laborers, with expectations that one successful model could be replicated among any similar groups.[15] The attention paid to industrial education revolved around its usefulness for meeting the missionaries' goals of timely world evangelization and cultural change.

This kind of emphasis on the control and alteration of potential converts can make it difficult to notice diversity among the missionary personnel or the ways that missionaries changed during their careers. David Hollinger focused on personal and cultural transformations led by American ministers to Asia and their descendants in his recent book *Protestants Abroad*. His analysis shows how previous experience in foreign missions set the groundwork for later interest in diplomacy, humanitarianism, and desegregation. The activist tendency that Hollinger traced among individual missionaries and some organizations through the 1960s wielded broader significance by influencing American policies and public sentiment. African American leaders in the Young Men's Christian Association factored into the narrative of *Protestants Abroad*, revealing part of the legacy of nineteenth-century black missionaries summarized in an earlier chapter.[16] Despite the widespread segregation of Protestant mission boards that Hollinger noted, these organizations remained aware of how Christians of African descent influenced the mission movement. *A Higher Mission* expands the topic of cultural change among African American missionaries and their significance within the first half of twentieth-century American history by tracing their connections to the largest source of race-specific education policy in that era: the Phelps Stokes Fund.

Since 1911, the Phelps Stokes family has focused much of its philanthropy on improving "the education of Negroes both in Africa and the United States."[17] Cultural adaptation became the hallmark of the recommendations developed by the educational specialist appointed to work with the fund, Thomas Jesse Jones. As a former Hampton Institute faculty member, Jones claimed to advocate the same industrial education ideals that Booker T. Washington had popularized since his graduation from Hampton. Jones toured black schools, colleges, and universities in the southern states before publishing a 1916 report designed to define effectiveness in "Negro education."[18] Instructors and administrators who worked to provide educational strategies distinct to the perceived lifestyles of black communities could be suggested by Jones to receive Phelps Stokes Fund grants.[19] As the historian Kenneth King has noted, this philanthropic process transformed the preexisting concept of industrial education into a segregated pedagogy with international implications. The 1922 and 1925 commission reports designed by Thomas Jesse Jones and supported by Anson Phelps Stokes applied previous findings about African American communities to prescribe a similar focus on agricultural and vocational training in eastern and western Africa. Meanwhile, criticism of the racial essentialism at the core of these commission reports remained rare and costly; as Jones and the Phelps Stokes Fund gained reputations for making black education efficient, African American academics who endorsed a different professional vision lost philanthropic support.

Though the public backlash that erupted after W. E. B. Du Bois and Carter G. Woodson denounced Thomas Jesse Jones had long-term consequences for the development of their academic institutions and organizations, these problems did not define the spectrum of African American leaders' reactions to the Phelps Stokes Fund. Partly because Jones and his colleagues worked so diligently to dominate the spokesperson roles in black education, it is important to identify those teachers, ministers, and lay leaders who subverted the Phelps Stokes Fund image while working behind the scenes. Robert R. Moton, the second president of Tuskegee Institute, fit this trend when he accepted praise from Jones for the on-campus agricultural programs while also inviting Du Bois, Marcus Garvey, and other Phelps Stokes Fund critics to speak at commencement.[20] Through his links to Tuskegee and agricultural missions, Alonzo Edmiston also altered the typical expectations regarding African industrial education during the early twentieth century. He showed how black leaders could pursue professional opportunities through white philanthropic organizations while still raising awareness of the cultural diversity within the African diaspora and the various academic methods used to promote cooperation at the Congo Mission.

Symbolically, the Edmistons' marital partnership represented the ways that the forms of education championed by Washington and Du Bois complemented each other. Unlike Althea Brown, Alonzo Edmiston did not earn a university degree or attend an institution with a wide variety of academic courses. His Stillman Institute seminary degree was designed for application among African Americans in southern towns, as was his additional medical training at Tuskegee Institute. The difference in their levels of academic prowess showed in their handwriting; Brown demonstrated evidence of additional penmanship and spelling lessons that Edmiston lacked. His published books were agricultural lessons designed for immediate classroom use, without the broad scholarly potential of Brown's dictionary and grammar.[21] Both missionaries, however, experienced childhood poverty and observed American racial prejudice before joining the Congo Mission. They perceived education as their means to help themselves, their children, and their African neighbors find alternatives to bare subsistence. A shared tradition of self-help and community survival instincts inspired them to give priority to the goal of strengthening local communities over the goal of uniformity of their own methods.

Just as the romantic relationship between Althea Brown and Alonzo Edmiston provides an underlying theme of family for this study, the techniques of industrial education set a framework for recognizing the Edmistons' ministry projects as familial endeavors. This could be seen in a literal sense as Brown and Edmiston took in foster children and enrolled them in the mission station schools. But in a figurative sense, industrial education strategies provided the interactive settings where a community atmosphere could be developed. The potential for gathering mission students and converts through shared work commitments took on religious and political significance in this colonial context.

The Kasai region in Central Africa, where the American Presbyterian Congo Mission started in 1891, had been associated with a powerful kingdom for centuries before the Americans' arrival. The Kuba kingdom produced distinctively patterned cloth made of raffia palm leaves. Because Kuba people relied on wearing or selling this cloth instead of manufactured alternatives, the kingdom remained isolated through the mid-1880s from the types of extended trade networks inspired by the earlier transatlantic slave trade.[22] The kingdom was surrounded by villagers who claimed Kete heritage and by a growing number of Luba migrants escaping wars and slave raids in their former territory. This displaced group later became a popular source of enslaved labor within the Kuba kingdom and the main source of potential converts for the Congo Mission.[23] A common route for slave traders from the Middle East and Angola led through the Kasai region, which also attracted attention from a group called the Zappo Zap that competed with the slave traders for resources and captives.[24] The existence of regional slave trading helped provide an early rationale for European traders, explorers, and missionaries interested in settling beyond the port cities of Central Africa.

King Leopold II of Belgium created the Congo Free State through negotiations at the Berlin or "West Africa" conference of 1884 and 1885. This conference was designed to settle land claims among five European countries that already had commercial interests on the African continent, and it became known as a key factor in "the scramble for Africa."[25] The Belgian king obscured his plan to maintain personal control over the natural resources in the Congo Free State by publicizing the region's new political status as a humanitarian effort to oppose Arab slave traders.[26] Leopold II authorized European trading companies to force local Africans to gather rubber and ivory as "taxes" to the colonial government, but most of the public infrastructure in the Congo Free State remained limited to construction projects that served the financial interests of the companies.[27] Some facts about the atrocities that Africans experienced in the colony were exposed by the African American journalist and historian George Washington Williams in 1890.[28] But the relative lack of international travel and correspondence through the interior of the Congo Free State ensured that there was little publicity about violence and death there before the 1899 publication of *Heart of Darkness*, Joseph Conrad's novel about Congo River travel.[29]

The migration of missionaries into central Congo hastened two major developments: it provided an incentive for European and American business interests to expand further into the colony, and it provided additional opportunities for witnesses to publicize the destruction caused by the rubber trade. The American Presbyterian Congo Mission was one of nine Protestant organizations that started ministry in the Congo Free State before 1900 and the first of those groups to choose the western part of the Kasai region as its base. The location had been suggested by King Leopold II for reasons that also applied to most of the Belgian Catholic and Protestant groups seeking territory away from the Atlantic coast.[30] After gaining control of the territory as his private colony, the Belgian king relied partly on religious travelers to expand Western settlement throughout the areas of the Congo Free State where his official representatives had not yet ventured. The British Baptist Missionary Society set an early model for the Southern Presbyterians by investing in a steamship that could travel upstream into the interior of the colony. These ships brought additional European and American travelers as well as incentives for construction and trade. The early Congo missionaries met their practical need for local craftsmen and farmers and their goal to reduce Muslim influence in the region through cooperation with the Belgian king's stated interest in freeing Africans who had been kidnapped into the domestic slave trade.[31] By 1908 it became common for both Catholic and Protestant mission organizations in the

Congo Free State to grow through the incorporation of former slaves.[32] The vulnerability of this landless population heightened the competition between missionaries of different Christian factions. The first APCM station, Luebo, grew quickly in the 1890s by redeeming people from the slave trade, but Belgian Catholic groups such as the Scheutists at Luebo gained numerical advantage by receiving larger groups of redeemed children through government intervention.[33]

The historian James Campbell attributed the population growth around the APCM stations after 1896 to the increasing rates of violent oppression in the region. People created new villages near the missionaries in the hope of developing a safer social structure.[34] The disastrous effect of the forced labor system in the Congo Free State remains the most studied aspect of the Congo Mission's early history because its leaders helped expose the torture, murder, and harassment sanctioned by colonial agents and rubber companies.[35]

Competition with local Catholic missions for land claims and potential converts led two of the APCM leaders to investigate and publicize signs that the Free State authorities might have acted against the best interests of the Presbyterians. In 1898 the Reverend William M. Morrison started noting his objections to the aggressive behavior of the Force Publique soldiers who collected taxes and appealed an official temporary closure of the Ibanche mission station.[36] The Reverend William Henry Sheppard left the reopened Ibanche station in 1899 to investigate atrocities committed against people in a different part of the Kuba kingdom. Both ministers later wrote evidence that Congo Free State authorities directed African soldiers or allies to destroy villages and search a Congo Mission for revenue and for workers for the rubber companies.[37]

Sheppard provided graphic details about amputations and other signs of torture when he visited churches, auditoriums, and historically black colleges in the United States.[38] Morrison used his furlough time in London to publish an account that inspired E. D. Morel to organize the Congo Reform Association.[39] After King Leopold II granted control of all the natural resources and potential workers in the region to the Compagnie du Kasai in 1906, the company filed a libel suit to prevent further allegations by Sheppard and Morrison. The 1909 trial against the Presbyterian missionaries led to the dismissal of the charges and inspired the Belgian colonial minister to require economic reforms within the Kasai. The historian Stanley Shaloff credited Morrison and Sheppard with helping motivate international interest in promoting "justice and decency in the Congo" against the interests of the Belgian king.[40]

The African communities near APCM stations continued to be transformed after the resulting human rights campaign compelled King Leopold II to concede his authority over the colony in 1908.[41] The Kuba kingdom remained under the surveillance of Belgian officials, and its villagers struggled to satisfy the tax and labor requirements on the Kuba king's behalf.[42] Landless individuals and families from the Luba and Lulua ethnic groups relocated en masse, seeking employment with the missions in order to pay colonial taxes.[43] The expansion of European trading posts through the Kasai region created the long-term demand for additional forced labor to construct roads and railroad tracks.[44] Intermittent draft raids seeking to fill quotas of soldiers, miners, and cargo porters destabilized APCM station communities, as did the additional burden for villages and families to meet state-mandated cotton harvest quotas after 1917.[45] This exploitative economic system left many villagers in the Kasai region with reduced social time, fewer child-care opportunities, less available land for growing edible crops, and fewer outlets for questioning colonial rule.[46]

African villagers and workers interacted with the APCM in ways that made the mission a potential alternative to the dehumanizing approach of the Belgian Congo government. In a system that quantified all Africans as potential industrial or agricultural workers, the founding of the African Presbyterian synod suggested a chance for local people to develop a community that defended their spiritual and intellectual lives from political threats. The trend of increased cooperation between the Presbyterian missionaries and Belgian officials after 1910 delayed the accomplishment of this goal. Yet to represent the type of humanizing perspective that African Christians introduced at the Congo Mission, this book avoids terms like *native* that preserve a dichotomy between the African and American participants in the African synod that was transformed into the Communauté Presbytérienne au Congo.

Part One of this book covers the chronological scope of the Edmistons' academic lives and careers until their final decade in the Belgian Congo. Chapter 1 introduces Althea Brown and Alonzo Edmiston in the context of their community of African American colleagues to identify shared religious and cultural motivations behind the black missionary movement to Central Africa. In conversation with the work of her mentors, a synopsis of Brown's Fisk University experience guides the explanation of how she planned her ministry objectives from 1902 to 1908. Likewise, the chapter presents Edmiston through the ways that Stillman Institute introduced him to overseas ministry. The story of how the couple married in the aftermath of a Kuba uprising highlights how and why the Edmistons started to design their ministries, including their industrial school, in relation to the interests of people in this specific kingdom.

Chapter 2 extends the chronology through 1936 to trace how shifting perceptions of Fisk University, Stillman Institute, and Tuskegee Institute led the Southern Presbyterian Church to circumscribe or eliminate the status of its African American mission staff. An increasing emphasis on professionalization and efficiency helped shift these perceptions, as did the expulsion of black Southern Presbyterians into a segregated synod in 1916. For Althea Brown and Alonzo Edmiston, the period from 1908 to 1936 represented a transition from establishing their own ministry approaches to making their presence indispensable to the Congo Mission. As a representative of Tuskegee-style industrial education, Alonzo Edmiston adjusted to a mostly agricultural workload while trying to avoid making manual labor the sole focus of his school- and church-related activities. Meanwhile, Althea Brown developed new ministry opportunities to overcome administrative arguments that her academic background and her linguistic pursuits were unfit for PCUS ministry. Some of these projects that she developed on her own or with her husband are analyzed in additional detail throughout the following chapters.

Part Two revisits specific developments in the history of the American Presbyterian Congo Mission for the twenty years beginning in 1916. Close reading of each event reveals complications in how the various groups residing in that part of the Belgian Congo related to one another. The analysis of certain time spans mentioned in Part One reinforces the influence of political, economic, and religious factors beyond the missionaries' control. As the African villagers in the region adapted to shifts in the colonial cotton industry and Belgian officials increased community surveillance, the Edmistons' ministry projects helped spur social changes beyond the issue of Christian conversion.

Chapter 3 provides a close reading of the Edmistons' plans for their most prestigious academic initiative at the Congo Mission: the Luebo Agricultural College. The curriculum, layout, and schedule of the college drew on specific features from the HBCUs that Althea Brown and Alonzo Edmiston had attended. But the comparative analysis shows that the couple's

goals extended beyond trying to re-create aspects of these American institutions. The Agricultural College provided the clearest depiction of how
Brown and Edmiston combined classical and industrial education to meet
specific needs of African students who were finding financial incentives to
leave rural villages for urban employment. The choice to accommodate that
interest was unique among the industrial school programs at the Congo
Mission.

Chapter 4 highlights how Althea Brown and Alonzo Edmiston learned
the perspectives of local people and applied that feedback to their mission
work from 1916 through the 1920s. Experimenting with making church
and school supplies from local vegetables and fruits helped ensure the longevity of the American Presbyterian Congo Mission overall. Likewise,
Brown developed an innovative linguistics style by turning her dictionary
into a celebration of Kuba political and social structures. On a personal
level, the broader concept of family among their Kuba neighbors in Ibanche
was a source of comfort to the missionaries.[47] Beliefs in ancestral spirits
connected to African American visitors inspired a sense of loyalty that led
neighbors to continue inquiring about the health of the Edmiston boys and
to celebrate Brown's return from an extended furlough. Finally, paying
attention to the concerns of local people helped Alonzo Edmiston carve a
niche of authority at a time when his Presbyterian leadership titles were
being curtailed by his white American supervisors.

A different perspective on the Edmistons' interactions with local people
is explored in chapter 5 by focusing on challenges to the authority of African American missionaries. As the African pastors and evangelists started
to consolidate their ministries in an African Presbyterian synod in the
1930s, they expressed more resentment of continued oversight by American
missionaries. Reduced professional recognition for the Edmistons by this
period made them easier targets for African Christians' public criticisms of
the APCM and Belgian colonial governance. The chapter explains how
racial segregation in the Congo Mission helped spur the development of a
more assertive role for African church leaders. And it concludes by following the Edmistons through their final furlough in Selma, Alabama, to analyze how their HBCU alumni network connected the missionaries to signs
of 1930s civil rights activism.

The book concludes with a consideration of the Edmistons' final years
in the field and their contributions to the educational policies developed for
the Belgian Congo and the PCUS from the 1940s to 1963. The legacy of

Brown's emphasis on language, music, and community building is evident in the reactions of the African Christians who mourned her. Edmiston's decision to retire and return to Selma in 1940 was complicated by race-based travel restrictions that prevented him from taking the safest sea route during World War II. The readjustment from leadership overseas to second-class citizenship in segregated Selma was also a trial. Signs that the academic visions of Althea Brown and Alonzo Edmiston would be applied to promote African independence rather than to strengthen colonial authority were delayed until after the deaths of both missionaries. But when those signs came, they were accompanied by increased Southern Presbyterian willingness to recognize and welcome African American professionals.

PART ONE

Education Goals throughout the Edmistons' Career

Before William Henry Sheppard cofounded the American Presbyterian Congo Mission (APCM) in 1891, he had already established personal and professional networks within several historically black colleges and universities in the United States. Most of the African American staff at the APCM were recruited through those networks and shared a sense of duty regarding outreach to the African continent. Part One shows how three institutions of higher education promoted the type of racial uplift ideology behind the early twentieth-century African American missions movement while also becoming the targets of efforts to alter or eliminate this style of Protestant ministry.

The explanation is guided by the chronology of how Althea Brown and Alonzo Edmiston established their lives at the APCM, starting with their connections to HBCUs. Chapter 1 analyzes some of the motivations shared by black missionaries from various denominations before detailing how the legacies of these missionaries helped enable Brown and Edmiston to move abroad in 1902 and 1904, respectively. In terms of their educational goals, 1908 was a pivotal year for the couple because they became the first of nine African American staff dismissed or retired from Southern Presbyterian foreign service during the denomination's first two decades in central Africa. Chapter 2 places the Edmistons' efforts to remain employed at the Congo Mission within the context of shifting theories regarding the roles of African American professionals in colonial societies. Major changes in the ministry duties of Brown and Edmiston through 1936 are explained as reactions to new denominational and political policies as well as partial conformity to the international rise of race-specific industrial and agricultural education. Part Two analyzes shorter periods during the careers of Brown and Edmiston in further detail.

1

Industrial Education and Symbolic Home Building in the Congo Free State, 1898–1907

> By certain favors to the Bakuba, [Congo Free State officials] are also trying to prove to them that they are their real friends and we their enemies. However, this is exceedingly hard for them to do.
>
> Althea Brown Edmiston, 1906

The marriage of Althea Brown and Alonzo Edmiston at the American Presbyterian Congo Mission was announced in the United States by a rumor. A newspaper article claimed that Brown was actually an anonymous central African woman who had convinced Edmiston to forsake his American habits. Since the article was attributed erroneously to a former missionary named Samuel Verner, his rebuttal (titled "Edmiston Did Not Return to Savagery") became one of the first published accounts of how the couple intended to use their academic skills to establish a new family home. He described Althea Brown as a Fisk graduate who was "the equal in intelligence and character of any colored woman in America." And Verner closed with an eyewitness account of the "splendid establishment built up by Edmiston's energy and common sense" at the Ibanche station. He expected that the mission movement would benefit from more African American ministers like them.[1]

The testimony of this former employer of Alonzo Edmiston highlighted the combination of moral conviction, liberal arts training, and practical labor that became a hallmark of ministry for these two missionaries. But, as the rumor suggested, the contributions of Brown and Edmiston could remain obscured unless they adapted and publicized an appealing narrative. They found models for their missionary careers—and hope for future ministry support—among the alumni of historically black colleges and universities.

Around the turn of the twentieth century, two men were celebrated as the most famous African Americans in the world.[2] One of those men founded Tuskegee Institute and became a champion of black industrial education. Booker T. Washington's plans to promote the self-sufficiency of black Southerners through entrepreneurship gained additional recognition following his 1895 Cotton States Exposition address and his partnerships with white philanthropic organizations.[3] The second-most famous man was his fellow alumnus from Hampton Institute, the Reverend William Henry Sheppard. He earned the nickname "the Black Livingstone" as a hunter, explorer, diplomat to a secluded African kingdom, and cofounder of the American Presbyterian Congo Mission.[4] Sheppard's intent to establish a thriving African American and central African Christian community in the Congo Free State was threatened by the regime of King Leopold II and by the race-based recruitment policies of Sheppard's denomination.

Both men sought to defy literal and ideological boundaries in pursuit of a future that recognized the humanity and leadership potential of their race. This chapter explains how Althea Brown and Alonzo Edmiston planned to maintain that ambition into the next generation of Southern Presbyterian mission work. Like their mentor Sheppard, the couple tried to protect the employment opportunities of their African American colleagues and expand the unique projects they had pioneered at the mission. And, like Washington, they encountered both the recognition and problematic racial stereotypes that accompanied a reputation built on industrial education expertise.

For all the rhetorical emphasis on the practicality of industrial education, much of its appeal was grounded in abstract ideals. Washington promoted it as a path toward recognition, self-respect, and the eventual dismantling of racial discrimination. A statue at his institute celebrated the teaching strategy as an essential step in the abolition of slavery. Other industrial institutes and colleges touted themselves as cornerstones of self-help and racial uplift through innovation in various trades. And Yekutiel Gershoni attributes a mythical status to Tuskegee-style industrial education as envisioned by African enthusiasts in the early twentieth century, describing the development of its reputation as "a magic formula by which Africans hoped to bridge the gap between themselves and technologically advanced Europeans."[5] The teaching strategy promised to keep attention on tangible, reproducible steps for success without losing its element of faith in results not yet realized.

Within the American Presbyterian Congo Mission (APCM), industrial education plans advanced the ideological interests of certain African American missionaries even when they did not claim to use vocational curriculum officially. Three industrial schools in the APCM were founded on the basis of plans that originated with the Executive Committee on Foreign Missions. The mission station that most of the black missionaries claimed as their home base hosted the first industrial school from 1905 to 1908; Alonzo Edmiston served as its director. Four female missionaries also oversaw unofficial vocational programs for orphan girls that began at the Congo Mission about ten years earlier. These initiatives served the symbolic goal of promoting status and leadership opportunities—a cornerstone of historic racial uplift work. The historian James Campbell linked the image of the APCM stations as "vehicles for the introduction of Hampton-style industrial education into Africa" to William Sheppard's experiences there. Campbell argued that, for Sheppard, a Hampton education "affirmed his faith in himself and his race."[6] Though the expectations for industrial education at the Congo Mission did not always originate with the African American Presbyterian ministers, this group shared a motivation unique to their context within a white-led denomination based in the American South. Incorporation of industrial education methods represented one way for the black missionaries to protect the place they considered their home.

In his analysis of the twenty-first-century black church, the theologian Walter Fluker defined *home* as a site where past injustices are met with acknowledgment and a plan to design a hopeful future. Historical memory provided the metaphorical location for the "home" built and preserved by continual efforts to respond to memories in innovative ways.[7] The mission movement contributed to the symbolism of "home" in African American religious history by offering an additional outlet for ambitions to escape Jim Crow oppression. The fact that this outlet became reality for relatively few did not diminish its appeal or influence. The Ibanche mission station, with "the Black Livingstone" as its supervisor and a primarily African American staff, represented religious and political authority sustained through its connections to African leaders and to black institutions in the United States. More so than the physical location of Ibanche, this social network itself became the figurative home for African American Presbyterian missionaries. Industrial education served to strengthen that social network through the sharing of curriculum strategies and resources while recognizing the historic obstacles that had made these strategies necessary.

The men and women of African descent who joined the APCM as staff from the 1890s through the 1930s represented a spectrum of educational experiences. Five of the men (William Henry Sheppard, Lucius DeYampert, Henry Hawkins, Alonzo Edmiston, and A. A. Rochester) were graduates of Tuscaloosa Institute, a southern Presbyterian seminary later called for some years Stillman Institute and now called Stillman College. Edmiston and Sheppard had additional experience at institutions known for popularizing industrial education. Their ties to Tuskegee Institute and Hampton Institute, respectively, played significant roles in how their later ministry work was publicized. Two of the first African American women to join the APCM (Lucy Gantt [Sheppard] and Lilian Thomas [DeYampert]) attended Talladega College, a liberal arts–centered program founded by former slaves with support from the American Missionary Association (AMA). A sister AMA university, Fisk, offered a scholarship to Althea Brown and inspired her commitment to overseas ministry. Annie Katherine Taylor (Rochester) graduated from the all-black Scotia women's college before committing to the mission.[8] Joseph Phipps was the only African American missionary at the APCM to travel without experience at a historically black college or university; he attended Moody Bible College. And Maria Fearing was the first of this group to have her application to the Executive Committee on Foreign Missions challenged because of her educational background. Though she took classes on the Talladega campus, Fearing completed the normal school rather than the collegiate program.

The willingness of these black missionaries to cooperate in the mission field without respect to their academic differences signaled that they shared a concept of success atypical among ministers for a Presbyterian denomination. Most of the individuals described above were recruited by the Reverend William Henry Sheppard to help maintain the original Southern Presbyterian station in the Congo Free State and start a second one in 1898. Sheppard designed the Ibanche mission station as an outreach to the Kuba kingdom that was also a demonstration of his unique evangelization capabilities. His status as the first Westerner welcomed into the Kuba capital city, Mushenge, increased Sheppard's confidence that he could also plant the first Christian ministry there with royal permission. The diverse educational experiences among this team of missionaries, all with this goal in mind, offered some advantages for drawing the attention of their African neighbors while also improving the Americans' quality of life.

Industrial education methods brought early recognition to the African American female missionaries. Maria Fearing earned her salaried appointment

Figure 1.1   Portrait of Lucius DeYampert, Lilian Thomas DeYampert, Alonzo Edmiston, Althea Brown Edmiston, and Sherman Kueta Edmiston at the Congo Mission, ca. 1907. From the A. L. Edmiston Papers, RG 495, box 8, Presbyterian Historical Society, Philadelphia.

to the APCM by providing room and board to orphaned girls. Her self-funded project continued to grow as an official component of the mission partly because the young residents worked cooperatively to complete domestic chores within the foster home. Lilian Thomas co-managed this Pantops Home and helped prepare Lucy Gantt Sheppard and Althea Brown to operate a similar program at the Ibanche station. As was the case at most other mission stations in the Congo Free State, the staff at the two APCM stations needed a pool of local laborers to help establish the infrastructure.[9] But the foster homes stood out by treating domestic training as a community-building tool rather than just as individual acts of servitude for missionary households. At the Pantops Home, girls lived together in small households and performed their sewing, cleaning, and meal-preparation duties for each other. It was a style of domestic training reminiscent of the way that students completed chores in the Talladega College female dormitory, where Fearing had served as a matron.

The opening of an official industrial school at Ibanche in 1905 brought further opportunities for African American missionaries to apply their expertise and gain recognition. At the time, the destruction of the Ibanche station during the 1904 Kuba uprising required the quick and efficient replacement of its chapel and all other buildings. Still, their approach to offering official industrial education defied some of the typical expectations within the region. First, the students were not trained exclusively to complete projects that would meet the needs of mission staff. The principle of self-help guided the plans toward projects that also addressed the concerns of local villagers. Second, the missionary appointed to lead the school (Alonzo Edmiston) did not have industrial expertise. He approached the assignment with little confidence in his own preparation but much confidence that his colleagues' welfare depended on the restoration of Ibanche. Understanding the role of industrial education in the first fifteen years of the APCM requires further explanation of why Alonzo and Althea Brown Edmiston treasured the Ibanche mission station and how they differed from other African Americans who served there.

Defining Evangelistic Success in the "Garden of Eden"

The twenty acres of land that constituted the Ibanche station symbolized achievement, reconciliation, and autonomy for the staff of the American Presbyterian Congo Mission. The founding staff of the Ibanche station fit within what Ogbu U. Kalu characterized as the generation of African American missionaries with utopian goals. Combining popular narratives of racial uplift with the global Great Commission, these leaders invested in educational, social, and political strategies to produce not just individual but societal change. Kalu explained their motivation as "a sacred duty to make Africa the garden of Eden again [and] to enable the black person to prove his or her worth and ability."[10] Models of specific interventions that encompassed that "sacred duty" had been set from the 1860s through the 1890s.[11] Edward Blyden, the first leader of African descent appointed to lead Presbyterian outreach in Liberia, argued that "non-Westernized Africa" made unique contributions to culture and society without accepting the premise that further progress depended on Christian conversion. He approved of African American missions as a means of publicizing more sensitive portrayals of communities on the continent.[12] A pattern of respecting African independence was also set by the predecessors of the black Congo Mission cohort. The historian Walter L. Williams identified three African American missionaries who were appointed to Baptist service in the Congo Free State before the APCM started: Theophilus E. Samuel Scholes and Mr. and Mrs. John E. Ricketts. The married couple helped expand the Native African Church in Nigeria between 1890 and 1893, and Scholes published calls for the creation of autonomous states for the British colonies in Africa and other parts of the British Empire.[13]

The black Presbyterian missionaries also worked within a religious context that celebrated millenarian approaches to African travel. The denomination formerly known as the Presbyterian Church in the Confederate States of America received aid for its foreign missions program from at least one high-profile advocate of African American mass emigration schemes. Senator John Tyler Morgan endorsed federal recognition of the Congo Free State and helped recruit Samuel Lapsley to cofound the Congo Mission as part of his plan to reduce the freedmen population in the southern states.[14] As Adam Hochschild noted in *King Leopold's Ghost*, Morgan argued that the Congo "was prepared for the negro as certainly as the Garden of Eden was prepared for Adam and Eve."[15] His racial ambitions meshed with "providential design" theories regarding the evangelistic benefits of the slave trade.[16] Outreach to central Africa was one of the means touted as proof that enslavement had prepared African Americans for ministry to others of African descent. Supporters of the APCM tended to make much of Maria Fearing's enslaved childhood, her service redeeming African girls from the domestic slave trade, and the familial connections most of her colleagues had with former slaves or slave owners.

As part of the second set of African Americans working at the APCM, Althea Brown and Alonzo Edmiston shared an interest in racial uplift and the consequences of slavery. Yet the selfless rhetoric undergirding such theories of African American leadership masked the incorporation of tactical decisions in behalf of the leaders' well-being. The historian Kevin Gaines analyzed some of the benefits of a reputation for "uplifting the race," such as an assumed middle- or upper-class status regardless of actual income.[17] Similarly, one of the foremost studies of black missionaries enumerates the additional leadership opportunities and social status that they acquired abroad.[18]

International Education Strategies and Black Churches

The choice to combine academic interests with Christian service and independent black leadership was significant in the international outreach of the black church. The African Methodist Episcopal (AME) Church, as the oldest Protestant denomination with black leadership, led the way in analyzing pedagogy in order to combine religious and racial community building. And the missiological emphasis within African American churches and colleges in the nineteenth century lent itself to the development of early educational institutions on the African continent. Though it was not the first Methodist organization to sponsor mission schools in western or southern Africa, the AME Church set a precedent for planning Christian education as a response to local needs.

The establishment of international missions schools by independent black denominations (particularly the AME and National Baptist churches) between the 1870s and the 1920s was significant for shaping the kinds of educational strategies available to black missionaries in this period. The black church combined religious, political, and social interests in a way that inspired its missionaries to criticize oppression through their ministries. The first AME schools established outside the continental United States were requested by African American church members who expatriated to independent Haiti in the wake of the successful revolt against enslavement to France. The church sent its first missionary couple, Elder and Mrs. Charles W. Mossel, to Port-au-Prince in 1879 to fulfill the long-standing requests for "moral and spiritual education" from trained and ordained leaders.[19] And though the original requests came from Americans seeking a spiritual connection to their homeland, the first AME day school signaled its broader intentions by offering instruction in both English and French.[20] The bilingual language format offered American students better familiarity with the working language of their adopted nation while also making basic education available to black Haitians. The AME mission stations in the Dominican Republic and in Sierra Leone that followed in the 1880s also boasted primary schools as part of their initial plans. In particular, church property in Freetown, Sierra Leone, was donated to the denomination by local Christians who expressed confidence that the African Methodists could offer better management of the chapel and its schoolhouse than other missionary organizations had since the 1830s.[21] The outreach in each case involved support for freedpeople and optimism in the future of their new societies.

In western and southern Africa, African Methodist educational offerings gained a reputation as favored options for local religious protest. Most the denomination's first congregations within the Union of South Africa were founded and supervised by Wesleyan Methodists in Britain until the members sought independence and a new affiliation.[22] Likewise, the mission schools started by the Dutch Reformed Church in Malawi faced increasing competition after 1924 from school programs started by African Christians and affiliated with the AME Church.[23]

Bishop Henry McNeal Turner's nationalist appeals and visits to southern Africa in the 1890s helped draw attention and support to African protest as an aspect of AME ambition for racial self-determination.[24] That sentiment had also been apparent in the perspectives of earlier black Methodist leaders who had served outside the AME denomination. The first two African American bishops appointed within the U.S. Methodist Church blamed the denomination for failing to support and expand its Liberian missions adequately.[25] It was not unique for mission supervisors to complain of a lack of adequate funding, but it was unique that Bishop Francis Burns and Bishop John Roberts made these appeals as long-term residents of Liberia who claimed the right to protest the denomination's financial priorities. In particular, Bishop Roberts was aware that the denomination was redirecting funds to support outreach to emancipated people in the U.S. South, but he did not want this racial concern to distract from the interests of Africans in the Liberian interior and the potential benefits of additional schools in that region.[26]

The pedagogical goals of the AME Church were less distinctive than the denomination's sense of urgency in the perceived need for their implementation at denominational schools within the United States and abroad. The most in-depth summary of the denomination's goals for schools named concerns for moral, religious, physical, and mental advancement in the face of ongoing legal slavery in the United States.[27] Calls to provide schoolhouses as soon as a new African Methodist congregation was established outside the United States indicated a desire to ensure that illiterate leadership would play a shorter role in the denomination's international history.

The National Baptist Convention likewise confronted the consequences of enforced illiteracy among many of its early leaders and members. The denomination expanded in the United States partly through the creation of local women's mission study groups that fulfilled an educational role.[28] The National Baptist Convention first became productive as a missionary-sending agency in the mid-1920s, but its constituent organizations still sponsored the founding of the denomination's second-largest school (the Bible Industrial Academy) and the resettlement of several American teachers in Liberia between 1883 and 1912.[29] Shared pride in the leadership

of Americo-Liberians motivated these black Baptists to incorporate patri-
otic displays in the schools.[30]

The historian Jeannine DeLombard interpreted these Baptist missionaries' signs of support for the Liberian colonial government as an expression
of racial solidarity distinct from the consciousness of shared American identity or shared African ancestry. The National Baptist Convention wanted to
promote spiritual conversion through education while boosting confidence
that Liberia had a society worth the social investment.[31] Analysis of missionary educational history in India suggests that missionary education systems
there left a legacy of inability to meet "indigenous pedagogical requirements"
because of the overriding focus on church evangelization.[32] These African
American denominations might have found more success at meeting local
academic needs by conceiving of education as a tool to ameliorate past
inequalities.

The romantic and professional partnership between the Edmistons
included a shared sense of commitment to uplift. Though they were not the
first or only married couple serving together at the APCM, the Edmistons
showed less interest in claiming a familial home in the United States during
their tenure. Unlike the Sheppards or the DeYamperts, the Edmistons never
established a permanent household together outside central Africa. Unlike
the Rochesters, Althea Brown and Alonzo Edmiston did not return to
America shortly after their wedding to meet their respective in-laws. All
family decisions other than health crises were scheduled around the timing
of their ministry duties or their desire to restart those duties as soon as possible. And the Edmistons' shared sense of mission was a beacon motivating
the couple to defy attempts to end their ministries and to risk more sacrifice
when they felt weak.

The dominant theories of what African American missionaries would
accomplish at the APCM depended on assumptions that their acculturation to the United States would help them bring religious and cultural
change to the African continent. The Edmistons' writings reveal a similar
embrace of civilizing missions but with less emphasis on a pressing need for
wide-scale social change among the African villagers. Althea Brown and
Alonzo Edmiston did want to establish something new as a sign of their
influence, but they also did not intend for that new structure to mimic the
United States as much as possible. An unsigned 1906 *Missionary* journal
article about the Ibanche Industrial School implied that its growth would
contribute to the colony's development so that "as the years go by, their

country will become more and more like ours."[33] But, in practice, the Edmistons organized the school schedule and curriculum around skills and resources that African villagers perceived as useful to contemporary local conditions and their long-term interests as colonial subjects. This kind of adaptation to promote the survival and well-being of subjugated people was central to American historically black education yet remained controversial and underfunded within the United States.

Classical Education and Adaptation

Three broad themes arise in studies of classical education among African American students in the nineteenth and early twentieth centuries: political analysis, personhood, and protest. Curricula featuring literature in Greek and Latin offered insight into the histories and policies of respected empires. The requisite language studies demanded intellectual rigor that was often considered definitive of human achievement. But it was the controversy over how classical studies would be applied to students' lifestyles that made protest a lasting part of educational discourse in African American history.

The question of whether a curriculum based on the classics could be adapted successfully to the needs and interests of African American students is almost as old as the United States. The scholars Kenneth Goings and Eugene O'Connor traced it to Thomas Jefferson's arguments against the premise in 1785 and to David Walker's warning about educational deprivation in 1830.[34] Though Jefferson based his case for innate black inferiority on his interpretation of Greek and Latin literature, Walker turned to the classics for insight into African antiquity. Identification of northern African leaders such as Cleopatra and Saint Augustine in these texts bolstered arguments that people of African descent shared an ancestral claim and an obligation to learn the classics as part of their heritage. Legal and social barriers to education enforced by race-based slavery brought consequences for African Americans beyond high rates of illiteracy; the barriers prevented this group from recognizing the leadership potential within what Goings and O'Connor termed "an Afrocentric model of classical education."[35]

Protestant missions service on the African continent empowered some graduates of historically black colleges to display their enthusiasm for classical studies on multiple levels. They proved its value for leadership development through their own achievements while proving its adaptability to foreign classrooms. Relevant examples can be found in the work of most

African American missionaries who engaged in translation work or taught fine arts like music. In general, the promotion of literacy in an African language showed recognition of that society and optimism that the language would remain necessary in the future. But the teachers who specialized in the Bushoong language at the APCM faced an additional political meaning behind their classical studies; they had to decide whether it was worthwhile to learn and teach about an independent central African kingdom that was often at odds with the colonial authorities. The brutality of the Congo Free State economic system threatened to strip the villagers in the Kasai region of any social identity other than their labor status. In that context, classical education became a tool for black missionaries to defy subjugation in both tangible and symbolic ways.

Between 1898 and 1932, Lucy Gantt Sheppard and Althea Brown Edmiston pioneered written ministry to the Kuba kingdom by publishing lessons, songs, and a dictionary in the Bushoong language. Both women had graduated from a classically focused American Missionary Association institution. Gantt Sheppard's alma mater, Talladega College, specialized in providing interdisciplinary training at the high school and bachelor's levels. Talladega gained recognition by the 1880s as one of the few colleges in Alabama where African American adults could learn basic literacy on a work-study basis. Its graduates gained further recognition by providing academic and support services that continued to expand black education in the state. Many of them worked as rural teachers, nurses, or carpenters during and after their coursework. In the 1890s Talladega students engaged in "self-help" as a matter of community solidarity and practical necessity; they maintained buildings, washed laundry, and provided meals in the dormitories to help the institution survive its tenuous financial status.

Before she married William Henry Sheppard, Lucy Gantt's nine years at Talladega College familiarized her with the types of funding challenges that she would also face overseas. Like most of her classmates, she worked for at least two summers to cover expenses. Her specialty in vocal performance allowed her to travel on a concert tour that may have offered compensation, but students more often relied on the resources and job opportunities around the campus.[36] Frequent cuts in campus provisions left the student body particularly disgruntled during this period. Mandatory on-campus chores increased without accompanying improvement in provisions for students.

In the meantime, Talladega continued its tradition of supporting missionaries and encouraging students to seek foreign missionary appointments. The religious commitment to service provided a shared goal, yet it did not assuage concerns about on-campus conditions. Like other American Missionary Association college administrations, the leaders of Talladega reached out to community members for financial and spiritual aid through invitations to chapel services and other events. But some community visitors posed additional risks in the context of post-Reconstruction Alabama; occasional attacks by white supremacist groups threatened expensive damage to the campus physical plant and harmed students' morale. Life in Talladega, Alabama, taught Lucy Gantt Sheppard to recognize the interconnectedness of academic experiences with local tensions and student well-being.[37]

Althea Brown pursued classical studies through her coursework and extracurricular activities at Fisk University. Her time at a historically black university taught her never to question the viability and practicality of literary education. After enrolling in 1892 as a normal (or high school–level) student, she quickly embraced the institutional motto that their "lives are ever on the altar" for missions service. It is notable that Brown chose to prepare for her life dream of African ministry by delving deeper into Greek and Latin curricula and joining the Fisk music program. In addition to learning how to translate classical texts, she founded a women's group called Duodecem Literae Virgines to practice literary analysis and public speaking. She also practiced with the Fisk Jubilee Singers for a year, learning the troupe's repertoire of classical music and Negro spirituals. Brown became one of ten Fisk students to engage in full-time overseas missions service before 1930, and, like most of this group, she did not complete a degree in theology.[38] She remained confident throughout her career that the challenges of teaching and organizing church work in central Africa could be met through application of her arts skills, classical expertise, and the additional medical training she received during a postgraduate year in Chicago.

Before they met in the Congo Free State, these missionaries shared two extracurricular activities that motivated their abiding interest in translation work. First, both participated in Jubilee ensembles as students. Experience with these later versions of the Fisk Jubilee Singers familiarized them with the troupe's reputation for fund-raising; the original Jubilee Singers raised over $50,000 in cash and library supplies in 1872.[39] Both missionaries carried on that legacy by incorporating American hymns and spirituals into their evangelism work abroad. Lucy Gantt Sheppard performed some translated hymns during a fund-raising tour through Virginia. Althea Brown took the further step of starting an Ibanche mission station Jubilee choir to perform during church services and preaching tours.[40] It became a popular and emotionally moving part of the ministry among Kuba villagers.

The two missionaries also shared experience teaching in rural one-room schools during the post-Reconstruction era. The scant resources at Lucy Gantt's small school in Grayton, Alabama, and Althea Brown's school-house in Pikeville, Tennessee, offered daily reminders that political senti-ment at state and federal levels was shifting toward defining black students by their agricultural labor status rather than by their academic pursuits.[41] Both women emerged from those challenging assignments committed to making learning accessible and engaging to the children they met abroad. Language studies provided the means to that goal by enabling these mis-sionaries and their colleagues to communicate the aspects of arts and humanities that had engaged them.

Lucy Gantt Sheppard continued her passion for music by making a translated hymnal her first publication for the Congo Mission. She fol-lowed up that 1898 book with two basic readers and part of a second hym-nal in the following decade.[42] In keeping with the domestic focus common to this era of "woman's work for woman," Gantt Sheppard more often pub-licized her work to teach Western-style housekeeping skills to the residents of the mission girls' home. Yet her ongoing interest in providing songs and primary lessons in African languages also provided opportunities for mis-sion students and church members to put a distinctive spin on what they learned at the mission rather than just mimicking American habits. The historian and librarian Robert Benedetto credited early Luba language texts like Gantt Sheppard's hymnal with sparking "the growth of literacy" in a prominent regional language sooner than if such work had been left to Belgian government intervention alone.[43]

Lucy Gantt Sheppard mentored Althea Brown for about two years fol-lowing Brown's arrival at the Congo Mission in 1902. Her focus on women and girls prepared Brown to manage the girls' home, lead the day school, and participate in village evangelism after the Sheppards left on furlough. The enthusiasm for classical languages and literature that Althea Brown had acquired at Fisk was manifested in her ministry as enthusiasm to ana-lyze the Kuba kingdom. She incorporated cultural observations into her published articles from her first six years at the Congo Mission, including descriptions of African traditions that met her approval. Brown also showed precise cultural sensitivity in her Tshiluba lyrics to the spiritual standard

"Swing Low, Sweet Chariot."[44] Considering the overarching pressures for missionaries to show evidence of conversion and cultural change, it was unusual for Brown to chronicle positive developments that did not begin with Protestant intervention. Ira Dworkin analyzes the broad scope and influence of Brown's language work as an extension of the Fisk University atmosphere.[45] Inhumane colonial conditions and her professional partnership with Alonzo Edmiston also shaped that approach.

One explanation for Brown's continuing interest in cultural analysis is that her classical education predisposed her to question some customary dichotomies between religious and social recognition. For example, her best-known publication introduced the Kuba as "one of the most interesting people of equatorial Africa" who had "a wonderful history."[46] She made this assessment in 1932 with the understanding that Presbyterian evangelism among Kuba villagers had not achieved enough success to make it a primary focus of the Congo Mission.[47] Brown staked over twenty years of research for her dictionary and grammar book on the premise that this particular language and society were worth studying for reasons other than their potential for the Protestant missionaries. Evidence of her interest in Kuba affairs was evident in the timing of her first published book as well. Brown's Bushoong-language catechism was released the year after a regional uprising forced the Ibanche mission to close temporarily. The release of a catechism designed for the Kuba kingdom in 1905 spoke less to demand than to her expectations that the kingdom would recover and show future interest in Presbyterianism.

Althea Brown continued that theme in articles that she wrote for a denominational magazine in the following two years. Acknowledging the lack of recent baptisms, she still found encouragement in the facts that some church attendees were using her catechism, and 250 students "seem[ed] very anxious to learn" at Lucy Gantt Sheppard's day school.[48] She explained at length the hindrances that the Protestant missionaries in Kuba territory faced but argued that few of these problems originated with the villagers. The prospect of an alliance between Congo Free State officials and the Catholic priests starting new stations nearby caused more trepidation than her lingering concerns about the recently disgruntled Kuba king.[49] Even when Althea Brown expressed concern that the king (called Lukenga) might have ordered targeted killings in surrounding Kuba villages, she claimed "no special alarm" over the incidents. To the contrary, her graphic description of the way one of the bodies had been disfigured suggested some intellectual curiosity about the symbolism of these wounds.[50] In the same article, Brown made a professional claim that she and her husband would repeat later in their careers: that they were friends to the Kuba people in ways that political opposition and regional instability could not change.

Ongoing colonial exploitation in the Congo Free State made the political implications of classical education more poignant for Althea Brown Edmiston. She arrived in central Africa about three years after the Congo Mission began its formal investigation of human rights abuses committed in the name of King Leopold II of Belgium. The evidence of torture that Lucy Gantt Sheppard's husband had collected had not yet been publicized to an international audience of human rights reformers.[51] As the reform movement gained popularity during Brown's first years in the Congo Free State, the debate over political and economic improvements hinged on arguments that imperial subjects deserved reasonable living and working conditions. Like her fellow Fisk alum W. E. B. Du Bois, Althea Brown Edmiston had prepared to address that issue through her writing and her other work.

When Du Bois chronicled the summer teaching experience from his university years, he recalled two ways that analysis of literature contributed to his expertise. Du Bois drew on his previous coursework translating Cicero to build a convincing case for sharecropping parents to send their children to his school. The Latin text *Pro Archia Poeta* (*In Defense of Archias the Poet*) provided theoretical insight for how acquired artistic skill could overcome ethnic biases in perceptions of citizenship.[52] Classical training also prepared Du Bois to look for theoretical implications in how parents and students perceived the issues of citizenship and race. Those observations supported his well-known metaphor of "the veil" and generational strategies for opposing racism.[53]

In the context of the Congo Free State, Althea Brown Edmiston helped preserve historical memory of Kuba traditions partly as a reminder that this society had offered admirable living conditions before Belgian intervention. Her speech to the American Missionary Association annual meeting in 1908 expressed regard for the "neat" rectangular planning of the large villages in the Kasai region, the "excellent blacksmiths," "beautiful baskets" and other handmade craftwork, and abundant local fruits and vegetables.[54] These features enhanced a society with distinct government levels, stable marriages, and "remarkably high" moral standards.[55] The artistic traditions of the Kuba kingdom drew additional praise when Brown compared graceful local dances to the dance theories of François Delsarte.[56] The reference to this nineteenth-century French philosophy of bodily expression revealed the extent of her artistic background while taking direct aim at assumptions of European colonial superiority. Though Althea Brown Edmiston echoed other missionaries' imagery of African societies' being in "darkness" for lack of the gospel, her classical studies led her to show American missions supporters some social attributes that were familiar and held positive connotations.

This missionary's tendency to compliment a central African kingdom on the basis of its embodiment of certain Western traits could raise the question of whether she appreciated African culture on its own objective merits. The historian Carter G. Woodson posed this issue as a potential consequence of classical studies at the beginning of his volume on reforming black higher education. He argued that "in their own as well as in their mixed schools Negroes are taught to admire the Hebrew, the Greek, the Latin and the Teuton and to despise the African."[57] Two aspects of Althea Brown Edmiston's writings suggest that she appreciated unique aspects of Kuba society and remained open to "the possibility of originality in the Negro" that Woodson worried had been lost in favor of "a nominal equality" for African American university graduates.[58] In the last decade of her career, Brown used the introduction to her Bushoong dictionary to credit the Kuba kingdom for setting a precedent long before American politics made the step. Following the passage of the Nineteenth Amendment, she informed readers that "woman suffrage has existed among the Bushonga for many centuries" through female representation in their parliament and judicial courts.[59] This revision to her 1908 speech about Kuba society seemed designed for her audience of female missions supporters. Some of these supporters were social activists with likely ties to the Woman's Christian Temperance Union and its rhetoric linking female suffrage and prohibition to the preservation of American civilization.[60] So the historical fact about Kuba women became a way for Althea Brown to add respect for the political advancement of this central African society to her list of reasons this language was significant.

After two years spent following the example of ministries founded by Lucy Gantt Sheppard, Maria Fearing, and other early Congo Mission personnel, Althea Brown started using her classical training to organize and publicize the Ibanche Industrial School. She did so in partnership with Alonzo Edmiston as their first joint venture following their wedding on 8 July 1905. And, though the call for such a school in the Congo Free State did not start with them, industrial education became a means for Brown to further display her confidence in African and African American originality. A common complaint against industrial programs in the United States was that the curriculum too often consisted of mechanical tasks that were not marketable for nonwhite students.[61] That fault remains amplified in historical memory through contrasting portrayals of Booker T. Washington and W. E. B. Du Bois that overshadow educational leaders who continued to merge liberal arts and industrial training through the early twentieth century.[62] Black clubwomen claimed special authority to oppose academic dichotomies because they championed both domestic science and teaching as professional options for working wives and mothers. As part of their support for women's higher education, these leaders advocated training that "enforced codes of morality and thrift," whether that led to a terminal degree in Latin or to opportunities for maids to earn higher wages while avoiding sexual harassment.[63] The historian Paula Giddings argued that this enthusiasm for female industrial education harmonized with the rhetoric of Washington but originated with "a very pragmatic concern about the relationship among training, the purity of the home, and economic survival."[64]

Recent books by Andrew Barnes and Andrew Zimmerman draw attention to the pressing issue of dwindling financial and administrative support for diversified black education in the United States while industrial education programs expanded in West Africa after 1901.[65] As one of the earliest industrial schools founded in the Congo Free State, the Edmistons' program contended with the increasing popularity of educational programs designed primarily to meet the needs of Western economic and religious leaders. These missionaries attempted to follow the tradition of African American educators who adapted both approaches in pursuit of financial and cultural self-help. And the couple would later face serious challenges to their careers because of denominational concerns that their balance of classical and vocational preparation was inadequate for Presbyterian ministry.

A few details regarding the distinctive features of the Ibanche Industrial School will precede an explanation of why Althea Brown and Alonzo Edmiston found their different academic perspectives compatible. First, unlike missionary-led industrial schools that recruited students only to fill the supply orders of church personnel, the Ibanche Industrial School taught boys to create items like tables and door frames that African villagers requested.[66] Students could also acquire basic literacy through daily study of the Presbyterian catechism that Althea Brown had translated. Alonzo Edmiston noted that the students were "very anxious to learn" by receiving other translated books.[67] Though one of their white colleagues claimed that two hours exhausted the attention span of African students, the Edmistons held their schedule of academic and religious classes for a half day before the mechanical or agricultural work was started.[68] The influence of Althea Brown's interest in political culture could be seen in the fact that regional African leaders were invited to tour each of their schools over the next fifteen years, starting with hosting the Kuba king and his family at the Ibanche Industrial School.[69] Combined, these features reduced the social distance between the students and their communities, helped expand an African crafts market that graduates could sustain independently, and provided reading and writing abilities that could also help graduates pursue colonial professions if they chose.

The ultimate goal that Althea Brown and Alonzo Edmiston declared for their industrial school—the equipping of African evangelists—encapsulated one of the main ambitions of classical education.[70] Several of the girls and boys who grew up practicing Lucy Gantt Sheppard's translated hymns or reading Brown's Bushoong catechism came to participate in traveling ministry as early members of what later became the Communauté Presbytérienne au Congo. The African synod that formed in 1920 issued some of the first effective group challenges against Belgian colonial oppression and overbearing missionary control. Educated Protestant pastors like them justified their financial and professional authority in the 1930s, setting the ideological stage for political self-governance.[71] Missionaries with degrees from historically black universities contributed to that process by modeling their faith in academics as an expression of shared humanity and shared capacity for achievement.

Industrial Education as Personal and Professional Partnership

Though the establishment of an industrial school marked their first joint ministry achievement, it is noteworthy that neither of the Edmistons had expected that goal as part of their careers. Both Althea Brown and Alonzo Edmiston pursued postgraduate medical training, anticipating that this skill, in addition to teaching and preaching abilities, would be advantageous. The influenza epidemic after World War I ensured that such training would indeed become instrumental in the expansion of the American Presbyterian Congo Mission. But, for reasons explored further in chapters 2 and 3, Alonzo Edmiston's long-term professional status with the PCUS was determined by the reputations of his colleges more than by the results of his specific training. His previous experience at Tuskegee Institute and the denominational African American seminary made Edmiston one of the few Congo Mission personnel chosen to model Presbyterian adoption of a popular and potentially lucrative education style. The literary scholar Ira Dworkin analyzed this shift in emphasis to industrial training as part of the denouement of Althea Brown's language work since it required transfers from Kuba territory to support her husband's new assignments.[72] The increasing demand for industrial projects at the Congo Mission did not, however, prevent Althea Brown from continuing her artistic pursuits. An examination of their shared goals up to 1911 reveals how and why the Edmistons found their distinct academic backgrounds compatible under the umbrella of "industrial education."

First, Alonzo Edmiston and Althea Brown shared an understanding of foreign missions service as a challenge to poverty. Childhood on the Edmiston plantation in Tennessee brought oppressive conditions similar to those his grandmother had endured before emancipation. He was selected to work with her as a house servant for the white Edmiston family from a young age, having previously lived with his parents and siblings in a small cabin with cornhusk mats for furniture. The household workload and the lack of a public school meant that Alonzo Edmiston had attended primary classes for only a few months of the year before the local Presbyterian church nominated him to attend Stillman Institute. This white congregation recommended him to participate in the recent expansion of the seminary, which had just moved to a new campus in 1898. Lacking a scholarship, Edmiston probably worked on the campus farmland as well as the Alabama State Hospital farm to pay school fees. The connections to the Congo Mission that he gained through classmates and faculty ensured that Edmiston and his descendants would never return to live in the family cabin. Following the death of his own father, Alonzo honored William Campbell Edmiston as the foster father who helped him gain a full-time education and exposure to the foreign mission movement.[73]

The Brown family also survived through plantation agriculture; their sharecropping work in Alabama and Mississippi supplemented the early years of their daughter's Fisk normal school scholarship. While living in Jubilee Hall during the winter of 1892, Althea converted to Christianity and pledged her life to service. In her words, when eighteen-year-old Althea Brown committed her life to Christ and missions, she "started out to win the fight in

Figure 1.2   Jubilee Hall at Fisk University, Nashville, Tennessee, in 2018.
Photograph by the author.

spite of poverty."[74] That fight motivated her to start a hair-care business in the
Fisk girls' dorm to help pay her tuition. It strengthened her as she taught summer school to one hundred rural Tennessee children in one bare room.
Despite the fact that Brown and her parents had no income to spare, she
found ways to renovate the schoolroom with books and writing supplies
within a week.[75] The teaching position and domestic service for female faculty enabled Brown to pay the expenses for her bachelor's degree and apply to
the Chicago Training School for a year of missions preparation.

A background in poverty inspired Althea Brown and Alonzo Edmiston
to emphasize construction and house design even before their industrial
school began. Part of the focus on construction came from a practical need
to make the second Congo Mission station viable. The Reverend William
Henry Sheppard planned the Ibanche station layout to provide proximity
to the Kuba capital city while appealing to the expectations of potential
American donors. Its hilltop location of twenty acres, large church building
with a bell tower, central square, and house-lined thoroughfares made the

first rendition of Ibanche resemble a town.[76] Lucy Gantt Sheppard enhanced the project by trying to re-create a comfortable southern guesthouse, as she had done previously at the Luebo station. The Sheppard home filled the social role of an embassy by welcoming American, European, and African guests to share Gantt Sheppard's cuisine.[77] For Althea Brown, being assigned her own small house upon arrival at Ibanche meant a chance to create her own version of the Fisk Jubilee Hall experience. And the dream of maintaining and expanding Ibanche helped Alonzo Edmiston earn his full-time ministry appointment.

While Edmiston was seeking medical training to strengthen his chances of being accepted to a mission team, he received an opportunity to travel abroad sooner than he had expected. Samuel Verner, a former Stillman Institute professor and Congo missionary, contacted Stillman alumni for help with planning a business trip to a village in the Kasai region called Ndombe. Verner had left the mission in the 1890s under controversial circumstances, yet he remained interested in the Congo Free State for the economic and political opportunities that King Leopold II's control had enabled. Verner started working as an agent for one of the European companies based there and facilitating trade networks in the United States. Edmiston joined his staff in 1904 as Verner made a major "purchase" for the upcoming St. Louis World's Fair; his mission was to help Verner acquire several Congolese pygmies and transport them to America.[78] Edmiston's cooking abilities during the excursion made a positive impression on Verner, who credited a delicious meal to his "characteristic skill."[79]

Edmiston's willingness to give precedence to his Stillman Institute alumni network over his employment indicated that his interest lay in the destination of the expedition rather than in its original goal. Soon after arriving at Verner's destination, Edmiston wrote to his former classmate the Reverend Lucius DeYampert to let him know that he was near the Presbyterian mission station. As he expected, DeYampert invited him to visit there. Ira Dworkin has suggested that discomfort with Verner's human trafficking plan led Edmiston to leave the expedition and visit the Congo Mission instead.[80] His unwillingness to transport people from Congo for business purposes also had a precedent in the earlier work of African American Presbyterian missionaries who rescued enslaved people being transported through their area.[81] But another motivation behind Edmiston's shift in course lay in the "delighted" feeling he had while visiting his classmate.[82] He was embodying the ethic of racial uplift common to historically black colleges by reaching out to professionals in his community to find new ways to offer service. He later listed his dates of missionary service starting from the time of Verner's arrival, as if appointment to the American Presbyterian Congo Mission had been the intended purpose of the visit all along.[83]

As a young man, Alonzo Edmiston was known for his tall, thin stature and an introspective expression in his eyes.[84] He tended to display a remarkable openness about his emotions in his letters and journals, and his first published report from the Congo Free State was no exception. The contrast between his positive emotions and the physical demands of his journey are evident in his reaction when DeYampert's invitation to visit the mission arrived. Edmiston reported in the *Kassai Herald* mission journal: "So delighted was I at the opportunity of seeing him again that I walked forty miles in one day, alone, through the jungle. I could not speak the language of the people, and had to make my wants known through signs. Having passed over many hills, and down into many valleys, and through many streams, I finally arrived where my friend lived. Luebo was to me what an oasis in a great desert must be to the weary traveler."[85] This report and the only published account of his courtship were preserved when he contributed to a colleague's 1947 biography of Althea Brown.[86]

After a short visit, Lilian Thomas agreed to accompany him on the forty-mile hike to the place he called "an oasis even more beautiful than the first."[87] Edmiston was provided temporary accommodations in the Sheppard home. It was there that his professional and personal interests began to merge; while the Sheppards were on furlough, Althea Brown remodeled the home and hosted him for meals at her own "Jubilee Cottage." Edmiston summarized his first day at the all-African American Presbyterian mission station by writing, "I was touched by the happy faces of the Mission people and by the earnestness of the two lone workers, Miss Brown and Mr. Phipps. My own heart longed to be at once in the work with them."[88]

Alonzo Edmiston quit his St. Louis Exposition work without pay and joined the APCM mission team early in the summer of 1904. Contributing to Ibanche became his first assignment; he helped Brown and the Reverend Henry Hawkins fulfill William Henry Sheppard's mandate. Sheppard intended for the Ibanche team to build an alliance with the Kuba kingdom, make the Christian message accessible to its subjects, and establish an eventual mission station within the Kuba capital city.[89] One part of that mandate had been fulfilled by establishing schools, a foster home, and churches in the villages around Ibanche. Althea and Lucy Gantt Sheppard worked on the second part of the mandate by writing lessons and songs in the local languages for their students.[90] Edmiston understood his duty as a new colleague to include completing some of the evangelistic and administrative work that languished while the Sheppards were on furlough. He also helped compensate for the recent sinking of the mission steamship that had caused a shortage of food and supplies. His five years of experience at Stillman and additional work at Tuskegee became the resource Edmiston drew from to tackle any requested tasks at the Congo Mission with "great earnestness."[91] And, when a crisis called for it, Edmiston also risked his life for the station and its personnel.

The original Ibanche station was burned in an uprising against foreign businessmen and missionaries that started on 2 November 1904. The Presbyterian missionaries fled just before armed men burned and demolished their houses on the orders of the Kuba king, Lukenga Kot aPe. When Althea Brown "barely escaped" from the station ahead of the impending attack, Edmiston was with her. He had been overseeing renovation work on the roads and the church within the station when a messenger arrived with news that one of the African mission workers had been killed in a nearby village.[92]

For the rest of the day, Edmiston coordinated with local Christians from the Luba, Lulua, and Zappo Zap tribes who had gathered to keep any Kuba attackers at bay.[93] As each side of the mission station was attacked, Brown focused on the types of crisis intervention that she had prepared for; she made her foster children and the displaced neighbors feel welcome on the front porch of her home, she nursed the wounded through the night, and she led them in a morning prayer.[94] The arrival of Lucius DeYampert with a warning that additional protection from Free State officials would not arrive until the following week prompted Edmiston to escort Brown and the group of about five hundred women and children to Luebo. He then repeated the twelve-hour march to and from Ibanche with his colleague Henry Hawkins in hope of salvaging any unbroken keepsakes.[95] The strain of enduring that journey three times within three days was enough to contribute to the fatal heart attack of the Belgian rubber trader who had accompanied the two men.[96] Yet Edmiston continued to give priority to the needs of Brown and her foster home residents above his own comfort and security.

The Ibanche mission station held life-altering symbolic value for Brown and Edmiston because it was the primary spiritual and physical home for both of them. Unlike William Henry Sheppard or Lucius DeYampert, they had no previous record of Presbyterian Church membership. What limited experience these missionaries had with Presbyterian congregations in the American South before 1904 had related to racial exclusion. Edmiston could claim the church that recommended him to Stillman Institute only as the church of his white foster father's relatives, not his own.[97] His probable temporary participation in the black Presbyterian congregation near Stillman engrossed Edmiston in the early stages of denominational segregation; the PCUS had encouraged its dwindling percentage of African American members to found and maintain the Afro-American Presbyterian Church as of May 1898. Salem Presbyterian of Tuscaloosa remained a site of contention when it hosted a meeting that reconnected black Presbyterians to the PCUS but only within a separate, race-based synod.[98]

Meanwhile, Althea Brown had received the sponsorship of two all-white congregations that she could visit only under rare circumstances. One of the PCUS churches of Nashville had commissioned her for missions with a secret Thursday night membership ceremony. The congregants "made arrangements for her to slip in" unnoticed because "a colored person dare not step inside the churches of the white people in that city."[99] Her memory of this process as "distasteful" may partially explain why Brown visited First Presbyterian Church of Selma, Alabama, only once in the first twenty-eight years of her time as a recipient of the congregation's financial donations.[100] While living in Selma during most of their furloughs, Brown and Edmiston attended a black church that Lucius DeYampert had once led called Sylvan Street Presbyterian. Facing multiple signs that the denomination kept them at arms' length, Brown and Edmiston clung tighter to the prospect of rebuilding their adopted African home and building a future together.

During her years at Fisk, Brown had earned the top spot in a beauty competition along with top marks in her degree program.[101] Some credit for the former went to her sewing skills and the wardrobe she created during her university years, most of which burned during the uprising. When the destruction of Ibanche forced him to return to Luebo empty-handed, Edmiston shared in her grief. Likewise, he shared her joy when she used her remaining fabric for a new project: a wedding dress and a pair of white trousers for the groom.[102]

The inner longing that Edmiston experienced during his first meeting with Brown found its match in her own recollection.[103] According to her short autobiography, the arrival of the new missionary brought an unanticipated gift into her life; she wrote, "Being in the heart of Africa, I thought I

Figure 1.3   Portrait of Althea Brown in her wedding dress, 1905. From the A. L. Edmiston Papers, RG 495, box 8, Presbyterian Historical Society, Philadelphia.

was invulnerable to Cupid's bow."[104] She seems to have been impressed that Edmiston would take on so much personal risk and inconvenience in her behalf. Though she did not mention him by name in 1904, Brown told her American supporters that "one of the other missionaries" had walked with her through the battle zone to Luebo.[105] And Edmiston's first report from Ibanche referred indirectly to her "magic touch," which turned his temporary lodgings into a "little palace" once he received permission to join the mission staff. He brought with him no furniture or decorations from his previous home, but the prospect of his new life was bright enough that he was ready to start from scratch. They married the following summer with a bridal "aisle" of palm leaves, an American-style cake courtesy of Maria Fearing, and fellow black missionaries forming the wedding party.[106] A tent pitched among the ruins of Ibanche provided their honeymoon destination.[107] As Althea put it, "Looking beyond the ruins, we beheld the glorious manifestation of God's love and presence about us. In our mind's eye, we saw again a most beautiful station."[108]

Being invested emotionally in the memories of Ibanche compelled Brown and Edmiston to analyze how local conditions could be improved to ensure the station's future. Both missionaries published articles notifying other Americans about the full context of the conflict. They concentrated on the roles of African authorities and colonial representatives in ways that foreshadowed the Edmistons' later career trajectories.

Edmiston published an article in the January 1905 issue of the Presbyterian *Kassai Herald,* two months after the Kuba uprising. His eyewitness account captured the grief and confusion of the time without failing to pinpoint its precedents. The article starts with a description of the Kuba king's annual visit to the Congo Free State authorities in Luebo. All the regional leaders were summoned to pay the taxes placed on their subjects by the Belgian king and determine the tax rates for the following year. But because King Kot aPe (or Lukenga) arrived later than expected, the state authorities imprisoned him and required an expensive bail. A loan provided by the Presbyterian missionaries at Luebo escalated the crisis because Lukenga considered both the bail and the repayment as contributions to a system that belittled his elite status.[109] After commanding his subjects to attack Africans of other ethnicities, Lukenga sent his kingdom to war against all Europeans and Americans.

From Edmiston's perspective, it seemed that Kot aPe's fixation on insults was too sudden. The king demanded "the hearts of traders [and] the heads of missionaries" after planning in silence for about four months. Only a few rumors and isolated attacks had suggested trouble in that time. To a recent immigrant with no personal memories of local precolonial politics, silence before a major attack denoted intentional dishonesty on the part of Lukenga. Alternatively, Edmiston praised the Kuba Christians who defied their king and tried to protect the mission station. He expressed confidence in the final paragraph "that this means a brighter future for the Bakuba, a firmer establishment of the gospel in their midst, and their eternal salvation!"[110] This

Figure 1.4   A portrait of Kuba Christians who joined the American Presbyterian Congo Mission between 1898 and 1908. From the A. L. Edmiston Papers, RG 495, box 8, Presbyterian Historical Society, Philadelphia.

early foray into local politics left Alonzo Edmiston inclined to pursue a mediator role as he gained more administrative influence with the APCM. He would continue Sheppard's style of approach by meeting with the Kuba royalty but not to the extent of forging an alliance with a specific African leader.[111] Likewise, his sense of camaraderie with Congo Free State officials varied depending on his observations of how colonial intervention influenced local Christians and the ministry itself.

In the following three years, during which Althea Brown more than once published her perspective on the uprising, she placed it within a broader context of educational progress, Presbyterian expansion, and community building. She did not mention the silence in the Kuba kingdom as malevolent in itself. Lukenga's secrecy fit a tradition of isolationism that had protected the Kuba capital for generations before William Sheppard entered it. By then, Brown had researched most of the Kuba political traditions that she would feature in her book's introduction, and she characterized the kingdom as "the most highly developed, intelligent, and yet most conservative people among whom our Mission is working."[112] While she mourned the destruction and bloodshed, Brown interpreted the Kuba uprising as a foreseeable reaction to the breach of trust when Congo Free State authorities imprisoned the king. She implied that representatives of King Leopold deserved reproach when she wrote: "We do not know whether this means any remuneration for the mission or not, for the State officials are trying in every way to put the blame of the revolt upon the missionaries. By certain favors to the Bakuba they are also trying to prove to them that they are their real friends and we their enemies. However, this is exceedingly hard for them to do. The smallest rumor of State officials coming in our midst fills the Bakuba with terror."[113] Brown had published her first translated hymns the previous year, and she found colonial visitations disruptive to the social interactions that had made her language study possible.

A degree of hindsight played into her willingness to tell an audience of American Congregationalists in 1908 that the "terrible revolt" happened "because of oppression."[114] Brown presented this speech about two and a half years after the couple reopened the Ibanche station with the help of their Kuba allies. The half a paragraph devoted to the uprising paled in comparison to the page and a half that included her descriptions of the culture and politics of the Kuba kingdom. Brown expected that the future success of her ministry would involve the rebirth of her mission station and its expansion into Kuba villages. Her articles implied that these ministry goals would be accomplished in the wake of the attack only through deeper analysis of this African society, not through rejection of it.[115]

After their return to Ibanche, Brown needed regular access to the Kuba villages and the capital city to study the linguistic, historical, and cultural context for her grammar and dictionary. Likewise, Edmiston's construction projects and church-planting agenda depended heavily on establishing and maintaining relationships with local people. He also recruited the African workers who would help him develop an award-winning agricultural program later in his career. This pattern of interaction influenced the way the couple pursued "self-support" goals for the industrial school. In 1907 Edmiston expected that the housing and clothing costs for students could soon be compensated entirely by the profits from school projects that were purchased by missionaries or African villagers.[116]

After the concept was introduced to the United States in 1869, the term *self-support* started to gain popularity among Protestant leaders in the 1880s.[117] Alonzo Edmiston adopted the original meaning with his decision to include products requested by Africans in his fund-raising scheme.[118]

The choice to expand inventory beyond the items that appealed to American missionaries offered a first step toward the increased distinction between Christian training and Western culture that the mission theorist Rufus Anderson envisioned.[119] The missiologist David W. Scott argued that values-defining power also factored into understandings of "self-support" in overseas missions.[120]

By that interpretation, a threat to Southern Presbyterian authority loomed within the Edmistons' industrial education pedagogy. African Christians could potentially exert power over the activities of the mission school as student producers and village-based consumers. Later industrial programs led by Alonzo Edmiston bolstered the financial interests of African villagers by including plans for new products specific to the needs of African congregations, business ventures with local crops, budgeting advice for students, and an on-campus savings bank. As the following chapters will show, these plans often met resistance from the Congo Mission executive committee or were ended prematurely.

With their partnership established through marriage, the Edmistons anticipated a lifetime of service in the rebuilt Ibanche station. Althea Brown was convinced that "the second Jubilee Cottage is even more pleasing than the first, for now it is an ideal home occupied by a host and hostess bearing the name of Edmiston."[121] Her optimism would be tested three years later, during the first attempt to dismiss the couple from service as Southern Presbyterian missionaries.[122] The process of recovering from that crisis pushed Edmiston and Brown to relocate to other mission stations and adopt new ministry responsibilities. Neither fathomed how these changes would threaten their professional reputations and disrupt their working relationships with African students and villagers.

2

Congo Missionaries and the Perpetuation of Manual Labor, 1908–1936

> Young men and young women, there is no escape. If we would be great,
> and good, and useful, we must pay the price.
> Booker T. Washington, *On Mother Earth*, 1902

Near the end of his mission career, six students from the Mutoto station boys' home made a public accusation against Alonzo Edmiston that disturbed him. They "spoke bitterly" against his management style to a committee of missionaries and African pastors, starting with a complaint that Edmiston "was always telling them that here is a place of work and not school."[1] Though the committee directed the boys to apologize, Edmiston remained concerned because of the kernel of truth in their statement. He knew that the boys could have heard him say something similar while he forced them to work off demerits at the farm. And Edmiston still hoped to avoid seeing his prediction from 1929 come to fruition; as a professional minister, he believed he "should have more to do with the boys than just working them in the fields, growing food, and feeding them."[2]

This chapter analyzes the Presbyterian mission reassignments, managerial practices, and Belgian initiatives that challenged the Edmistons' careers from their first extended furlough until their last full year of joint ministry. These changes were part of a broader shift in how Protestant denominations and colonial governments regarded education and professionalization for people of African descent. Criticisms of Althea Brown and Alonzo Edmiston that were based on their academic backgrounds led to their temporary dismissal from Presbyterian ministry in 1908. Their status as reinstated APCM staff was secured through a process that involved diversification of their mission work; each one engaged in less instructional work and more vocational and manual labor. As some of the techniques that had helped the Edmistons and their predecessors maintain a distinct African American mission station lost strategic value after 1910, black missionaries dealt with increased pressure to continue their work without asserting expertise.

As I noted in the previous chapter, the methods that Althea Brown Edmiston and Alonzo Edmiston used in overseas ministry were stimulated by the academic institutions they had attended. Evaluating the professional status of these missionaries also requires evaluating the reputations accorded to their institutions. In particular, the Southern Presbyterian Executive Committee on Foreign Missions expressed strong opinions about Stillman Institute and Fisk University. This committee paid the salaries of each of the missionaries and provided living and school expenses for their dependent children who remained in the United States. The educational philosophies of these institutions fit opposite sides of the spectrum in terms of what the denomination hoped to achieve with racial diversity at its Congo Mission. And part of their long-term success as missionaries depended on the Edmistons' abilities to adopt professional personas that did not reflect either institution fully.

The original mission of Stillman, founded as Tuscaloosa Institute in 1876, mentioned outreach to black Southerners specifically with implicit expectations for foreign missions. The small faculty expected African American pastoral graduates to return to their own communities, but those segregated communities were not expected to remain static.[3] The seminary constituted part of the home missions outreach of the PCUS Committee on Colored Evangelization. As former slaves and their descendants left Southern Presbyterian churches for independent black denominations, the PCUS created an institution that would help extend its influence over the growing trend of African American congregations. Despite the relative lack of growth in its black membership base, the denomination continued to claim progress in its race-based initiatives. These initiatives led to a plan for Presbyterian racial segregation with a separate synod for black members starting in 1916.[4] The segregated synod was based at a church close to the Tuscaloosa Institute campus, and the seminary graduates were expected to serve either that synod or other Protestant ministries for black communities in the U.S. South or abroad.[5]

William Henry Sheppard was the first Tuscaloosa Institute alumnus to volunteer for foreign missionary service, and his ambitions represented a significant religious and political opportunity for the Southern Presbyterian denomination. First, Sheppard set a model for an "interracial policy" at the APCM by traveling with his younger colleague Samuel Lapsley.[6] When Sheppard returned to the United States to recruit more students from historically black colleges to join the Congo Mission, his successful efforts brought the denomination closer to fulfilling contemporary political goals regarding emigration. Senator John Tyler Morgan of Selma, Alabama, issued appeals from the 1880s through 1898 for the U.S. government to aid emigration of African Americans to the Congo Free State as it had done for Liberia. In support of Jim Crow legislation, Morgan hoped that educated African American leaders would become the main expatriates; by moving overseas with their families, they could reduce the number of black professionals willing to challenge de jure segregation.[7] Indeed, most of the new African American missionaries who joined the Congo Mission in 1896 had earned bachelor's or seminary degrees.

As Sheppard and his colleagues from Stillman Institute (Henry Hawkins and Lucius DeYampert) worked to expand the Congo Mission between 1896 and 1904, denominational interest in the campus reached a plateau. The institute relocated to a former Tuscaloosa plantation site with farmland and a classroom building, yet financial donations remained insufficient.[8] Administrators and supporters complained of the crippling lack of support and occasional hostility displayed toward their work with African Americans.[9] It seemed that the PCUS expected little more than continued existence from the institution. Perhaps the most notable signs of this trend happened between 1908 and 1911, when the denomination started to change its official policies regarding Stillman.

From its founding in 1891 through 1910, the operations of the seminary had been overseen by members of the PCUS Committee on Colored Evangelization. This underfunded committee never had adequate resources to meet its goals for expanding Stillman Institute or for supporting the Presbyterian churches that its graduates led.[10] The committee, however, did offer a forum where black Presbyterian leaders' interests and concerns would be publicized on at least an annual basis. And the committee echoed black ministers' arguments that they needed a range of social and financial issues addressed within their communities to maximize their leadership potential.[11] Committee leaders read these arguments into the published minutes of the annual meetings of the General Assembly of the Presbyterian Church in the United States.

For church members and leaders who could access these volumes, the published minutes offered a means to track long-term accountability on the status of black congregations and religious education. This potential accountability ended in 1910. After the Committee on Colored Evangelization was subsumed under the umbrella of the Executive Committee of Home Missions, its annual reports on Stillman Institute and the activities of black ministers were no longer collected or published. That change eliminated a primary way that African American issues were publicized within the denomination.[12]

The new categorization placed the education and church work of African American Presbyterians as a product of the denomination's missionary outreach rather than as a long-term initiative with a specific goal. The drastic reduction in the amount of printed space dedicated to colored evangelization updates in the minutes of the PCUS General Assembly symbolized the denomination's reduced concept of the committee's purpose. Details regarding developments at Stillman Institute were replaced with summaries indicating that operations had not ceased completely.[13] Applying the label of "missions" to the work of black Presbyterians and their allies drew attention to the presence of activity rather than to the quality of those activities.

In the meantime, the Southern Presbyterians' reduced confidence in the quality of the seminary for African Americans prompted the first major challenge to Alonzo Edmiston's career. He had lived at the Ibanche station for about four full years when he was informed in 1908 that he should leave the mission field with no expectations of returning. Althea Brown could offer no guidance on the matter since she had left on furlough earlier in the year to seek medical care for their son, Sherman Kueta. Later correspondence indicates that multiple reasons—a few unspoken—had led to his dismissal, starting with accusations that his education was inadequate. And none of the denominational officials expressed confidence that further academic pursuits could solve the problem.

Believing that his forced resignation might be temporary, the Edmiston family settled in a small house about two blocks from the Stillman Institute campus. They lived there for about four years while they pursued strategies they hoped might lead them back to the mission field. Edmiston enrolled as a full-time student, pursuing the academic program at Stillman in addition to his seminary degree. As he wrote to the Executive Committee on Foreign Missions, sacrificing time to recuperate from four years of continuous service or visit relatives was worth it if the additional training would make him a qualified representative for the Southern Presbyterian Church.[14] And Althea Brown, confident in her academic qualifications and ministry experience, offered to depart for the Belgian Congo alone while her husband completed his studies.[15] The Edmistons remained unaware that their denominational supervisors had disqualified both of them for future mission service because of the supervisors' opinions about their institutions. As secretary of the PCUS Executive Committee on Foreign Missions, Samuel Chester expressed private misgivings that either Stillman Institute or Fisk University could produce ministers who would perform cost-effective work in a congenial way.

The correspondence from Chester and other leaders of the Executive Committee on Foreign Missions reveals much about the devaluing of historically black education in their efforts to avoid discourse on the subject. In the two years following the Edmistons' dismissal in 1908, two other Stillman graduates were also removed from the Congo Mission. Both Sheppard and Hawkins were accused of adultery with African women, and Sheppard was reassigned to pastor a black congregation in Kentucky.[16] In the meantime, Chester and an APCM missionary, James McClung Sieg, had requested that Alonzo Edmiston accept an upcoming ministry position within the United States, specifically a staff position with a black YMCA in Winner, Mississippi.[17] The committee kept the specific reasons for the reassignments of the Edmistons, Sheppard, and Hawkins private, their stated goal being to avoid publication of "embarrassing problems"; but the implication for the Stillman student body was left unaddressed.[18] The seminary witnessed the reassignment of its most famous alumnus and the reenrollment of one of its youngest African missionaries without any public statements from the denomination regarding Stillman's future role in Presbyterian mission work.

Althea Brown stepped in to fill the vacuum of official guidance by giving a 1909 newspaper interview about her husband's academic study of "industrial work that he wishes to introduce in the mission" and assuring her Congregationalist sponsors that she would return to the Congo Mission soon.[19] She also visited the Executive Committee on Foreign Missions offices to discuss her case in 1908.[20] Still, the arrangement of a YMCA position for Edmiston and the secretary's personal confidence that the couple would never return to mission work indicates that the committee no longer saw Stillman Institute degrees as qualifications for an overseas post. Because Chester requested confidentiality, neither the Edmistons nor other members of the Stillman Institute community were informed of the committee secretary's argument "that our committee will deem it wise to send out only white reinforcements to Africa for the present."[21]

Southern Presbyterian leaders' confidence in Stillman Institute theological and academic degrees continued to decline through the 1910s and 1920s. The Executive Committee on Foreign Missions began a search for at least six "first-class" and well-educated recruits to the Congo Mission before the Edmistons' appeals to return could be considered.[22] In 1915 Dr. Egbert W. Smith, then executive secretary of the foreign missions board, defined as "first-class men and women" those with demonstrated "scholarship" at their academic institution and positive results from the "rigid and comprehensive" missions examination.[23] Notably, Smith offered recommendations of degrees from Louisville Seminary as advantageous for ministry service without mentioning Stillman Institute.[24] Though the PCUS continued to expect college degrees from its African American recruits, internal correspondence suggests that those degrees were not seen as adding value to the organization.

The Southern Presbyterian missions program administrators were changing their guidelines in the aftermath of attending the 1910 Edinburgh conference, the first effort to coordinate foreign missions plans among Protestant denominations.[25] The conference agenda promoted optimism that worldwide evangelism could be accomplished in the near future through targeted study.[26] These plans were made within a group of over a thousand delegates that included just two representatives of an African American denomination, one African attendee, and nineteen other Christians who did not originate in Europe or the United States.[27] The missiologist Francis Anekwe Oborji characterized the resulting conference reports as seeking "to meet the challenge of carrying the gospel from Christian lands (Christendom) to non-Christian lands (heathendom)" without allowing sufficient representation from those who could question such dichotomies.[28]

By 1923 the minimized diversity modeled at the Edinburgh conference also became part of standard policy for the International Missions Council and the Foreign Missions Conference of North America. Both organizations limited future commissioning of African American missionaries to eastern or western Africa after that year.[29] Those who remained as ministers on the African continent, including Althea Brown and Alonzo Edmiston, became less likely to receive recognition for their service in denominational or educational reports; either administrators neglected to list their names or emphasized their mistakes as reasons to reject other African American missionaries.[30] In the following years, lay staff and volunteer positions within the African American branches of the YMCA and the YWCA became prominent ways for black leaders such as Max Yergan, Elizabeth Ross

Haynes, and George Edmund Haynes to circumvent this exclusion and remain affiliated with the Protestant mission boards.[31]

Additional Southern Presbyterian Executive Committee consideration of the leadership skills of Stillman seminarians would be delayed until 1934, when a retiring missionary named Joseph Savels recommended A. A. Rochester as a potential leader for a Presbyterian higher education program in the Belgian Congo.[32] Savels claimed to recommend Rochester because he was "educated" and "beloved," but the omission of the Edmistons implied that Rochester's origins in the Caribbean influenced the choice.[33] A graduate of the seminary for African American men seemed more likely to gain recognition at the Congo Mission if he was not born in the American South.

Whereas Presbyterian leaders' attitudes regarding Edmiston's alma mater were suggested through omission, the concerns regarding Althea Brown's university were clarified in greater detail. The Executive Committee on Foreign Missions was based in Nashville, where the co-secretaries had observed the activities of the American Missionary Association and Fisk University community members for years. The familiarity with Fisk left a strong impression on Secretary Chester in particular. He worked through the Executive Committee to block the reappointment of Althea Brown Edmiston in 1909 and to discourage the applications of other potential missionaries from her alma mater.

Secretary Chester expressed his concerns in a series of letters to Dr. William Morrison regarding what became known as "The Edmiston Affair."[34] Though the exact charges against the couple were not preserved in the mission station minutes or correspondence, Chester listed lack of interpersonal skills and "self-conscious piety" as reasons to support calls for the Edmistons' dismissal.[35] In a later letter he mentioned the controversy while referring to the influence of "a certain institution in this country" that he believed left its graduates ill-suited for service abroad.[36] Secretary Chester suggested that this personality flaw reinforced his previous decision "that I would discount heavily, in considering anyone's application for appointment to Africa, the fact that he or she had received training at Fisk University."[37]

Brown's persistence in contacting financial donors and denominational leaders proved a source of "great embarrassment" to the Executive Committee on Foreign Missions.[38] The coordinating secretaries preferred that personnel matters receive as little publicity as possible, especially in cases that were attributed mainly to interpersonal conflict.[39] It is also likely that the committee wanted to avoid drawing attention to the racial implications of the official reasons for the Edmistons' return. Memories of the Edmistons' controversy led the Executive Committee to delay a request from APCM Supervisor William Morrison for reinforcement by "only really efficient people" after the forced resignations of two more black colleagues, Lucius and Lilian Thomas DeYampert.[40] Through the early 1920s, the APCM requested recruits with training in agriculture, industry, printing, secondary teaching, and nursing. No mention was made of the years Althea Brown and Alonzo Edmiston had devoted to filling some of these positions.[41]

The leadership expectations at the Congo Mission became more specialized, and the mission staff were expected to reflect that trend. Yet Althea Brown, with her vocal training and her specialization in classics, exemplified the product of the kind of broad-based liberal arts education that distinguished Fisk University from HBCUs that emphasized industrial education. Her ability to minimize or erase this legacy in her work may have been the key to what Presbyterian administrators interpreted as a necessary level of humility. As of 1910, the Executive Committee and the Congo missionaries acknowledged the contrite tone of Althea's appeals for reappointment and continued salary payments to the Edmistons as if they were on furlough, but the consensus in the Nashville office remained firm that the family's missionary endeavors were complete.[42]

Economic modernity also exerted some influence on Southern Presbyterian policies. "New South" initiatives promoting industrialization and urbanization expanded the need for supervisors and technical research in the region.[43] Though agricultural trade remained the norm in the region after the turn of the twentieth century, landowners faced increasing difficulty retaining sharecroppers in competition with the cash wages offered by industrial positions.[44] Southern towns and cities were at the cusp of permanent demographic change as the urban middle class grew and invested in the kinds of specialized education that ensured their professional advancement. In the religious realm, demands that ministers gain technical and academic expertise fit the tenor of the times.

The context of the "New South" also influenced the ways that missions leaders in the PCUS discussed the financial role of racial integration. Though none of these leaders mentioned Booker T. Washington's 1895 Cotton States Exposition Address in their correspondence, Congo Mission Supervisor William Morrison did seek Washington's support for the reform campaign against King Leopold.[45] And he was probably also aware of William Henry Sheppard's reputation for being, like Washington, a famous speaker. Both Sheppard and

Washington had gained recognition while advocating for interracial cooperative ventures, and both men had raised financial support successfully with
their messages. Though Morrison's interest in Booker T. Washington seems to
have sprung from his passion to improve governance of the Congo Free State,
public solidarity with "the Wizard of Tuskegee" could have also been part of
the internal strategy to alter governance at the Congo Mission. Speeches like
his 1902 address "On Mother Earth" helped Washington promote an image
of African American progress starting from material sacrifice and menial status.[46] William Morrison continued appealing for white male recruits through
the 1910s, but the need for support staff made him reluctant to dismiss any
additional African American missionaries during that decade.

The search for "first-class people" to lead programs at the stations did not
imply that these people were expected to make up the entire population of
the Congo Mission. Staff who would not have qualified for the "first-class"
designation, including African American colleagues, were still employed in
supportive roles at the original mission station. By cooking, running a girls'
home, and teaching classes in close proximity to white colleagues at Luebo,
three of the five remaining black missionaries (Maria Fearing, Lilian Thomas
DeYampert, and Lucius DeYampert) came closest to symbolizing the type of
interracial workplace cooperation that had been celebrated at the founding of
the mission.[47] And their work was expected to help make the Congo Mission
more efficient over time.

Colonial Industries and the Congo Mission Cotton Plantation

Sometime in 1911, Alonzo and Althea Brown Edmiston returned to the
Ibanche mission station under unusual circumstances. Neither the family nor
the denomination preserved the documentation explaining why they returned.
The flaunted goal of recruiting six white male missionaries had not been fulfilled, the YMCA still sought to hire Edmiston, and the unofficial ban on
hiring Fisk graduates had not been lifted. Yet the Edmistons worked for about
two more years as the full-time Presbyterian representatives in their favorite
part of the Kuba kingdom and welcomed their second son, Alonzo Leaucourt
Bope, on 27 May 1913. The personnel shortage compelled the Congo Mission
to consider retaining experienced candidates.[48] But the justification for their
return—and the relative denominational silence about it—also resulted indirectly from the increasing convergence between humanitarian reform movements and standardized labor demands.

Dr. George Washington Carver's emerging research on the means for starting and expanding cotton plantations and the Tuskegee cotton expedition in Togo contributed to making Tuskegee a global model for African American industrial education.[49] The German colonial government hoped that labor methods similar to those used to control black sharecroppers in the New South could be applied to maximize the production of subjugated "Negro" villagers in this West African colony.[50] Andrew Zimmerman noted in *Alabama in Africa* that the cotton expedition garnered additional interest in the Tuskegee model by Germans in East Africa, British growers in Sudan and West Africa, and French textile manufacturers with plans to start cotton production in West Africa.[51] Edmund D. Morel, one of the British leaders of the humanitarian reform effort against King Leopold II's government, provided one reason for the transnational appeal of Tuskegee-style industrial education in his study *The Black Man's Burden.* Though he condemned the torture and exploitation instigated by that regime, Morel preferred alternatives that still relied on white supervision of African workers.[52] Within the Belgian Congo, political reform translated into shifting rhetoric about the colonial industries and their labor requirements. The cotton and mining companies were embedded within an educational network through the eventual addition of agriculturalists, agricultural monitors, and government-sponsored schools that offered specified training for these industries. The American Presbyterian Congo Mission expanded its influence in the early years of the Belgian Congo by contributing to this educational network with its own renewed focus on industrial and agricultural schools.

Analysis of the Edmistons' second term of duty at the Congo Mission helps explain the implications of this colonial enthusiasm for cotton and for concepts of modern "Negro labor" after the human rights campaign against King Leopold II ended. They returned about two years after the king's private colony was renamed the Belgian Congo under the control of that nation's government. The Southern Presbyterian mission administrators were hoping for improved relations with Belgian officials in the wake of the 1909 libel trial, and there was a similar interest in change from the government's perspective. Belgian officials started promoting colonial agriculture partly because of its established popularity among other colonial powers. The association of German West African plantations with the Tuskegee Institute offered the partnership a semblance of systematic development and academic modernity. The developing ideology of "a colonial civilizing mission" that Zimmerman found as motivating European enthusiasm for industrial education seems to have also underlain the internal political plans to differentiate the Belgian Congo from its predecessor, the Congo Free State.[53]

After 1909 Belgian officials started to offer land grants for cotton plantations within the colony, and Alonzo Edmiston helped operate the first plantation venture for the Southern Presbyterian mission. The initial focus on cotton would soon increase the prestige of agricultural missions in the Belgian Congo and provide additional outlets for the work of black educators while also placing the Edmistons' diplomatic roles under additional scrutiny. A businessman named W. Laurens Hillhouse joined the APCM as the designated industrial missionary in 1913. He applied for a one-hundred-acre land grant near the Luebo mission station to start growing cotton in 1914.[54] The application listed his name as the sole proprietor, but the Congo Mission expected to access the land for ministry purposes.[55]

After the deal was finalized, the Edmistons were reassigned from the Ibanche station to Luebo, where Alonzo Edmiston worked the Hillhouse land while Althea Brown taught in the girls' school. Preaching, rural evangelism, and foster care for girls had remained the priorities of the Ibanche station in the four years since its founder, William Sheppard, had returned to the United States.[56] Since the industrial school program that Edmiston pioneered in 1905 had been discontinued in his absence, it is likely that he had devoted much of his time to traveling evangelism and the founding of outstation churches. So the move to a farm was a notable shift in Edmiston's career trajectory.

Reassignment to the Hillhouse land isolated him from most local church members and potential converts by keeping him on the border of the mission station throughout the workday. Full-time farming at Luebo also reduced the couple's potential for ministerial collaboration. Though Edmiston had been able to demonstrate the spiritual value of learning the Kuba language when he traveled as a preacher to Kuba villages around Ibanche, the move to Luebo made him one of several Presbyterian missionaries who did not regularly interact with Kuba speakers. The lack of demand for ministry publications in the language of the reclusive Kuba nation would be used to delay the publication of Althea's Kuba dictionary and grammar for about twenty years after she wrote it.[57]

The model American-style plantation that Laurens Hillhouse and Alonzo Edmiston tried to create in the Belgian Congo was part of a period of cash crop strategizing for the colony. The Belgian rubber trade was in sharp decline by 1914, and the Great War heightened that nation's need for another lucrative industry.[58] The Belgian government started to promote cotton agriculture during the final years of the war with a trade system that soon relied on mandatory harvesting quotas. Government-sponsored "agricultural experimental stations" introduced cotton to certain villages in the northern regions of the colony by offering reductions in tax burdens.[59] Through its organizational structure and long-term goals, Hillhouse Plantation functioned as an experimental station seeking government recognition at least through 1917. The Ad Interim Committee at the Luebo mission station expressed disappointment that the regional agricultural director did not show more interest in the endeavor.[60]

Hillhouse expected that a successful cotton harvest on his land would become the forerunner to widespread cotton cultivation in the Kasai region.[61] He understood that the broader agricultural scheme would be under the control of the Belgian government and reliant on local Luba workers. Hillhouse designed his plantation to demonstrate the means for plentiful cotton production and an amenable labor force. Knowing that forced labor had been outlawed after the transition from the Congo Free State, the missionary expected that Luba villagers would need access to food crops and regular profits from the cotton trade as incentives to continue in the work.[62] Besides his confidence in the eventual success of his farming methods, Hillhouse had legal reasons to expect an imminent increase in cotton agriculture in the areas around the Congo Mission. The Belgian government started requiring its colonists to complete two days of agricultural labor per week in 1917.[63]

Alonzo Edmiston devised two strategies that increased his leadership opportunities after he was reassigned to assist at the cotton plantation. He followed the model of the Tuskegee expedition in part, but with less emphasis on the commercial goals of cotton cultivation. First, he built popular demand for the plantation not to follow its original one-crop plan. According to a younger colleague, Roy Cleveland, Edmiston started circulating weekly produce lists to each household of Luebo missionaries.[64] They could choose which of the items from his fruit and vegetable plots they would like to have delivered to their homes at the end of the week.[65] He also started keeping goats and other livestock as a source of fresh milk and meat.[66]

The lists appealed to the Cleveland family as a refreshing convenience for themselves and their children, but they were also a subtle usurpation of denominational policy.[67] Since Laurens Hillhouse was the designated authority over the plantation, only he could authorize major changes to its goals. And Hillhouse envisioned a thriving cotton plantation that could be replicated eventually through additional land grants.[68] Appealing to commercial interests seemed like a clear way to ensure state permission for the future expansion of the Congo Mission. But Edmiston found power in appealing to the current personal interests among his colleagues: milk for the babies and vegetables that reminded them of home. As long as the other missionaries clamored for more of the farm assistant's weekly rations, Edmiston would not be told to focus all his time and all the acreage on cotton.

In May 1915 Edmiston planned a further expansion of his role at the Hillhouse plantation through the development of an experimental farm. He submitted a framework that listed his team's agricultural output over the previous year and suggested ways to increase the farm's usefulness to the foreign and African communities near Luebo. The document started with a list of the crops Edmiston's group of thirty-three workers had planted as experiments that year and ended with eleven recommendations to transform the farm into "an information bureau." All but one of the experimental crops (cotton) had been vegetables, and five of those vegetables had been used primarily to supplement the meals of resident missionaries.[69] Regarding the farm employees, Edmiston showed special concern for the underage boys who lived at the mission station and were hired at less than half the wages of the grown men in the same positions. He appealed for recreation time to be added to the boys' schedules as a way to designate the farm as "a place of instruction rather than a place of labor."[70] Edmiston's plan for fellow missionaries was that they would appeal to him and the farm employees for gardening advice that they would apply to starting small gardens near their homes. And local Kete villagers would continue to get advice on soil and crop maintenance through visits from the missionaries and farm employees. Edmiston hoped to enhance those learning opportunities through additional training in caring for livestock.[71]

Laurens Hillhouse's marginal comments on the typed draft of the experimental farm plans were revealing. He crossed out Edmiston's suggestion "that the Farm be made *purely* experimental" to recommend the phrase "largely experimental" instead, adding that this topic might be "better left to the Work Committee." The plan to teach villagers about "the raising of fowls and domestic animals" was also eliminated in favor of a specification that the use of "native fertilizers" should be taught by the farm.[72] The removal of these two provisions limited the potential for community empowerment in the original plan. Access to domestic animals could mean access to additional nutritional and financial options for African villagers. The ability to maintain their own livestock meant that the animals' owners could count on having meat for their families and other items to sell at the market besides the mandated cotton yield. This type of reasoning might have been what motivated Edmiston to include hogs, chickens, and ducks among the suggested experimental resources that the farm could help popularize.

The other change that Hillhouse made was significant for opposing Edmiston's goal for the farmworkers; if the Belgian government had granted permission for the Hillhouse farm to operate as a cotton plantation business, it would have become "a place of labor" primarily. So Hillhouse did not object to the parts of Edmiston's plan that called for improving the farm's harvests of vegetables or for adding fruit and local edible plants as long as the experimental farm would not commit to planting all crops "on a small scale." Hillhouse's suggested edit implied that the mission station farm might later proceed with a format that would encourage both increased cotton cultivation and an increased variety of edible crops. But the fact that the farm rented parts of its unused land to villagers at a charge of 25 percent of the harvest suggests that both visions for the farm could not have coexisted long-term.[73] Agricultural patterns throughout the colony in the following decades showed that demand for the cash crop would have probably compelled increasing use of the sharecroppers' and the experimental farmland for this purpose, to the detriment of nutritional concerns.

The Edmistons' next opportunity came through embracing the race-based assistantship role and applying it to fit Belgian political interests. In 1916, after working at the Hillhouse Plantation for about two years, Alonzo Edmiston started managing the defunct Ibanche station. Both sites were under scrutiny because of lack of productivity at the time. The first cotton harvest at the plantation had not been profitable, and Hillhouse foresaw continuing difficulties with the care and trade of the produce owing to wartime conditions. Meanwhile, the Congo Mission had closed the Ibanche station in 1915 to establish the new Bulape station closer to the capital city of the Kuba kingdom. The Edmistons might have received permission to run an officially failed mission station because of Laurens Hillhouse's continuing optimism for a cotton-based partnership between the Southern Presbyterians and the Belgian government. Though no records were preserved to document the goals that the Congo Mission set for Ibanche under Alonzo Edmiston's management, his journal indicates that he devoted much of his first year back at the Ibanche station to teaching cotton cultivation to villagers while producing food and agricultural supplies for his colleagues at the Luebo mission station.

Though the Hillhouse Plantation did not flourish in its first three years of operation, the government-sponsored agricultural experiment stations did yield cotton harvests large enough to calm lingering doubts about the expansion of the industry.[74] These stations were established with the participation of African chiefs governing villages under the influence of Belgian territorial administrators.[75] They were the forerunners of the system of corporate harvesting contracts that expanded throughout the colony in the 1920s. Such a widespread agricultural network depended on reliable information about the climate and labor capacity of each region, which was difficult for colonial authorities to obtain for the areas that remained isolated from cities and trade posts. So it is no coincidence that Alonzo Edmiston started providing details about rainfall and soil quality after he returned to managing Ibanche in 1916; the details were valuable to Belgian authorities and investors interested in maximizing profits from cotton grown in the Kasai.[76] His ability to gather those details in a remote location strengthened Edmiston's position as a regional leader.

The Ibanche mission station employees and local Christians worked through 1917 and 1918 to produce cotton, food crops, and building supplies according to Alonzo Edmiston's specifications. Local instability incited throughout 1916 by tax collection and the military draft prevented the Ibanche station from sending reliable shipments of surplus produce or supplies during that year. And Edmiston did not start planting cotton at the mission station and teaching cotton cultivation in the surrounding Kuba villages until January 1918, about seven months before the couple would be instructed to leave Ibanche again.[77] Yet the lack of a profitable cotton harvest from Ibanche did not diminish the significance of Edmiston's agricultural projects there. His report showed a reliable trend of increased productivity from 1917 to 1918 through the items grown, gathered, created, and purchased in behalf of the missionaries.[78] Without replicating the results of a cotton-based agricultural experiment station, Edmiston helped prove such experiments could flourish in Kasai.

As I explain further in chapter 3, unique agricultural experiments flourished at the Ibanche station under Edmiston's supervision. The mission station workmen helped him design affordable ways to produce syrup and sacramental juice from local fruits. He also started observing which local and foreign vegetables thrived in the climate. Both activities drew attention from his Congo Mission colleagues at the Luebo station, but it was the ability to fill supply orders that defined the role of Ibanche station in its final years. Edmiston and his workmen harvested and prepared most of the *malala* (local straw) that was used to create new roofs for Luebo station buildings, and local market women provided corn that Edmiston was directed to purchase for use at the Luebo station.[79] And regional chiefs also helped in the supply endeavor by directing their villagers to provide additional labor at the mission station in addition to maintaining their family gardens. These efforts provided for the growing population of staff members at the Luebo station and were compensated by the Congo Mission on the basis of the market value of the produce.

The scheme of relying on labor from the Christians who lived near Ibanche station without including their community as an active part of the Congo Mission suggests that its status was more akin to that of a colonial government agricultural experiment station. Through the fulfillment of periodic orders, the APCM kept track of the physical capabilities of these villagers rather than following up on their spiritual development. Even after an aggressive 1916 military drafting campaign that led most of the local population to flee into the forest for days, the track record for successful harvest and delivery of supplies from Ibanche remained strong enough that the Congo Mission hoped to continue the strategy after the Edmistons were relocated back to Luebo.[80]

Alonzo Edmiston had nursed concerns over the years that the supply orders caused too much disruption of the villagers' private harvest schedules, but he justified the difficult process as part of obedience to the ministry.[81] Once his ministry at Ibanche ceased for the final time, however, Edmiston did not mask his opinion that the system exploited the local workers. When the local chiefs informed him that they intended to relocate their villages farther away if the mission station was closed indefinitely, he noted simply that "the old men are hard to fool."[82] At the end of their tenure at Ibanche, the Edmistons grieved over leaving their preferred work venue and not being allowed to accomplish more there. Yet Alonzo Edmiston had achieved a lasting accomplishment by setting a model of efficient labor management in the central region of the colony. That model of organizing villagers' labor through chiefs and concentrating their efforts on fields near foreign stations or trading posts would be replicated throughout Kasai over the following decade.

After 1920 the Kasai region became one of the concessionary zones in the Belgian Congo controlled by different companies for the purpose of cotton production.[83] The government company, Compagnie Cotonnière Congolaise, or Cotonco, held the contract to profit from the arable land in Kasai as well as from the labor of its population.[84] Counting and locating that population was important to the financial plans of Cotonco; though men were expected to make up the agricultural workforce, entire families often needed to participate in order to meet planting and harvesting deadlines.[85] As the government company consolidated its control over the region and started to require the establishment of additional cotton fields, the APCM became instrumental in the implementation of its plans. Specifically, both Edmistons took on increasing responsibility for managing the manual labor of children. Alonzo Edmiston also gained additional visibility with the state through his supervisory role in the native court and in census planning.

Mission Station Towns and Child Labor

From the mid-1920s until Althea Brown Edmiston's death, the couple worked at the Mutoto station outside the Kuba territory. Besides traveling occasionally to preach or lead Bible studies for rural congregations, the Edmistons grew close to the residents of Kankalenge, the village nearest the mission station. Edmiston was assigned by the Congo Mission to supervise church development in this village, and both he and Brown shared responsibility for some of the village children living in the Mutoto boarding schools. Forced cotton cultivation affected these groups of potential converts in detrimental ways.

Unlike the villages that had flourished around the Ibanche station after its founding, Kankalenge village was a government-designed settlement with a controlled population. Its residents needed active labor contracts to remain there as well as permission from one of the local authorities to travel outside its confines. These types of monitored communities were especially common within the Cotonco concession as the means to keep a steady agricultural labor force in place near planned cotton plots. And, in their final decade of service, the Edmistons were among the missionaries whose work ensured that such settlements would produce the expected amount of labor for government investors.

The region around the Mutoto mission station became part of the extensive concession of Cotonco in 1920, when this Belgian company was founded.[86] The adult male villagers in this region were considered by virtue

Figure 2.1   The home of Alonzo Edmiston and Althea Brown Edmiston at the Mutoto station. Edmiston drew the mark to indicate the room where Brown died in 1937. From the A. L. Edmiston Papers, RG 495, box 8, Presbyterian Historical Society, Philadelphia.

of geography to be part of the potential labor force for the cotton company. This particular company claimed the largest amount of cotton territory in the Belgian Congo, so it also relied on a large network of cotton monitors, territorial administrators, and agronomists to monitor workers. In addition to this corporate surveillance, state officials sent police to conduct periodic patrols of villages, limit travel, and enforce compliance with rules regarding household layouts and social activities.[87] These were the constraints that the students, disciples, and evangelists of the Mutoto Presbyterian mission faced while continuing their searches for spiritual freedom.

Meanwhile, the APCM continued the reorientation of its working relationship with the Belgian government. New and returning missionaries were gaining French language and cultural knowledge through extended stays in Belgium en route to the mission field.[88] The political connections of Alonzo Edmiston's work also changed during his decades at Mutoto. He was appointed the head of the "native court" in 1931, after serving on the organizing committee the previous year.[89] With a panel of fellow missionaries and evangelists, he assigned punishments that included farm labor and public whipping.[90] Local evangelists participated in the deliberations, but Edmiston had to be present for the native court ruling to be considered valid.[91] Edmiston also shared responsibility for conducting the annual census of the Kankalenge village and reporting unauthorized residents.[92] He signed travel passes to permit these villagers to leave and reenter their communities, and he served as an occasional mediator when evangelists or chiefs from an outstation village were placed in the custody of state police.

Each of these tasks assigned to Alonzo Edmiston involved an essential aspect of power acquisition for the colonial government. The native courts have been called "the incarnation of repression" in the Belgian Congo for the ways they enabled quick, public retribution for dissent.[93] The original stated intent of providing a forum for Africans' palavers masked the influence of government officials and chiefs who could sway the judgments and the level of corporal punishment required. This potential for political influence was stronger in the Kasai region because its cotton company had a pattern of forging connections with retiring government officials in search of lucrative new positions.[94] The Mutoto station tribunal was one of at least twenty-seven native courts in the Congo-Kasai province as of 1931.[95] Local chiefs and cotton monitors could arrange for villagers to be brought before the native court. The villagers' level of cooperation with Belgian territorial officials and employers could then become a factor in the deliberations of guilt or innocence.[96]

The decision to keep Alonzo Edmiston at the head of the Mutoto native court resulted in two implicit complications that could favor the interests of the cotton companies rather than the villagers. First, his supervision of the mission station farm and his agricultural advocacy in the outstation villages ensured that Edmiston's relationships with evangelists and church members would include some observation of their labor habits. The meticulous notes in his journal regarding the size and condition of gardens in each outstation read as evaluations of each evangelist's effectiveness but also served as benchmarks by which potential defendants could hope to gain his favor.[97]

Though Edmiston did not say so explicitly, it is also likely that some of the evangelists he worked with around Mutoto served as cotton monitors for Cotonco. He had recommended some of his agricultural students to fill a commissaire's request for "agricultural teachers or instructors" in December 1919.[98] Presbyterian evangelists served on the judicial panel of the native court each year, and their connection to Edmiston gave them credibility for using labor and agricultural productivity to evaluate character in that court. That scenario would have been attractive to cotton monitors, whose willingness to use brutality, kidnapping, and extortion as labor-motivating techniques became notorious throughout the colony.

Second, the isolating influence of racial incidents among the APCM colleagues helped reduce Edmiston's mediating influence in political concerns other than agricultural productivity. While his ministry roles were constrained at the mission station and his notifications of significant APCM meetings diminished after 1926, the attention his work received from state agronomists increased. Edmiston received his first award from King Albert in 1926 in recognition of his agricultural work. It matters that the award honored Edmiston's farm ministry as service to Belgium. His second government commendation was awarded in 1932, when both the Edmistons were celebrated for more than twenty-five years of service in the region.[99] He was also invited to become a member in the National Geographic Society because of his experiments with local crops. During his years with the native court, Edmiston received increasing government recognition for a specific facet of his work while the rest of his Presbyterian ministry seemed to face indifference or outright opposition.

This wave of political affirmation preceded by a few years an official policy change toward the use of awards and incentives to motivate cotton growers in the Belgian Congo.[100] Likewise, the efforts that state officials and agronomists made to laud Edmiston as an agricultural expert might have been arranged with regional agricultural productivity in mind. It's possible that these officials calculated that Edmiston would focus harder on agriculture as his sphere of influence and use the court to punish those who were accused of taking it lightly.

The National Geographic Society

Through the Board of Trustees at a meeting held in Washington District of Columbia in the United States of America on the *fifteenth* day of *June* 19*23* has elected

Alonzo Lmore Edmiston

of

Luebo Congo Belge, Central Africa

a member of that Society

In Witness Whereof, this certificate has been signed and presented

_____
Secretary.

Figure 2.2   A 1923 National Geographic Society certificate of membership for Alonzo Edmiston. Courtesy of Herbert Edmiston. Photograph by the author.

In the meantime, Althea Brown balanced assignments as a Mutoto hospital nurse, middle school teacher, and temporary girls' school matron. Her last few years as an instructor coincided with the implementation of an incentive-based corporate plan to increase cotton production for Cotonco. Her mentors, Maria Fearing and Lilian Thomas DeYampert, had introduced boarding school students to the use of sewing machines, one of the consumer items that the companies started to provide to families that met or exceeded harvest quotas.[101] The medical training that she had gained before joining the APCM helped enable the founding of two Presbyterian hospitals in the region, which were needed partly because the use of migrant labor throughout the colony had increased risks of epidemics such as the flu. But Brown's connection to the context of cotton production had more to do with contemporary controversies regarding child labor and corporal punishment.

Since child labor was illegal in the Belgian Congo, the APCM followed the precedent of other missions in classifying the work of young station residents as part of their educational duties or paying off demerits.[102] Brown sent students regularly to work off demerits at her husband's farm, but she also expressed concern about situations when students seemed to draw an inordinate amount of disciplinary work.[103] In particular, she defended students when it appeared that accusations of disobedience were false, and she advised that children who did not seem likely to follow the rules of the boarding schools should be allowed to return to their parents long-term. The APCM did not heed her advice in one case involving the Mutoto girls' school, which led to a significant controversy involving corporal punishment.

When the matron of the girls' school left Mutoto on furlough, the Edmistons co-managed the project in her absence. They shepherded several changes in the school during those two years, including the construction of a new school building. Althea Brown also hoped to change the age limit for the boarding school, thereby barring enrollment to teenage girls. She found this age group to be the least cooperative and the most likely to violate curfew. Her concerns came to fruition in 1934, when several of the older girls from the boarding school were caught skipping school with their boyfriends and encouraging fellow students to do likewise. Since Brown also served on the Girls' Home Committee, she joined in the recommendation for the girls' punishment to be spanking. The responsibility for carrying out the spankings was assigned to A. A. Rochester and Alonzo Edmiston, who complained that the energy required to hold down and slap twenty-five tall girls left him emotionally and physically drained.[104] The girls' parents reacted angrily; at least one demanded that the missionaries not keep his child if they could control her only with force.[105]

This incident was not the first time that Alonzo Edmiston had documented his use of corporal punishment while living in the Belgian Congo; he had used spanking as a disciplinary measure with students from the boys' home who had refused to complete chores in the past. But the choice to spank this group of girls agitated local Christians in a way that the other incidents had not. Church attendance in the nearest village declined drastically the following weekend.[106] The ritual of public whipping had become the dominant tool of military police and cotton monitors by the 1930s. This form of discipline was authorized for use in prisons in 1931, and results were fatal for some of the imprisoned rebels.[107] The illegality of using physical force on women did not prevent widespread rumors that officials could do so anyway without repercussions.[108] Internal correspondence for the Congo Mission indicates that the missionaries were aware of the reputation earned by any use of corporal punishment in this oppressive environment. All the missionaries were told to cease whippings of African youths after 1910.[109] When the black missionaries participated in the punishment of the teenage girls, their actions implied that this mission policy could be broken at will. The girls and their parents reacted to the unspoken message that the missionaries were a special group exempt from legal oversight.

The spanking incident at the girls' school was the most public controversy regarding the physical discipline of children at the Mutoto mission station. Yet the Edmistons had faced concerns over the role of labor in their education programs since 1919. At least fourteen boys left during the first year of the Luebo Agricultural College because of their concerns about the daily schedule. Most of these students complained that the recreation time was too short, whereas a few argued that the farmwork itself was too strenuous. One Kuba man withdrew his son from the school and returned with him to Ibanche. What was notable in Edmiston's reactions was that he focused on the offense against the facility—referring to the boys as runaways and the father as a thief—while contrasting these exceptions with the students "who want to learn."[110] The choice of punitive language was meaningful in a context in which the colonial government was in its first years of mandating agricultural labor from its subjects.

It was only after the closure of the Agricultural College that the Edmistons started to enforce fieldwork as an occasional form of punishment rather than an academic asset. The students who brought a formal com-plaint against Edmiston in 1936 based their claim that he had abusive intentions on his attitude regarding demerits. When other mission station teachers, including Brown, sent students to the farm, it was a form of after-school detention that would remove the demerits from the students' records. Edmiston's defense was that he had described the farm as "a place of work and not school" only when it involved the process of working off demerits. But his response did not grapple with the students' suspicions that the bal-ance of work and education at Mutoto had tilted permanently against their interests. Expectations of students' labor productivity were factored into the annual budget through the consensus that additional paid station workers were not needed.[111] Fees for required books, supplies, and tools increased, yet boys in the home were threatened with whipping if they neglected to bring their work tools to the morning chapel service.[112] And soon after the fees increased, Edmiston started planning construction of two additional boys' homes—each with a dedicated farm that was intended to help sup-port village churches.[113]

In 1931 the visiting PCUS executive secretary for the Committee of Foreign Missions recommended that the boys' home require more "per-sonal work" from its residents.[114] If Dr. Egbert W. Smith was referring to domestic service, then his advice harkened back to the labor practices of the first five years of the American Presbyterian Congo Mission. Luba children who had been displaced by the internal slave trade lived at the Luebo station in the homes of the missionaries who worked there in the early 1890s: the Sheppards, the Snyders, Samuel Lapsley, Maria Fearing, Lilian Thomas, and Henry Hawkins. After Fearing and Thomas started the first Presbyte-rian home for female orphans, these "house girls" started performing chores for households managed by older local girls rather than by American missionaries.

It remained customary for the missionaries' households to include domestic servants through the late 1930s, but the trend switched to the employment of adult maids or butlers. After the fall of the Congo Free State, the new government banned child labor. Edmiston might have declined to make the boys at Mutoto participate in domestic service for missionaries out of concern that the old system could be reinstated. He might also have wanted to avoid comparisons with the Roman Catholic missionaries, whose stations were charged with violating child labor laws in a 1936 report.[115] In either case, Edmiston made regular budget requests to hire additional adult workers rather than basing the infrastructure and produce needs of the station on the work of students. And he continued to recruit student workers and village volunteers to complete required projects when his requests for additional paid workers were not filled.

The Edmistons' options for promotion or additional autonomy within the mission station looked slim by the fall of 1932. The couple had served among the Luba people at their new mission station for about twelve years after closing down two initiatives that had been close to their hearts: the Ibanche station and the Agricultural College. Althea's dictionary and grammar had been published that January with financial support from Fisk University donors, but the APCM still released no plans to use the text for ministry.[116] Meanwhile, Edmiston's efforts to continue his semiannual evangelistic tours of regional villages had been curtailed after two rollover car accidents. The station committee had voted to prevent Alonzo from transporting other missionaries with him on the assumption that his driving skills were at fault.[117] Nevertheless, both Edmistons found another means to exercise their ministerial goals when he applied his reputation for supervising manual labor to a new initiative. They started traveling more often and interacting with more Kuba and Luba villagers by accepting produce as compensation for the Presbyterian mission churches.

As the missionary assigned to oversee Kankalenge village, Alonzo Edmiston decided to start accepting a tithe of the members' garden and farm crops as payment for their church dues. He advised evangelists throughout the region to follow this method of paying off church debts.[118] Edmiston created tables of common local crops such as bananas, manioc, and corn along with the estimated cash value of each.[119] Church members expressed their excitement and relief upon finding out that they had an attainable means of settling their accounts with the local church.[120] Even without having savings in Belgian francs, these people could remain Presbyterians in good standing simply by growing the types of plants that were already part of their domestic traditions. Community productivity became a literal part of worship for these villagers; they showed their spiritual devotion through their effort in home gardens and through the volume of their donations. Rural church members could join one of the "field committees" Edmiston organized to help their neighbors plant gardens as well.[121] And the Mutoto missionaries also benefited by having a dedicated source of produce for the Bible College, the boarding schools, and the staff at prices comparable to those at the community markets.

Figure 2.3   An example of the agricultural tithe system adopted by church members near the Mutoto mission station. From the A. L. Edmiston Papers, RG 495, box 8, Presbyterian Historical Society, Philadelphia.

Alonzo marketed the new giving system as a solution to the ongoing funding problem at Mutoto; enthusiasm for paying annual church dues had waned against the tide of state taxes, road construction, cotton harvesting, and tribute labor for local chiefs. Edmiston's ability to motivate regional church members to make in-kind donations made him valuable as a traveling evangelist again, which provided a respite from his duties with the mission farm and the boys' home. That benefit was even more pronounced in the context of the ongoing Great Depression, which had affected the economies of Belgium and England as well as the United States. Prices kept rising in the countries where Congo Mission representatives ordered bread and supplies, while Edmiston's farm struggled to feed all the students in the face of intermittent locust infestations.[122]

Edmiston also affirmed the integrity of the church members' intentions by challenging any attempts to corrupt or invalidate the system. When one of the local pastors decided to reduce the value of his church members' peanut donations to one cent, Edmiston warned him that "if they give the people too little for their produce, we could not get them to come again."[123] He encouraged villagers to support the ministers, but not for the sake of any minister's personal wealth.[124] Ensuring honest dealings within the donation system was a way of protecting the integrity of this growing presbytery and celebrating early signs of its strength. Edmiston amplified the visual effect of this alternative tithing ritual by sharing photographs of the piles of donated produce with his fellow missionaries and mission supporters.

The in-kind donation system lasted only about a year before the Mutoto station committee considered ending the practice. Despite the fact that this system cost less for the missionaries than relying on the local food markets, the Evangelism Committee preferred not to buy fruits and vegetables from outstation villages directly.[125] The traveling evangelism involved in publicizing the call for produce as tithes had enabled Alonzo Edmiston to get to know more of the villages around Mutoto and to reunite occasionally with Kuba villagers whom the Edmistons had known at Ibanche. The temporary project did not alleviate his concerns about budget cuts and food shortages in the mission station. It may have increased the Presbyterians' association of Alonzo Edmiston with low-level chores, since a colleague considered Edmiston's status as a Bible College agricultural teacher questionable as late as 1939.[126] In the meantime, the official reports of agricultural ministry at the Mutoto station were filed by the Reverend William C. Worth, who had been appointed as an industrial missionary and was counted among the recognized American instructors.[127]

Incentives for Manual Labor

The designation of Alonzo Edmiston as a farmworker placed his ministry at risk of serving the interests of the colonial government more than those of potential church members. His duties intersected with Belgian demands for labor, village demographics, and cotton cultivation through a mutual desire to increase the productivity of the local soil. Even the plans that Edmiston designed with the intention of providing quality education and facilitating church rituals remained rooted in the exploitative political context of the region; the Agricultural College students could be recruited as cotton monitors, and the in-kind tithing system became strenuous in conjunction with state tax demands. In addition, the use of corporal punishment to enforce rules led to the withdrawals of increasing numbers of students from the mission boarding schools. In the last twenty years of his mission career, Edmiston started what became his best-known initiative in the Belgian Congo: a series of agricultural exhibitions designed to increase enthusiasm for local food cultivation. This initiative also had ties to colonial politics, but Edmiston distinguished his work by avoiding a focus on consumerism.

Agricultural exhibitions in the colony often had an atmosphere akin to a festival's. The state exhibitions included spectacles demonstrating the themes of profit and material success. Attendees could watch dramas, browse displays of model crops, and walk inside full-scale houses designed to show the lifestyles of local farmers.[128] Though a variety of traditional produce was collected to exhibit, the government agronomists always emphasized cotton and its commercial potential. That kind of messaging made sense for the context of the mid-1930s; the Belgian officials drew a crowd by showing off luxury items and implying that diligent cotton farmers could afford them eventually.

In contrast, the Edmistons started their agricultural exhibitions about a decade earlier and maintained a focus on subsistence production. The annual APCM meetings served as their venues, and the variety of their displays increased through Edmiston's experimentation. Sometimes the items on display were vegetables grown by Brown in their private home garden.[129] Most years, Edmiston made the Mutoto mission farm part of the exhibition to teach visiting evangelists about strategies for field preparation and planting. The switch to farm visits brought opportunities for different categories of exhibitions: local staple crops, American transplants like Tennessee watermelons, and student model plots. The results of the two agricultural textbooks that Alonzo Edmiston published gained recognition through these events, when he used banners, signs, and photography to prove the benefits of his methods. At the Edmistons' exhibitions, the crops themselves provided the spectacle, not expensive model homes or luxury vehicles. Prizes were awarded for domestic concerns; the Edmistons adopted a strategy popular in nineteenth-century American agricultural fairs and African American female reform work by hosting contests for "the mothers who bring in the finest and healthiest babies" to the conferences.[130] Edmiston's scrapbooks reveal that the exhibitions also provided a natural role for his younger son, Alonzo Bope, and other young children to fill; the little boys would stand close to giant manioc roots, squash, or watermelons to prove their impressive scale.[131]

The state agricultural exhibitions have been interpreted by the historian Osumaka Likaka as a significant part of the colonial government's attempt to win the compliance of the subjugated people.[132] Through entertainment and advertisement of seemingly attainable goods, the territorial administrators hoped to turn the local focus from mutual suffering to a mutual desire for finer things. Overall, the exhibitions network represented part of the rebranding effort to make the Belgian Congo government seem justifiable and sustainable. For similar reasons, the Edmistons' refusal to adopt a consumer focus in their agricultural exhibitions during the Great Depression was significant. Rather than encouraging attending evangelists and church members to value agricultural work for aspirations of a transformed lifestyle,

Figure 2.4   Alonzo Leaucourt Bope Edmiston and a Congo Mission student posing with a manioc root during an agricultural fair. From the A. L. Edmiston Papers, RG 495, box 8, Presbyterian Historical Society, Philadelphia.

the Edmistons emphasized the pressing goals of the present time. They displayed the crops that would be most nutritious and different varieties of the local staple crops that villagers relied on to survive. That change in approach was enough to show that the Edmistons observed and responded to the perspectives of local people even in the final years of their careers. The following chapter explains how academic institutions in the United States prepared the missionaries to follow this approach to agricultural education.

PART TWO

Specific Educational and Ministry Strategies

The fact that Althea Brown and Alonzo Edmiston devoted over thirty years of individual and joint ministry at the American Presbyterian Congo Mission made them unique in church history. They became the African Americans with the longest missions tenure among Southern Presbyterians and two of the few travelers of African descent to interact with the colonial governments in the Congo Free State and the Belgian Congo. The process of planning evangelism trips in the Kasai region and taking international furloughs over the decades also placed the Edmistons in situations in which they witnessed major global events, including the effects of world wars, the trade implications of the Great Depression, and increasing rates of racial justice protest.

To provide closer evaluation of how the Edmistons' careers reflected broader historical and cultural contexts, the following chapters focus on specific periods when they took on new projects. Part Two revisits the Luebo Agricultural College that Edmiston and Brown established in 1918, the regional crises caused by forced labor and food instability in the 1910s and 1920s, and the black Presbyterian missionaries' ambiguous professional status in the 1930s. In each case, changes in how local African students, villagers, and leaders reacted to conditions in the Belgian Congo led the Edmistons to adapt their own ministry strategies. Further adaptation was required as segregation policies changed within the APCM. These negotiations did not produce a cycle of cooperation among the various groups involved in the APCM. The exploitative conditions in the colony as well as the ongoing oppression in their home base of Selma, Alabama, combined to engross Edmiston and Brown in struggles to claim their parts of a dwindling sphere of influence.

3

Implementing Historically Black Education Strategies at the Presbyterian Congo Mission, 1918–1919

> Unless we are able to give to the masses the things for which their minds are craving, they are going to seek them elsewhere.
>
> Alonzo Edmiston, 1918

The first agricultural college promoted by the American Presbyterian Congo Mission opened in mid-1918 under the reluctant leadership of Alonzo Edmiston. This new position required him to discontinue "with a heavy heart" the Ibanche ministry that he called "my work so dear to me."[1] The new college also required him to extend the seven years of continuous service he had performed since the couple had been dismissed from the Congo Mission in 1908 and rehired quietly in 1911. Fear of disrupting the continuation of their joint ministry had kept Edmiston at his post. But this venture seemed less secure because he doubted that the initial funding would be sufficient to maintain the program.[2] Nevertheless, he envisioned religious and political benefits if the college flourished. The description and goals statement for the Agricultural College was probably drafted with detailed feedback from Althea Brown; the document includes hallmarks drawn from the ministries and expertise of both missionaries.[3] And the statement emphasized two principles that had been crucial to the longevity of the institutions where the Edmistons studied: maximization of resources and flexible academic preparation.

The founding document of the APCM Agricultural College incorporated educational and social benchmarks drawn from the traditions of the American institutions the Edmistons had attended. These specific institutions—Fisk University, Stillman Institute, and Tuskegee Institute—each earned recognition for establishing broader expectations for African

American and African education. This chapter analyzes the Edmistons' educational initiatives with a focus on what they learned from the curricula and reputations of historically black colleges and universities. These academic contributions to the American Presbyterian Congo Mission placed the Edmistons in the position of promoting mergers of industrial and liberal arts education in central Africa in the decade when that combination was deemed increasingly controversial.

Embodying the "Tuskegee Character" and the "Fisk Program" Abroad

The academic backgrounds of Althea Brown and Alonzo Edmiston placed them at the center of the most contentious political debates regarding African American missionaries. Colonial administrators and Protestant missions organizations coordinated to almost eliminate the options for African American leaders to travel to the African continent, basing their selection criteria on a dichotomy between pedagogical styles at Tuskegee Institute and those at the historically black universities that emphasized classical training. The ensuing rhetorical competition regarding the merits of each educational style masked the result that few graduates from either type of institution received permission to maintain careers in overseas missions.[4] A comprehensive analysis of the controversy surrounding HBCU pedagogy should include the perspectives of the African American missionaries who served in western Africa during the first two decades of the twentieth century.

With the influence of the institution's founder, Booker T. Washington, and the support of the Phelps Stokes Fund, the "Tuskegee character" came to represent the form of African American leadership deemed most appropriate for organizing educational and commercial endeavors.[5] Tuskegee's reputation as a model for industrial education under black administration flourished through Washington's promotional efforts, through the innovations of George Washington Carver and other faculty members, and through the community development endeavors of alumni. The infamous "Atlanta Compromise" speech inspired expectations that Washington's leadership would keep Tuskegee's industrial programs financially viable without posing threats to the racially segregated social order.[6]

On campus, the results of industrial education were more complex. Washington advocated for the Tuskegee Institute community to enact economic self-help strategies for the promotion of "simple survival instincts."[7]

The inclusion of liberal arts coursework through its first two decades suggests that a broad curriculum was not perceived initially as a threat to that goal.[8] And the campus continued to host W. E. B. Du Bois and other politically active guests through at least 1928.[9] Because Alonzo Edmiston graduated from a seminary with a working farm and attended the nursing program at Tuskegee, he applied similar self-help strategies to the educational programs he started through the APCM. The trajectory of his career also shifted dramatically because of the Southern Presbyterian leaders' expectations for how he would use his industrial education background.

Founded in 1866 by the American Missionary Association, Fisk University thrived on faith that formerly enslaved people and their descendants could create dramatic social change through creative applications of a liberal arts education.[10] Fisk alumni dominated the rolls of instructors at black schools and colleges throughout the South (including Tuskegee).[11] The "Fisk program" gained recognition among religious leaders in the United States and, eventually, on the African continent. The institutional name was not always attached to that recognition, but by 1900 a consistent counterimage featured prominently in most religious and academic debates regarding the Tuskegee model.[12] It was the counterimage of African American professionals eschewing manual labor and second-class citizenship. Althea Brown, Fisk class of 1901, demonstrated a career trajectory that avoided such a strict dichotomy. She led a rural school, earned a degree in classical languages, and became an accomplished linguist and nurse while also performing manual labor when necessary.

The political implications of West African travels by Tuskegee alumni have garnered scholarly attention. Collaborations between the Tuskegee administration and representatives of European colonial governments were planned in the first decades of the twentieth century, their goal being the expansion of commercial agriculture and mining programs in West Africa. The most extensive of those agriculture programs involved the Togo cotton plantation venture explained in Andrew Zimmerman's *Alabama in Africa*.[13] The historian Kevern Verney listed the expedition as part of the expanding advisory role Booker T. Washington adopted in colonial affairs; he sought to balance Africans' incorporation into European industries with occasional condemnation "of the excesses of European imperialism," especially in the Congo Free State.[14] But, for the specific purpose of evaluating the social significance of Tuskegee education strategies, it is more important to identify some of the Tuskegee Institute curriculum that was not permitted full expression in the United States or abroad.

There was a notable mismatch between the popular image of Tuskegee's industrial education program and the actual priorities of administrators, faculty, and alumni who espoused this academic goal. First, the practical unlikelihood of receiving adequate support for an equipped industrial program necessitated diversity in the ways that educators applied the concept. Segregated school systems, budget cuts, and political complaints against public school taxation in southern states ensured that the kinds of secondary schools that could provide training on factory or office machinery to African American children remained unauthorized or underfunded.[15] At the university level, "industrial education" sometimes became useful as a catchphrase to help administrators attract publicity and potential donors in the 1890s even when the actual curriculum varied.[16]

Likewise in western and southern Africa, African Christians' enthusiasm for "industrial education" seems to have functioned as a preference for high schools and colleges organized by black administrators with community prestige in mind. As the historian Andrew Barnes has emphasized, African Christians were less likely to envision as the only option the focus on manual labor championed by Phelps Stokes Fund representatives. And educators and students on the African continent wrote letters appealing for industrial institutes to be founded in their regions as a step toward expanding the African professional class.[17] They showed special interest in Tuskegee-style "scientific or practical agriculture" programs that were expected to prepare students for success in global markets.[18] Small industrial institutes in the southern United States also often incorporated academic training in order to update their engineering and mechanical programs to the conditions of modern factories.[19] The fact that state governments, colonial administrators, and a charitable foundation coordinated successful efforts to suppress broader interpretations of industrial education did not erase public confidence in the system's potential.

Likewise, the antipathy directed toward Fisk University focused on dismissing its curriculum as unmarketable or politically hazardous rather than valuing the professional flexibility that students gained through this training. After the 1919 Pan-African conference, Thomas Jesse Jones of the Phelps Stokes Fund competed against Du Bois and his potential for recruiting other alumni and students into a transatlantic discourse on black leadership and human rights.[20] But his status as a Fisk graduate did not mean that Du Bois was the only reason that colonial governments and denominational mission boards placed increasing restrictions on travelers affiliated with this university. Althea Brown's first near-dismissal from the Congo Mission in 1908 revolved around concerns that her college education had inspired a temperament incompatible with effective overseas ministry. And the Fisk community had been controversial decades earlier in the Nashville area; Ku Klux Klan members and masked vigilantes launched frequent attacks on Fisk student teachers and others who led small black schools around the region.[21] It was this tradition of making primary education and literacy—not just the postsecondary liberal arts studies—more accessible to rural African Americans that inspired the early attacks.

Yet the violent atmosphere did not diminish the willingness of Fisk students and alumni, including Du Bois and Brown, to teach part-time and during semester breaks. The legacy of the university through the teaching profession features prominently in its most extensive published history. What started as a means for about half of the Fisk student body to pay tuition and boarding fees flourished into a means for Fiskites to exert community leadership and fill prominent positions at some of the best-known industrial institutes.[22] Around the turn of the twentieth century, as rates of racist violence increased and funding sources for African American universities and secondary schools decreased, Fisk student teachers remained active by proving the diverse range of applications for classical studies.

Margaret Murray Washington, the second wife of Booker T. Washington, expressed her respect for the Fisk alumni on the Tuskegee faculty as "by far the best workers" at the industrial institute because of their academic preparation. Murray Washington's own Fisk degree prepared her to help acquire significant funding and endorsements for the university in 1908.[23] Althea Brown recalled the rural school where, about eight years earlier, she taught for two summers as a training ground for quick innovation; she had to create or purchase all the instructional supplies while serving students of various ages.[24] The attitude of Fisk alumni and students toward teaching seemed to follow the moral emphasis behind most forms of student work at American Missionary Association campuses; every teaching appointment offered an opportunity to practice cooperation, self-reliance, and perseverance.[25] The significance of these commonalities made the classical training of these Fiskites directly applicable even when their assigned schools had a very different academic environment.

Both Edmistons served as teachers or boarding school managers for most of their careers in central Africa. Though their Agricultural College existed for less than two years, their goals for the institution represented the foremost combination of their academic roots and ministerial aspirations. The difficult process of establishing the college was also important in revealing where the pedagogical strategies of Althea Brown and Alonzo Edmiston differed from those of their Southern Presbyterian colleagues. The following section analyzes the short history of the APCM Agricultural College as an example of how these two missionaries envisioned the extension of historically black education abroad.

The Congo Mission Agricultural College as a Merger of Black Education Ideals

Though the Agricultural College program was the most prestigious appointment that Alonzo Edmiston received during his missionary career, he did not want to accept it at first. It is striking that Edmiston seems to have been reluctant to claim expertise in such a high-visibility field when the Agricultural College opened in 1918. By that year, the attention paid to Hampton and Tuskegee at the 1910 World Missionary Conference had flourished into projects to expand similar institutions in India and eastern and southern Africa. The Phelps Stokes African Education Commission formalized these plans with the publication of its 1921–1922 and 1925 reports.[26] Having full management of an institution dedicated to that purpose, Edmiston was still careful in his second school report to reiterate that "certainly we do not emphasize the teaching of agriculture just for the sake of agriculture itself."[27] What was touted as a way to expand Presbyterian outreach and create "a truly self-supporting church" struck the Edmistons as an inadequate excuse for abandonment of their preferred mission field and a suspected threat to Althea's linguistics expertise.[28] Edmiston worried that his promotion as head of the new college served as a ruse "to give me a punishment" and to offer other Presbyterian missionaries control and credit over ministry "with the Bakuba language which my wife has worked so hard on all these years."[29]

Closing their Ibanche mission station permanently caused the couple hardship, yet it also motivated them to identify the aspects of their Kuba work that they considered essential to building a quality school elsewhere. These elements of the Edmistons' plans for the Agricultural College represented priorities drawn from their own academic experiences and ministerial observations: occupational flexibility, crop sustainability, community empowerment, and cultural preservation. And the combination of their

Figure 3.1   Inspecting the school farm at Luebo. From the A. L. Edmiston Papers, RG 495, box 8, Presbyterian Historical Society, Philadelphia.

different priorities under the designation "Agricultural College" enabled the couple to bolster Edmiston's ministerial status through industrial education without abandoning Brown's language-based academic ambitions.

The first claim that stands out in the 1919 progress report for the Agricultural College is the couple's conviction that the curriculum would "equip [students] for whatever other calling they may choose."[30] That goal indicated confidence that the new emphasis on farming could contribute to flexible education without becoming an end in itself. He continued to tout the academic venture as a means "to teach the natives how to do things well" and "count the value of time."[31] Edmiston's focus remained on the personality traits reinforced by agricultural skills—traits that he argued would develop "a higher level of Christian character and Christian living."[32]

And though the Agricultural College reports are not attributed to Althea Brown, her academic priorities influenced the emphasis on broad applicability. Against the preference of a Belgian colonial minister and unlike the Carson Industrial School operating at the Luebo station, the Edmistons' program required French and mathematics lessons.[33] The math instruction aided the students with their required participation in the "pupils' bank" and prepared them to keep business records.[34] And French lessons could help graduates seek professional positions with the Belgian colonial government, specifically as clerks, agricultural monitors, or traveling salesmen.[35] These two curriculum requirements brought the college closer to the status of an arts and science institution than any other academic programs at the APCM in the late 1910s, and they were key to proving that the Edmistons were interested in the financial upward mobility of the students.

Before Althea Brown made her first departure for the Congo Free State, she clarified the reasoning she would use sixteen years later to apply her liberal arts background to the task of founding a trade school for farmers. While being interviewed for a 1902 Student Volunteer Movement convention speech about opportunities for African American missionaries, she argued that "industrial work" was necessary to protect the future of African evangelists and mission school graduates.[36] Her specific observations about the Student Volunteer Movement also applied to the APCM schools at the time; the existing curriculum for African schools was limited to lower grade levels and lacking in professional networking opportunities. Brown endorsed industrial education as a foundation for a secondary or postsecondary institution—an incentive for promising students to extend their connections to the mission and consider ministry.

She said little about the expected technical aspects of the curriculum except that they would help graduates avoid becoming employed in a "demoralizing trade." She was probably referring to the type of trade activity best known to supporters of the Presbyterian Congo Mission around the turn of the twentieth century: the kidnapping and selling of enslaved people. This was the regional practice that her mentors had tried to combat by taking in many emancipated children and adults at the Luebo station.[37] Althea Brown implied that this approach of housing refugees and orphans was insufficient if it did not include a means of training and equipping community leaders. Her main argument for industrial education was that access to additional schooling could increase the number of African ministers with marketable skills—the type of men who she believed had a proven capability to "fill up the churches and govern them."[38] In contrast to the threat of social instability posed by regional slave trading, Brown advocated for American missionaries to do more to educate local leaders who could maintain stable religious centers. Industrial education was instrumental in sustaining the livelihoods of these African ministers, but she expected that these potential industrial students would show their merit by using a variety of other social and religious skills.

Glimpses of Althea Brown's Fisk-style liberal arts approach are evident in the original schedule and policies of the Agricultural College. The five and a half hours of fieldwork on weekdays were supplemented with half an hour of religious education, three hours of classroom time, and at least two hours of recreation.[39] The hands-on application time matched the amount of time given to interpretation of the students' work experience through lecture, catechism reading, and playtime. The schedule served as a reminder that the different activities were connected by a common purpose not defined fully by manual labor; besides working the farm, the students were also expected to understand and value their time at the Agricultural College through their own choices. For example, the stated objective of the recreation time was so that "no pains should be spared to make the pupils happy."[40] They could choose to devote that time to hunting, fishing, or free play, and the missionaries hoped to provide a variety of playground apparatus and musical instruments. Though budget constraints prevented them from acquiring all the equipment they desired, the Edmistons wanted to enable students to choose which recreational activities satisfied their interests and creativity.

Students' input also factored into curriculum development at the Agricultural College. Althea Brown probably played a significant part in translating the first agricultural textbook that Edmiston proposed for eventual publication, but in the interim the missionaries had to explain the book's contents in person and answer students' questions about the material. Edmiston wrote the following year that this process had been time-consuming, yet the results were a high retention rate and responsiveness among the student body.[41] The Edmistons seem to have felt invested in the project because they had helped shape its academic relevance.

It is notable that experimentation was encouraged in multiple activities at the Agricultural College. It was a pedagogical goal that capitalized on both missionaries' educational backgrounds and history of financial need. First, the original plan called for the eventual construction of small "model homes" assigned to some of the children from the dormitories. Each group of girls or boys assigned to live in one of the homes regularly shared responsibilities for cooking, cleaning, gardening, and laundry in the household. These mundane tasks depended on the problem-solving skills of the boarding students, who were expected to show evidence of their preparation to become "thrifty home makers."[42] The idea was an update on two teaching strategies important to Brown's background: the division of Fisk boarding students and teachers into "family" groups and the structure of the Pantops girls' foster home founded by her mentor Maria Fearing. Having observed that several Pantops alumnae had become respected evangelists' wives as adults, the Edmistons considered the group homes concept useful for the future of APCM programs.[43] And Brown had participated in the Fisk version of a model home system when she entered the university at age eighteen. Working cooperatively to complete chores in Jubilee Hall served as her foundational example for how students could help compensate the university for their expenses while contributing to an academic version of a family home.[44] But there were two major differences envisioned for the Agricultural College. Rather than starting with homes for girls, boys would also have the option to participate in domestic training at the college in separate model homes. Also, neither missionary served as a dormitory supervisor in the way that the Fisk University teachers or Fearing had. Students were given time and space to figure out their own way of completing a daily task and encouraged to switch responsibilities periodically.[45] As Althea Brown had done as a student, the Agricultural School students could expect to fill a wide variety of duties and activities in the pursuit of a reputation for resourcefulness.

The second means of experimentation dealt directly with the farm produce. Alonzo Edmiston continued the types of subsistence and commercial agricultural projects he had practiced at the Luebo farm and the Ibanche mission since 1915. Some of the African staff from Ibanche joined him as teachers at the new school.[46] Under his direction, the Agricultural College students planted and harvested corn, beans, pumpkins, and other vegetables. They found by trial and error that a regional type of peas called *kambulu* produced a better crop than imported navy beans.[47] Edmiston also restarted a cane syrup–making venture that had begun at Ibanche in 1917, possibly with the goal of supplementing the institutional budget. The notable omission in his plans for the college was wide-scale cotton cultivation; he mentioned planting the cash crop in 1918 but not the following year.[48] By emphasizing work with vegetables and local plants, Alonzo Edmiston built his case for agricultural missions as an asset for self-supporting churches, and he defied narrow interpretations of Tuskegee-style training.

Inspiration from Stillman and Tuskegee Institutes

A desire to explore the usefulness of non–cash crops characterized Alonzo Edmiston's agricultural work at Ibanche and through the college program. That educational approach was an outgrowth of the strategies he had observed during seminary. Edmiston had learned practical strategies for maintaining organizational self-support through farm produce. Lacking a full scholarship, he probably worked on the campus farm to help pay tuition, as most of his classmates did.[49] The institute itself faced chronic underfunding by the Presbyterian Church in the United States throughout its early history, which compelled its first director to recommend that the campus relocate to a rural area with potential for commercial farming.[50] The plan reflected the ongoing dominance of plantation agriculture in the region and expectations that graduates would serve rural farmers, yet it remained undercut by the relatively small campus landholdings of twenty acres until 1903 and forty-five acres until 1920.[51] Those limitations, combined with the need to have their tuition compensated, inspired the Tuscaloosa Institute (as it was still called at the time) community to enact President Stillman's call for "some practical plan for the self-support of the students" as a focus on what best met the students' social and financial interests.[52] The farm became known for housing livestock, growing fruits and vegetables to supplement campus meals, and selling surplus produce to benefit the institute's general fund.[53]

In the absence of denominational oversight or faculty supervision, the Tuscaloosa Institute farm came to be defined by the subsistence needs and fund-raising ambitions of the student body. Alonzo Edmiston arrived in Tuscaloosa around 1898, possibly just after the institute purchased the former farm that became its permanent location. And though the administration anticipated that the student workers could soon transform that plot of land into "a high state of productiveness," no evidence remains of a strategic plan to profit from those acres.[54] An instructor with farming expertise was not appointed until 1919, nor did a professor with industrial specialties join the faculty until three years later.[55] The absence of academic or administrative records makes it difficult to specify operations at the institute farm around the turn of the twentieth century, but some conclusions about its beginnings can be drawn from the habits and conditions that characterized it by the late 1940s. The campus dining facilities were known for offering high-quality and nutritious meals, its canned goods sold consistently, and the institute could expect earnings of at least $3,500 from the annual harvest during the late 1920s.[56] These outcomes were important for students like Edmiston, who arrived with no local family, outside income, or other ways to pay campus expenses.

An extensive 1947 campus study found that the farm included a general barn and several livestock pens, but the condition of most of these buildings was so dilapidated that they might have been established before the 1920 expansion.[57] What stands out about the continued use of these old buildings is that they had been sufficient for helping the student workers produce inexpensive food and feed crops typical of the region, including peanuts, soybeans, sweet potatoes, corn, and cowpeas.[58] But the layout included no designated space for housing or processing the farm's thirty acres of cotton, the only cash crop listed in the study as part of a typical harvest.[59] That lingering omission suggests that cotton was added to Stillman Institute farm after 1920, possibly as part of hands-on training led by the several farm supervisors who arrived during that decade.[60] That conclusion is strengthened by the fact that all the institute fields were still judged to be fertile by 1947; continuous cotton agriculture has a reputation for diminishing soil quality.[61] Yet, after almost fifty years of continuous use of the twenty-acre plot that Edmiston and other students had helped cultivate, the 1947 campus study found that only a small part of that land needed fertilizing. The student workers had chosen an agricultural plan that met their financial needs while protecting the long-term interests of the institute farm.

After earning his seminary degree, Alonzo Edmiston went to Tuskegee Institute for the nurse training program. Though his name was not listed in the official catalog, the autobiography of a family friend suggests that he enrolled between 1901 and 1903.[62] At the time, nursing coursework included a metallic chemical analysis course cross-listed with the chemistry program.[63] This program provided specified instruction for five different training divisions, including agriculture. Between his participation in a chemistry program that offered practice on the Tuskegee farm and his previous lack of financial aid, it is likely that academic or work-study opportunities led Edmiston to meet the best-known agricultural chemistry expert at the institute.[64] If so, then Edmiston became one of the last Tuskegee students to observe Dr. George Washington Carver's methods of agricultural experimentation while they were directed exclusively toward his original goal: maximizing the benefits of locally grown crops for the sharecropper population surrounding the Tuskegee campus. He also corresponded with Carver in 1926 to help continue that research.[65]

According to Andrew Zimmerman's *Alabama in Africa,* such willingness to expand the trading options of black Southerners was less evident within the Tuskegee agricultural program in the five years following Alonzo Edmiston's departure for the Congo Free State. During an institutional shift away from academic course offerings, Booker T. Washington and other administrators told George Washington Carver to redirect his famously inventive work toward the lucrative cotton cultivation techniques desired by the German and British colonial governments.[66] Having missed that phase of Carver's work, Alonzo Edmiston took to central Africa an expectation that Tuskegee-style agricultural education would help small-time farmers find accessible alternatives to exploitative economic conditions.

The scientific agriculture program at Tuskegee started in 1897 as part of a state-funded experiment station located on the campus. Starting in its second year, George Washington Carver wrote short bulletins designed to explain one of his two goals for the station: "the solving of many vexing problems that are too complex for the average farmer to work out for himself."[67] The findings developed from field research, analysis of other publications, and his preparation to teach courses such as agricultural chemistry and bacteriology.[68] The best-known solutions created through Carver's laboratory experiments included his peanut product inventions, which enabled the marketing of one of the region's most plentiful crops for nutritional and commercial purposes.[69] But it is the style of the scientist's explanations that seems to have influenced Alonzo Edmiston's teaching philosophy more than the specific products that resulted from Carver's work.

The bulletins were published by the Tuskegee Institute student press as a community service and written to avoid scientific jargon. Additional copies could be requested free of charge, and readers were encouraged to respond with relevant questions.[70] All the titles in the first decade were short and focused specifically on wild plants or farm products that were common in the region. That approach indicated that the experiment station was not founded on aspirational goals; it meant to offer "direct benefit to every farmer," depending on the farmer's current conditions.[71] Carver's early references to cotton show his emphasis on subsistence and resource building. His first bulletin advocated increased use of acorns to feed livestock partly as a reaction to the decreasing sale value of cotton harvests. He argued that acorn feed in lieu of corn would be more nutritious for hogs and cows while helping cotton farmers avoid the diminishing profit margin as corn prices rose. The same bulletin suggested reduced use of cottonseed for feeding livestock, which would likewise reduce the financial risk for sharecroppers purchasing the seed on credit.[72] These suggestions acknowledged the pressing need for financial alternatives to the cotton economy while offering a solution that could be implemented with little investment. It was a business strategy that Alonzo Edmiston adapted in 1917 at Ibanche and re-created the following year at the Agricultural College.

Edmiston's syrup "factory" had employed several men and boys to experiment with local pineapples and varieties of sugar cane to determine which produced the best-quality sweetener. Wild variants of red and black sugar cane grew plentifully near the Ibanche station, increasing the potential profits for the mission and for the local workers.[73] In addition to earning wages for starting the business venture, mission station workmen received assistance paying their taxes to Belgian Congo authorities. The experiments revealed that red sugar cane produced sweeter syrup than the black variety, and pineapple syrup had a lighter texture. The ability to offer different types suggests that the business could achieve longevity, and reliable cash flow helped villagers avoid imprisonment for tax debts.

Edmiston and his team of local workmen started the marketing process in mid- 1917 by shipping bottles of syrup from Ibanche to the Luebo mission station at a total cost of 400 francs per gallon, and they expected to sell the products in other regional markets.[74] After the announced closure of Ibanche, the "Aims and Policies" document for the Agricultural College included a plan to build a new facility where students and workmen could cook syrup for mass distribution. If the plan had not been preempted two months after the school's founding by a demand to produce syrup only for APCM missionaries, it might have become a funding stream for the Agricultural College.[75] In the long term, Alonzo Edmiston hoped that graduates would take agricultural strategies such as the syrup venture with them to help sustain self-supporting Presbyterian churches in the Belgian Congo.[76]

Though some of the advice given in the Tuskegee Experiment Station bulletins could help improve financial outcomes, Carver was reluctant to promise specific monetary values for his early experiments. Even in his first publication focused on improving cotton harvests, he preferred to compare the "crop-making power" of each fertilizing method rather than estimate a profit amount.[77] It was a cautious strategy that the institute's developing affiliation with the Phelps Stokes Fund would lead Carver to alter after 1905; thereafter his bulletins about cotton focused on growing techniques with the assumption that individual effort could make that cash crop more profitable.[78] International publicity for the new Tuskegee approach to commercial agriculture flourished through the following decade as the Phelps Stokes Fund encouraged similar educational strategies on the African continent, including the Belgian Congo.[79] Yet the APCM Agricultural College failed to embrace that trend, instead following the older approach of finding value in other types of productivity.

Alonzo Edmiston expressed his divergence from the curriculum changes at Tuskegee Institute implicitly when he listed the agricultural programs that could serve as models for his own venture. He commended the Presbyterian institute in Allahabad, India, and the Methodist Lovedale School near Cape Town, South Africa, for their ability to recruit students from far-flung regions. But he did not list either of his own colleges in the report or draw a comparison with the Lavras Agricultural College and Evangelical Institute, a Southern Presbyterian school in Brazil, other than to acknowledge its success.[80] Though one of the newer Congo Mission missionaries expressed hope that the APCM Agricultural College would develop eventually into a government-recognized Presbyterian industrial institution like the denominational college in Brazil, the Edmistons made no claim to seek sponsorship from the colonial government before the program ended.[81] While their colleagues valued the Lavras College program because the colonial government granted it authority to prepare boys for manual labor and polytechnical positions, Edmiston valued the other two institutions for their popularity among enrolled and prospective students.[82] And in his later reports, Edmiston emphasized any indications that African villagers considered the Luebo Agricultural College worthwhile. He recommended some advanced students for government service, but he did not record that validation from colonial authorities as necessary for the school.

The third strategy from George Washington Carver that seems to have inspired Alonzo Edmiston was his encouragement of community participation through resources that were readily available. The first bulletin from the Tuskegee Experiment Station included an invitation for farmers throughout the state to participate by visiting the campus or by shipping samples that could help students analyze the soil, insects, and plants from various regions.[83] These readers were not required to bring a theory or research technique of their own in order for their contributions to be considered valuable. Likewise, student contributions were not limited to those at a high level of scholarship; agriculture students with limited literacy skills could still assist in staging the photographs and copying the statistical charts that helped make Carver's findings accessible to readers.[84] Though only one photograph of the Luebo Agricultural College remains, Alonzo Edmiston followed that strategy by making scrapbooks and exhibitions of his agricultural experiments with later students. And, as the next section describes, community participation based on local interests and tools was built into the design of the Luebo Agricultural College.

Since the Edmistons took a long-postponed joint furlough in 1920, Alonzo's last duty in behalf of the Agricultural College was to describe its goals and curriculum at the Bulape mission station church.[85] The setting represented the central role that community participation played in the original policy statement of the college. If the college had been allowed to endure, the missionaries planned for village leaders to be involved in recruiting efforts and annual campus conferences. That long-term involvement would have started with the appointment of "big chiefs" from most of the ethnic groups in the region as "honorary members."[86] Their input would help determine which children from regional villages showed the most promise as future students. In addition, these chiefs and their representatives would be invited to visit the campus and share their own ambitions for regional development. Edmiston started by envisioning different village leaders encouraging one another to improve their farming and gardening habits, but he also suggested future exhibitions of African arts, crafts, and farm tools accompanied by a permanent museum of similar Western artifacts.[87]

Art and Inspiration from Fisk University and Stillman Institute

This plan to collect and celebrate a variety of art and objects merged the legacies of Fisk University and Stillman Institute in an African context. A direct inspiration can be traced to the Fisk museum collection that, by the year of Althea's graduation, had grown to over three thousand items related to natural history and ethnology.[88] Implicitly, the plan also spoke to the inspirational symbolism of William Henry Sheppard's Kuba artifacts, and it represented an outlet for Althea's interests in cultural analysis. Moreover, the intent to stage annual arts-and-crafts contests with prizes indicates the Edmistons' commitment to the continued flourishing of regional arts and crafts that would be compared with—but not replaced by—American and European offerings.

Though the most extensive parts of William Henry Sheppard's African art and photography collections were donated to Hampton Institute and the Presbyterian Historical Society, some Kuba sculptures and jewelry from his collection are at the campus now known as Stillman College. In the setting of this Southern Presbyterian campus, the theme represented in these donated items has special meaning. The library exhibits carvings of the Kuba king and the types of textiles and beadwork that would have been used to decorate his throne—items that honored Sheppard's status as the

Figure 3.2   Memorial statue of a Kuba king. From the collection of Dr. and Mrs. Walter D. Sheppard, William H. Sheppard Library, Stillman College, Tuscaloosa, Alabama. Photograph by the author.

first Westerner welcomed by the Kuba royal family. Sheppard enabled aspiring black Presbyterian ministers to see evidence of the political authority he had gained as a missionary. And, though available records do not indicate whether Alonzo Edmiston saw these specific art objects, his journals reveal a consistent interest in forging his own special relationship with a succession of Kuba kings after Sheppard's dismissal from Ibanche. Art provided a possible method of communicating the social and political interests involved in central African mission work to the next generations of potential ministers.

On the other hand, Althea Brown's interest in providing a meeting space for central African political leaders resulted more from her exposure to European classics than from art collections or exhibitions at Fisk University.[89] The Duodecem Literae Virgines (DLV) campus organization that she founded in 1900 continued for over fifteen years as an exclusive training center for the development of leadership skills and "aesthetic and literary tastes."[90] Her choice to associate civic engagement and cultural literacy with the Fisk classics curriculum was significant. As one of the foremost enthusiasts for a classical liberal arts curriculum, Brown personified the most distinctive academic feature at Fisk. Since its founding, the university had defended the need for former slaves and their descendants to have access to mentally rigorous degree programs. Mastery of Greek had been said to symbolize the benchmark proof of equal ability, and it stood in well-publicized contrast to arguments that African Americans were best equipped for a basic, hands-on education.[91] Althea Brown's student club offered a testament to Fisk students' enthusiasm to interpret their Greek and Latin coursework as a preparation to master a variety of new cultural challenges.

The DLV club was among three Fisk women's organizations credited in the campus catalog for encouraging students to practice quality writing, presentation, and political negotiation skills.[92] Students of the Agricultural College could have watched these last two skills modeled by familiar chiefs and village leaders if the annual conferences had started as planned. In addition to affirming the students' connections to their own communities, the school conferences would have encouraged regional dialogue about land development and cultural preservation. The conferences could have also provided physical space for chiefs invited from different ethnic groups to compare the effects of Belgian colonialism throughout central Congo. In these ways, the Agricultural College promised to promote consciousness of broader African identity according to the perspective and priorities of

African leaders—an educational outcome that was not expected from industrial schools in that era.[93]

The literary scholar Susan C. Jarratt credits late nineteenth-century classics curricula at certain historically black universities with sparking students' interests in transnationalism and political resistance. Familiarity with ancient empires and their conflicts offered these students a broader perspective regarding their place in the modern world. They were charged with learning languages for the sake of their patterns and aesthetic qualities rather than for utility in the workplace. And campus oratorical contests encouraged students to combine mastery of classical history with analyses of current events and controversies such as racial and gender equality.[94] Althea Brown had incorporated the student oratorical tradition into her women's club and her summer school teaching while enrolled at Fisk.[95] Her Agricultural College plan created further potential for political consciousness by inviting regional leaders to speak for themselves as honored participants.

Health Concerns, Budgeting, and the Closure of the Agricultural College

Historically black colleges and universities shaped the educational ideals that Alonzo Edmiston and Althea Brown implemented as managers of the Luebo Agricultural College, and the memory of campus hardships also influenced the couple's responses to the budgetary problems and early closure of the college program. Specifically, the couple had prepared for the prospect of operating an underfunded institution because of the personal and organizational poverty they had witnessed at Fisk and Stillman. The perceived financial failure of the Agricultural College left the Edmistons facing the prospect of permanent dismissal from Presbyterian service because of doubts about their leadership qualities for the second time in their careers. Yet the lack of profit had not prevented the Edmistons from making institutional changes that protected their higher priority: the welfare of the students and each other.

Student sacrifice in response to budget crises had been enshrined in the history of Fisk University through the memory of the first Fisk Jubilee Singers; the campus remained open in the 1870s mainly because they had persisted through a grueling international fund-raising tour schedule at a risk to their own health.[96] Likewise, the labor of impoverished students helped keep Stillman Institute solvent for decades while its requested appropriations from the Presbyterian Church in the United States were slow in coming, if they came at all. The need to work off most of her own tuition bills motivated Althea Brown to work for five years either on or near campus. Notably, her jobs served the goal of improving others' material circumstances in the midst of budgetary problems. She provided domestic service for a Fisk faculty member and styled classmates' hair in Jubilee Hall in addition to her rural schoolteaching. These activities set a precedent: Althea Brown and Alonzo Edmiston reacted to budget crises at their mission station by addressing the livelihoods of community members.

The most devastating budget crisis for the Luebo Agricultural College started because of the global flu epidemic of 1918. Travelers and returning Great War soldiers spread the disease to the Belgian Congo; in this case, the virus spread through travelers on the Presbyterian steamship that December. The Edmistons were among the first at the college to become bedridden owing to the influenza virus, partly because neither had recovered fully from malarial fevers they suffered shortly after the move from Ibanche.[97] An infestation of tsetse flies near the farm may have exposed Althea Brown to the sleeping sickness that eventually caused her death. Out of concern for their own safety and the well-being of the students, Alonzo Edmiston started appealing to his colleagues for a better location and better facilities within a few months of the students' arrival. The proposed alternative location was farther away than expected and less well equipped, but the Edmistons agreed to change the school's location temporarily.[98]

After about nine months of classes at the Luebo station farm, the Agricultural College relocated to the Bulape mission station. The move interrupted the second harvest and forced the students and workmen to clear virgin fields with inadequate tools.[99] Edmiston abandoned the original plan for students to plant cotton in favor of a focus on vegetables, probably to replenish the school supplies after the move. The choice of the new location also proved emotionally difficult for the Edmistons, who did not want to commit to another ministry in the Kuba territory unless they could anticipate when it would be uprooted.[100] The college continued operating for about another six months, but it never had sufficient farm acreage or livestock after the relocation.

On 10 November 1919, the APCM committee in charge of finances, business, and industrial work decided that the results of the school did not justify continuing its budget. Two committee members agreed that the proposed closure of the school jeopardized the continued employment of Mr. and Mrs. Edmiston at the Congo Mission; the school's financial woes made them doubt his qualifications as its director.[101] Comparison with the newly reopened APCM Industrial School did not help the case for the Agricultural College. Alonzo Edmiston remembered J. Hershey Longenecker implying "that I was not worth the money that the church was spending on me out here."[102] Longenecker was one of two newer colleagues hired after 1914 to lead work projects at the Luebo station.[103] Under the direction of Carroll Stegall and Longenecker, the Carson Industrial School emphasized some lessons similar to those of the old Ibanche program. The classes in shoemaking, tanning, tailoring, cabinetmaking, carpentry, and bricklaying were intended to produce bed mats, stable doorways, thick boots, and dining tables for the sake of local public health.[104] Longenecker considered it a discouraging sign that several graduates relocated to the colonial cities to receive wages from European companies instead.[105] By extension, he faulted the Edmistons' educational program for emphasizing the students' access to personal finances, professional flexibility, and the colonial language. Such goals were not targeted to the potential of a self-supporting local church as much as his industrial program goals intended.

The 10 November meeting turned out to be one of the lowest points in the couple's professional history; the losses incurred during the relocation had exacerbated older concerns about African American missionaries elevated beyond an assistantship role. Edmiston interpreted the resistance as a sign that "it is not my efficiency or the way I spend the mission's money but my color that makes the way hard for me."[106] He had anticipated the budgetary concerns and even considered retiring from mission service to avoid the contention about finances.[107] The choice to sacrifice a harvest season and the main asset of the Agricultural College (its access to fifty acres of the old Hillhouse plantation) made sense only from the perspective that the students' well-being outweighed the expected benefits of their farmwork.

"A Real Month of Jubilee"

If the Agricultural College had continued as planned, Alonzo Edmiston envisioned that each school year would feature a time to celebrate the accomplishments and goals of students' home communities. This "month of Jubilee" would have coincided with the annual conference of regional chiefs and village representatives on the campus and offered them time to encourage one another in farming, arts, crafts, and home management.[108] The biblical reference also involved the celebration of nationwide debt cancellations.[109] Edmiston's use of the phrase "month of Jubilee" showed undue optimism that regional cooperation under the guidance of the Congo Mission could succeed despite the economic turmoil in the region.

A brief overview of the student population at the Luebo Agricultural College reveals some of the social and cultural factors that altered the missionaries' plans. Of the 150 students who enrolled initially, a little fewer than half had left the school by its second term. Their reasons for leaving varied from illness, family obligation, and inability to relocate to the new site to disappointment with the farming schedule. Originally, most students were sent by parents in regional villages, so those whose parents had not expected the work requirement returned home. The ethnic demographics on campus fit trends in other APCM schools, as Luba and Lulua students attended in greater numbers than their Kete and Kuba counterparts.[110] As many as seventy students attended during the 1919 school term at the new site. Only thirteen of the students had failed to advance beyond the basic reading course by November 1919, even though most of the students had started at that level upon arrival. These statistics indicate that students from the regional ethnic group least likely to control large landholdings—the migrant Luba tribe—were among the most numerous Agricultural College attendees.[111] Considering that a harvest was lost because of the relocation, the increase in literacy rates was possibly the most dramatic change that resulted from student work at the college. In other words, the Edmistons' Agricultural College seemed on track to produce many advanced bilingual readers with training in the government language but fewer farmers prepared to work in their village.

These findings did not mean that the campus had isolated students from the surrounding communities. Personal connections in nearby villages remained important to the Agricultural College students; losing permission to visit a village during recreation time was a severe punishment. Parents visited often, sometimes to bring gifts and compliments for the program.[112] Public punishment was reserved for occasional theft of tools or clothes—usually committed by a group of male students who wished to take those items back to their own villages.[113]

Yet it was the pattern of theft and student withdrawals that indicated the looming threat that colonial taxation posed to the villages and by extension to the college. The students who complained about the rules and the required workload might have sought to avoid the least advantageous labor rather than avoid manual labor itself. As the Belgian government started monitoring colonial cotton production in 1917, enrolled students left their parents' homes during the first years that villages faced increased pressure to complete agricultural work quotas.[114] The penalties for failing to fulfill this type of colonial tax burden included imprisonment, additional fines, and forced labor. The historical context suggests that students who left the college or stole supplies during these years would have probably expected to find similar tasks in their home villages; the addition of an extra worker or extra tools could have eased the burden on their families.

The Edmistons envisioned annual conferences at the Agricultural College as a time for mutual encouragement by regional leaders, but in practice the campus community developed through shared grief over illness and inadequate provisions. The developing crises of forced labor, abuse, and starvation in the villages around the APCM stations would complicate the remainder of the missionary couple's careers. What remained of the college after its closure was its interventions that had the potential to alter how students and graduates related to the Belgian government. At least two of these interventions offered students an advantage. Making office work training and French lessons—not just the domestic science courses—available to female students was an unusual approach that helped Althea Brown's students prepare for success in a coastal city.[115] And the school requirement to deposit cash or invest in chickens made it more likely that each student could leave the campus with tangible savings.

After 1899, access to cash was relatively rare for Africans in the Kasai region under Belgian governance. The Compagnie du Kasai maintained its monopoly over local rubber harvesting by compensating African workers with low-quality goods or small crosses made of solid copper. The Congo Free State required these copper crosses to fulfill the Africans' tax obligations. The company purchased these crosses from state authorities at rates up to two-thirds higher than the value credited when state tax payments were calculated.[116] Such practices limited the villagers' buying power.

But the most lasting part of the Luebo Agricultural College policies would link the Congo Mission to one of the most oppressive systems of colonial supervision by the mid-1920s. Alonzo Edmiston planned to "train good wide awake native leaders and teachers" as "native superintendents" to districts throughout the Kasai region, especially to areas near new railway stations and public works. These superintendents would provide advice and direction to help ensure plentiful harvests of every sort of typical local crop, including cotton and one of the most important staples for the traditional diet, manioc.[117] Seven young men were preparing to graduate when the APCM ended the program in December 1919, and they might have been the same students Edmiston chose for a related opportunity. No longer able to start this program through the Congo Mission, Edmiston adjusted his native superintendent plan by recommending some of the promising male college students to Belgian authorities to work elsewhere as agricultural monitors.

He did not provide a follow-up on these specific students' progress in his journals, but the agricultural monitors in the Belgian Congo became notorious. The colonial agricultural monitor position was created as part of the expanding Belgian cotton industry.[118] The monitors required cotton cultivation above all other pursuits to the point of compelling villagers to abandon family vegetable gardens. As agricultural monitors' work demands became increasingly complex and more monitors started using physical force, starvation rates in the region around the Congo Mission also increased.[119]

The appointment of Alonzo Edmiston as director of the APCM Agricultural College lasted about a year and a half before the program was declared a budgetary failure. Yet the Agricultural College succeeded in representing a highlight in the careers of both Alonzo Edmiston and Althea Brown because it embodied their different academic ideals and experiences within a single institution. The couple took an industrial education mandate and proved that it need not exclude a classical studies approach. Edmiston brought agricultural experimentation and subsistence farming experience to complement Brown's goals for increasing community empowerment, regional cooperation, and cultural literacy. They continued some of this work on a less prestigious scale after their reassignment to the Mutoto station in the early 1920s.

Though their Agricultural College ended prematurely, the Edmistons succeeded in promoting the cultivation of food crops while increasing literacy rates. Those results stood in tribute to the historically black education strategies that shaped Tuskegee Institute and Fisk University; the Luebo program encouraged the type of agriculture that met local needs while also promoting innovation and cultural literacy. Though the APCM had expected the new school to reflect the vocational skills focus prescribed by the Phelps Stokes Fund specialist Thomas Jesse Jones, Edmiston and Brown provided a vision of artistic and musical exploration within a flexible curriculum format. The forthright blend of industrial and classical education styles that the couple produced defied contemporary arguments that only one form of pedagogy worked for students of African descent. Independent black denominations that sponsored similar overseas missions projects in the late nineteenth and early twentieth centuries set some of the precedents for this work. Through these denominations, African American ministers and HBCU graduates merged evangelism and justice concerns by designing outreach that responded to the requests and interests of local people. Chapter 4 explores how opportunities to learn from African villagers and students started to shape the Edmistons' careers before 1918 and continued to do so into the 1930s.

4

Neighbors Recognizing and Redefining Identities in the Belgian Congo, 1916–1935

The Jubilee songs seem to appeal to the very soul of the people. . . . They were running away, but when they heard "Swing Low Sweet Chariot," they came back to listen, and made friends with us.

Alonzo Edmiston, 1918

In November 1934 Alonzo Edmiston implemented a new way for Congo Mission evangelists to communicate with African Christians in the region surrounding the Mutoto station. As one of the missionaries overseeing congregations in rural villages, he recommended that Presbyterian evangelists appoint one elder from each family of church members. Each elder would share church information with his *deku* (clan) on behalf of the ministers.[1] The plan represented a significant departure from the youth focus that characterized the early years of the APCM. When he and Althea Brown began their industrial school at Ibanche, Brown wrote that their hope for ministry expansion was in the Kuba children.[2] Almost thirty years later, Edmiston placed his confidence in the leadership abilities and kinship networks of the older generation.

This shift in his approach developed as the missionary couple gained a better understanding of what local communities expected from their cooperation with American Presbyterians. It also developed through the Edmistons' observations of the social and political consequences of Belgian colonial labor policies. The industrial education strategies discussed in previous chapters created the venues for Edmiston and Brown to witness the destabilization of the Kuba kingdom as it developed over three decades. And their marriage and growing family also made the couple vulnerable to emerging policies against African American international travel.

The combination of personal and regional instability pressured Althea Brown and Alonzo Edmiston to accept their continual status as students as well as teachers; they valued what they learned from their African neighbors while developing their own professional credentials. This chapter focuses on the Edmistons' activities between 1916 and 1935 to explain the outreach strategies that local people helped these missionaries adopt. The journal entries, letters, and articles written by Brown and Edmiston during this period indicate four categories of interactions that were added to the Congo Mission at this time and then remained important to the ministry and its personnel. Some of these interactions can be traced to expressions of African traditional religion, whereas others developed as defenses against the Belgian colonial system. As cultural habits changed among African villagers who were defined increasingly by their labor outputs, the local people placed more emphasis on how the Congo Mission reaffirmed their humanity.

The measure of the Edmistons' work in the Belgian Congo depended on several factors beyond their control, including the reception of the local people and the environmental and medical conditions in the area. Like the early phases of educational planning at Tuskegee Institute, industrial education at the Congo Mission considered the survival of the community by producing items intended to promote economic opportunities or public health.[3] The hands-on techniques in industrial education created the setting for cooperative learning among missionaries, their employees, and village residents. Published accounts of the Congo Mission industrial schools by their American directors remain examples of how missionaries tended to focus on whether their own specific plans succeeded.[4] But the results of industrial education did not depend only on the missionaries' initiatives.

Much can be learned by considering how the people who were targeted as potential converts influenced these new arrivals and encouraged them to consider unanticipated issues as parts of the ministry. Through their reactions to changes within mission churches, schools, and the colonial tax system, African villagers taught Althea Brown and Alonzo Edmiston that physical well-being and communal identities needed to be factored into effective Presbyterian outreach. The significance of these interactions between the missionaries and local people can be interpreted through comparison with the work of early African theology scholars. The political climate surrounding the birth of African theology in the late 1950s hinged on definitions of justice, as it had during the transition period after King Leopold II relinquished control of the Congo Free State. Scholars have analyzed traditional religion and missiology to envision a culturally distinct spirituality that would complement decolonization on the continent.[5] The futuristic vision in this work held special meaning for African women theologians, who advocated liberation from misogynistic elements in both Western and African traditions.[6] Likewise, the crucial aspect for making Presbyterian ministry in the Belgian Congo relevant did not depend solely on the missionaries' recognition of African traditions predating the colonial era. Brown and Edmiston learned which types of values and activities helped local people cope with their current circumstances in ways that also respected historical memory.

Identity Formation and Claims to Authority

Though the Ibanche mission station was listed officially as a closed site after 1915, Alonzo Edmiston worked there for the next three years as a station manager, a pastor, and a supply chain director. In cooperation with the station workers and local villagers, he purchased or made the food and construction equipment essential to the sustenance of the older Luebo station. Althea Brown joined him as a teacher until she and their younger son, Bope, returned to the United States on furlough in 1916. Control of an unofficial mission station brought their work little recognition except in response to political controversies. The location of Ibanche, about forty miles northeast of Luebo, meant that Edmiston represented the mission among the villages closest to the Kuba capital during a period of suspected rebellion against Belgian colonialism. Meeting often with the regional chiefs, the Kuba ruler, and local villagers influenced Edmiston's views about authoritative communication styles and about his own leadership status.

The decision to conduct Ibanche mission station business in part through negotiations with African royalty and village chiefs was inspired by a Kuba ancestral tradition. William Henry Sheppard received a royal welcome to the Kuba capital city during his first visit there in 1892 because the king referred to him as the spirit of a former ruler.[7] Sheppard acknowledged that perception throughout his career in the Congo Free State by establishing a long-term alliance with a prince from that kingdom.[8] His choice established a model for how his younger colleagues approached the political implications of their religious work.

Receiving royal permission to proselytize in Kuba territory gave the Ibanche mission station a corporate mandate that the older APCM station did not share. The Edmistons and their colleagues understood that Presbyterian longevity in the region depended at least in part on their ability to negotiate with African authorities. Political issues were less pressing at the Luebo mission station because a larger percentage of the local population claimed Luba identity. This landless ethnic group depended on migrant labor for survival and could therefore respond more freely to individualistic appeals for salvation, such as recruitment of orphans and requirements to live apart from the local villages.[9] Althea Brown found that similar strategies proved ineffective for expanding the school programs at Ibanche. Instead, the Presbyterian program leaders had to explain their appeal not just to one convert's soul but also to the welfare of nearby communities. In doing so, Brown and Edmiston adapted to an African traditional worldview that questioned dichotomies between the sacred and the secular.[10]

During the Congo's first three decades of colonization, the typical recruitment strategy for Christian missionaries there involved a large operations base set apart from African villages. Neighboring children, migrant laborers, and former captives of the domestic slave trade would be encouraged to reside in or visit these mission compounds.[11] One study identified this centralized strategy as the basis for "the most successful pattern of educational development" in what became the Belgian Congo, yet it also reinforced the geographic and social isolation of African participants.[12] When the APCM was founded in 1891, it followed this pattern through incorporation of former slaves and children with the intent of sending them out later to establish village churches and schools. Most of these European or American organizations assumed that periods of physical separation were necessary to promote eventual conversion among the broader African population.

But William Henry Sheppard's leadership style suggested a different theological concept of religious space. He chronicled his meetings with Kuba rulers as factors in his ministry that held no less religious consequence than the establishment of school and church buildings at the Ibanche station.[13] Even in his absence from the mission field, his colleagues continued to discuss the Kuba territory and the Presbyterians' political status within that territory as aspects of ministerial planning. The enrollment of individual villagers in programs held at Ibanche did not fulfill Sheppard's vision unless it also signaled increased cooperation from regional African leaders. Emphasizing the interests of non-Christian rulers and village leaders made the missionaries conscious of how their mission station community remained linked to its broader context despite religious differences.

Recognition of a broader social and political context was a significant process in the face of colonial abuses. First, it reinforced the foundation of social justice work established by the early leaders of the Congo Mission. By chronicling the torture and exploitation that led to at least eight million deaths there by 1909, Sheppard and William Morrison gained recognition within the human rights campaign against the leadership of King Leopold II. Following the departures of William and Lucy Sheppard and most of the other African American staff by 1916, Alonzo Edmiston took a more prominent role in condemning the ongoing violence and deprivation that villagers faced under Belgian colonialism. His efforts to encourage fellow Southern Presbyterians to confront the Belgian Congo government defied two of the driving narratives behind the transition from the Congo Free State system. Noting the continuance of human rights abuses questioned the image of dramatic change after the political transition of the colony. And highlighting cultural characteristics of various groups in the Belgian Congo worked against the dehumanizing consequences of forced labor in the regional villages.

The anthropologist Jan Vansina identified the decades between 1900 and 1920 as a definitive period for cultural identity formation in the regions that came under the control of King Leopold II and the Belgian government. Policies outlawing the practice of divination and initiation rites accompanied the expansion of colonial authority during and after the height of the rubber trade.[14] Efforts to abolish traditional hierarchies also began during this era, replacing local authorities with a smaller number of African leaders who reported to Belgian officials.[15] This political climate exacerbated other fractures in rural societies caused by labor conscription, urbanization, village relocations, and establishment of separate communities for Christian converts. Given such factors, the recognition of instability defines the cultural significance of the Edmistons' work with African villagers in the central Kasai region. Local people helped the missionaries recognize that, despite recent humanitarian efforts and political transition, the Belgian Congo societies could not be expected to return to precolonial norms. New strategies for survival and inspiration were needed, and comparison with Western norms would not constitute the only source.

Among the Kuba royalty and village elders around Ibanche, adjustments to different concepts of African authority under colonial rule often played out in conversation with local missionaries. Vansina described exchanges between the Kuba king and Congo Mission representatives as

Lukenga's attempts to play the missionaries against one another and thereby thwart their expansion into Kuba territory.[16] Corroborating evidence for this interpretation is clear in the accusatory tone of Edmiston's description of one such negotiation in 1918.[17] Because he intended his daily journal to be a public record of the mission's affairs, Edmiston often wrote the responses of chiefs and other leaders in dialogue style to show that he followed administrative protocol.[18] This habit of recording local leaders' views contrasted sharply with overall Congo Mission policy: African evangelists and church members were not invited to speak at its business meetings until 1919.[19]

Edmiston argued that two of his white colleagues were trying to ruin his relationship with Lukenga out of jealousy. Edmiston noted the irony of his colleagues' rules that they alone could speak to the king on behalf of the mission when neither of them could converse fully in the Kuba language. Edmiston observed: "The boy Maluci whom they had to interpret for them could not speak Bakuba, and they made all manner of fun of him. The king's men, some of them looked as if they would fall over laughing."[20] The inclusion of the Kuba dignitaries' inside joke indicated that Alonzo Edmiston credited his leadership status partly to a sense of common insight with local authorities. It also suggested one method by which African leaders in the Belgian Congo used unique aspects of their society to criticize or at times curry favor with foreign leaders.

In 1922 Alonzo Edmiston relocated briefly to start building the long-awaited new station that had inspired this meeting with Lukenga.[21] Aid from the Reverend Hezekiah Washburn and one of the APCM nurses during two outbreaks of dysentery and influenza had prompted the next Kuba ruler to open his capital city to American residents for the first time.[22] But the inability to gain Belgian permission for long-term settlement in the city meant that Bulape, the station managed by Washburn, would remain the only APCM post still functioning within Kuba territory.[23] Edmiston joined Lukenga in objecting to the concentration of Presbyterian activity at a location other than Ibanche, partly because the proximity of the newer Bulape station seemed to diminish the strategic importance of the Kuba kingdom. The ruler's concern that the Presbyterians' relocation would cause "the Bakete to be ahead of the Bakuba" hinted at a broader conviction that the American missionaries' intervention would affect the political status of African communities in the colony.[24] Alonzo Edmiston incorporated this perspective into the ways he acted out his authority as the last Ibanche station leader.

Mediation Strategies and Hospitality

On 15 July 1917 Alonzo Edmiston received news that Belgian Congo officials had ordered five of the villages near his Ibanche mission station to relocate on short notice.[25] This demand followed a year of "hard times," including increased tax burdens, confinement of some local chiefs in prisons run by Belgian officials, and removal of men and women as forced laborers and soldiers.[26] Some villagers were drafted as soldiers for the Force Publique in behalf of the colony while others were drafted for the Kuba king, feeding rumors that he sought to declare another war on Europeans.[27] These destabilizing events had taken a noticeable toll on religious activities at Ibanche mission station, causing the atmosphere at Sunday services to feel "dull" as the congregation worried about their imprisoned leaders and relatives.[28] Edmiston observed that the success of his ministry would require strategies beyond religious education and church management; his mission station needed also to promote emotional health and community stability.

Considering that the APCM had never finished rebuilding its original station in the Kuba territory after the 1904 regional uprising, the guiding vision for stability in that area could not be attributed solely to the Presbyterian influence. Postcolonial African theology offers a comparative means to identify the cultural influences that shaped the development of the Ibanche station in its final decade of operations. Like the initial years following the transition from the Belgian Congo government to the Democratic Republic of the Congo, the decade following the Kuba uprising brought increased outside scrutiny regarding the legitimacy of African leadership styles. African theology since the 1950s has also contended with the ongoing need to identify and address social injustice in a political context that was expected to represent freedom. The theme of hospitality provided one way for theologians to evaluate traditional leadership and advocate for oppressed groups. Alonzo Edmiston learned different mediation strategies partly by accepting the interpretations of hospitality offered by the villagers near Ibanche.

In April 1916 Edmiston canceled a church service to host "only prayer services to-day for our Bakuba friends who are in chains."[29] The decision was a response to community members' concerns about the increasing demands for soldiers and laborers from Kasai. He noted that "some mothers had to be cheered and pacified, some fathers talked to, [and] some chiefs are mad because another has gotten some of his people and sent as soldiers to the State."[30] The sudden removal of relatives and neighbors sparked distrust of the colonial authorities and of some Africans who seemed to cooperate to the detriment of another village. The crisis festered while Edmiston followed the overall policy of the APCM and encouraged the Christian villagers to obey the colonial laws. He reported that "the people seem[ed] to take [it] all right" when he preached on the duty to pay taxes and volunteer for military service faithfully.[31] But the acquiescence of church members did not ease the social consequences of the draft system.

A primary goal in some of the earliest African theology texts was, in the words of Harry Sawyerr, to "seek to interpret Christ to the African in such a way that he feels at home in the new faith."[32] That statement was published in 1971, in the first decade following a wave of successful nationalist revolutions against European colonial rule. The concept of creating a stable "home" carried physical and spiritual significance at the time, as it did for those members helping establish an African Presbyterian synod in the 1910s. Gwinyai Muzorewa, one of the most prolific scholars in the field, argued that Christian ministries thrive in these types of settings only to the extent that "the community of believers takes collective survival very seriously" by using the African traditional concept of humanization.[33] He explained it in his familial context as a linguistic preference for speaking of shared ownership and relationships and compared it to John Mbiti's summary of the *ubuntu* principle; Muzorewa concluded that African humanity could not be understood separate from the conviction that each community played a defining role in the identities of individuals.[34] By extension, dangers to the community could not be isolated from individual well-being.

Evidence suggests that the villagers around the Ibanche mission station embraced traditional ideas of humanization and used those ideas to alter Edmiston's perspective on community-wide hospitality. For example, the missionary chose to mediate in behalf of draftees' families through the summer and fall of 1916 even though his specific congregation did not face imminent danger. After recruiting thirty men to help the state representative travel with supplies between Ibanche and Luebo, Edmiston expressed disappointment that these men were not expected to return home in the near future. The state officials had drafted each man into military service and sent him to a different region in the Belgian Congo. Edmiston confided in his journal, "It was through my influence that these people agreed to go to Luebo at all as the State man requested and I feel that I should do all I can to help them."[35] His sense of responsibility motivated more direct opposition

to Belgian authority in the region, even though it complicated his administrative interests. The APCM was seeking permission from the governor general of the Belgian Congo to renew its claim to the Ibanche station property
in 1916.[36]

The shift in Edmiston's leadership style that started during the forced
labor crisis at Ibanche lingered throughout his career as an impulse to analyze religious or political interventions according to their effects on local
people. Edmiston reacted to the removal of local villages by placing it in the
context of the African residents' agricultural and domestic traditions:

> So strange how the State is putting the people here and there to make
> new villages, especially at this time when everybody is in distress. This
> is the time when the people are making their fields; to pull them up
> and set them down at a new place means that hunger is bound to fol-
> low. The State has no mercy upon the poor people. They expect the
> people to leave their good homes which took some of them five and six
> months to build, to leave their fields of corn and ciombi still ungath-
> ered is hard on them. Also the State still calls for tax just the same.[37]

His years of farmwork in Tennessee, Alabama, and the Belgian Congo
made the missionary sensitive to the growing season and the risk of going
without. This perspective sometimes motivated Edmiston to act on the
basis of his neighbors' concerns before coordinating with other leaders.

During conflicts between the colonial authorities and African leaders,
the typical form of intervention from the Congo Mission was an appeal
directed to the territorial headquarters located near the Luebo station. This
strategy had resulted in a public letter to the district leaders and European
traders permitting a brief respite from labor demands in February 1916.[38]
But Alonzo Edmiston bypassed this protocol the following month by telling colonial soldiers to stop drafting additional men and refusing to allow
them to search for escaped draftees.[39] The following year, he ordered a sol-
dier to release four men who were held prisoner for alleged tax delinquency;
Edmiston suspected that extortion was the primary motive.[40]

These confrontations motivated a Belgian judge to interrogate Edmiston about his political loyalties. But what Judge Dumont interpreted as an
effort to make trouble for the colonial government Edmiston understood as
an attempt to prevent a potentially corrupt official from disrupting the
Kuba villages and circumventing the authority of local chiefs.[41] Represent-

ing the interests of local political leaders beyond the mission church rolls was a specific way that Alonzo Edmiston adapted a traditional definition of hospitality to the broader community during his efforts to maintain an effective ministry.[42] He continued that pattern by incorporating oversight of local village planning and commercial ventures into his Congo Mission role.

Expressions of sympathy for the African villagers facing oppressive labor demands or forced relocation did not mean that Alonzo Edmiston took their side in every political dispute. When a group of Kuba men sought his approval of their plan to free a Christian captured by the soldiers, he defused the situation by announcing: "I would not protect them in their wrongs, neither would I help the State against them. But I wanted to see all sides do right."[43] The missionary's strategies for ensuring that the outcome was "right," however, sometimes involved adjustments that villagers requested in response to colonial policies.

Edmiston started formal negotiations with state officials in 1917, asking them to provide advance notice and explanation of plans to remove people from the villages around Ibanche.[44] And, for those villagers who were able to remain in place, he experimented with local produce to develop marketable goods like sugar cane syrup. The agricultural projects at Ibanche mission station provided new paid positions and opened new financial possibilities for townspeople in grave need of cash to pay taxes.[45] But the factory enterprise ceased when one of the APCM supervisors forbade him to provide syrup anywhere else but the Luebo station.[46]

The Ibanche mission station employed at least sixty workers during its final full year of operation.[47] The standard wage ranged from seventy-five cents in francs per month to one franc per day, even though the mission stations sometimes paid wages in the form of barter items such as cloth.[48] Edmiston offered salt as compensation one month in 1917, but he provided francs as often as the colonial post would put cash in circulation.[49] The choice to pay wages in francs was made at the request of the Kuba and Luba workers, and the Edmistons' compliance was a way to invest in community empowerment. He might not have known that the trade of francs also reduced the workers' vulnerability to colonial manipulation.

The families that had savings in francs could bypass some of the restrictions that had made the tax code so onerous since the Congo Free State era. Like the copper crosses that were first distributed around the turn of the twentieth century, the kinds of manufactured goods used occasionally to compensate workers had no value except for variable rates that fit the government's interests at any given time.[50] Francs were more empowering since the value was recognized in transactions with both Belgian officials and non-state traders. And once an entire community, through the representation of its chief, pooled enough francs to pay its tax burden, the community was less likely to face drastic penalties like the annual requirements to pay debts by sending people as forced workers for the state.[51]

Gwinyai Muzorewa identified the need for "Africanization" as key to making African theology "capable of dealing with present African realities."[52] The empowering aspect of Africanization encompassed both spiritual and secular changes. In the late 1970s, John Mbiti characterized Christian liberation movements in southern Africa as part of the anticipated social services of future churches on the continent; these anticolonial movements complemented a general argument that "there is no permanent home for foreign Christianity in Africa."[53] That emphasis on social justice also factored into Mercy Oduyoye's explanation of African humanization in a 1979 publication. She described the process as "a two-way relation: with God and with our fellow human-beings."[54] The shared conviction in postcolonial African theology that Christian transformation according to traditional ideals would influence societal development suggests that African Christians found meaning in this principle earlier in the twentieth century.

In the case of the Ibanche mission station, the Africanization process within the congregation was represented best through the sacred use of a local plant. Edmiston experimented with local fruit juices to choose a suitable alternative to imported grape wine for communion.[55] He chose the berries of a common *belebele*, or miracle fruit tree, which resembled bright red grapes with clear pulp and hard seeds. This fruit earned its nickname because its pulp reacted with the taste buds to make sour foods taste sweet. The miracle fruit juice provided a key to future church growth through increased self-sufficiency and African leadership. In Edmiston's words, "This is the only and best fruit we can use for Communion wine and have something which the natives can use also."[56] After congregants started using the mission church as a prayer refuge during a crisis in 1916, Edmiston accepted the evidence that villagers found comfort in these gatherings. Using an abundant natural resource made it easier as well for African evangelists to carry that sense of comfort into remote village church services that the missionaries did not operate.

Another notable facet of the change to belebele communion juice was its ritual symbolism. The Presbyterian *Westminster Larger Catechism* explained the benefits of receiving the Lord's Supper in terms of "spiritual nourishment," renewal of "thankfulness," and "mutual love and fellowship."[57] The ability to produce communion supplies quickly and in abundance was an investment in the future for these mission churches. After baptism and the successful completion of catechism class, communion welcomed new church members into the fold, and the monthly observance helped preserve a sense of solidarity among the local Christians.

The use of belebele juice as part of a shared communal meal may have also signaled to African church members a significant part of traditional religion regarding hospitality. In his analysis of African family systems, the theologian Gerald Tanye described the perception of guests "as divine agents who bring divine blessing for the community that welcomes them." Because the preparation to host guests brought harmony to a home, he argued that "hospitality therefore emphasizes the African openness for life in its communitarian dimension."[58] The addition of a fruit recognizable to local people could be interpreted as a form of hospitality to the African "guests" in the mission church as well as a symbol that the American Presbyterian community was open to the advantages these guests could bring.

An immediate financial advantage offered by the switch in communion wine supplies came from reducing the Congo Mission's reliance on semiannual deliveries of supplies by river steamboat and personal couriers. The outbreak of the First World War had disrupted transatlantic shipping while raising prices dramatically. Edmiston's change to belebele berries reduced the shipping expenses and the risks involved in hoping that the grape juice shipments would last long enough for several months' worth of ritual services. The Ibanche church could claim to provide for one of its main monthly expenses without adding to the overall budget of the Congo mission, and it modeled a way to start Presbyterian congregations in the region while minimizing additional costs.

Agricultural choices and labor demands continued to guide Alonzo Edmiston toward an Africanized interpretation of hospitality after the Ibanche station was closed in 1918. As mentioned in chapter 2, the villagers and station workers at Ibanche provided agricultural provisions and construction supplies for use at the older Congo Mission station. Edmiston shared the local chiefs' suspicions that Ibanche villagers would still be expected to send food and supplies to Luebo after Ibanche closed but receive even less compensation.[59] Before his relocation, Edmiston envisioned several ways to make supply demands less onerous for the local farmers.

Since these farmers provided most of the produce, meat, and building supplies for two mission stations, strategies to expand fields and boost productivity seemed to promise mutual benefit. His final report from Ibanche urged the APCM to make crop rotation, gardening skills, and animal husbandry part of the regular script for evangelism tours. He reasoned, "Instruction along these lines will not only prove beneficial to the natives themselves but also to the foreigners, and also help to lay the foundation for a self-supporting church."[60] The concept of self-supporting churches promised to ease the budgetary concerns of American and British missions sending agencies during the Great War, and it implied eventual managerial control by local Christians.[61] By using this term, Edmiston hoped to ensure the long-term success of the APCM. He linked his ministry to one of the most modern concepts in his professional field while also keeping the proposed changes grounded in the interests of local people.

Alonzo Edmiston also designed new grass-covered buildings for the Luebo Agricultural College after the couple's move to Luebo. Most station buildings had been built with mud and waterproofed with *malala* and palm leaves from Ibanche. The shift to grass from a field outside Luebo saved funds during a crucial stage in the life of the college, and it helped reduce the mission's continued reliance on Kuba produce and labor after the Ibanche station was closed.[62] Finding and using local grass for construction allowed the Edmistons to display their interest in the local workers' input, and their decision to forgo the palm leaves might have eased the concerns of Ibanche residents that their resources were being exploited.

During the years that Edmiston and Brown worked at the Mutoto station, he learned to resolve complaints by being more attentive to students' concerns about the lack of variety in the food served at the mission boarding school. Students of the Bible College and the girls' boarding school boycotted in 1924 and 1927, refusing for an entire day to eat the food provided by the mission staff.[63] Budget constraints had led to reliance on manioc as the main or only ingredient in student meals. This root could be boiled and then served mashed like potatoes or in stick form like cooked carrots. Students tired of this starchy meal, especially when it was not paired with meat or other vegetables. Edmiston and the other missionaries showed little patience for the boycotters' demands; they tried each time to identify and punish the leaders of the protest. Nevertheless, he did take the crux of the complaint to heart. He started offering meal allowances and planting more fruit trees to supplement the students' diet.[64]

The types of produce that Alonzo Edmiston planted at Mutoto—such as peas and watermelons—created new ways to help African ministers feel welcome at the mission. The APCM stations hosted an annual conference for the African evangelists who had founded churches in villages throughout Kasai. The Edmistons worked with the other missionaries to plan conference seminars, administrative reports, and special church services. Tours of the fields were added to the conference itinerary, along with phototaking sessions.[65] Edmiston compiled visual evidence of the farm's productivity and the local evangelists' enthusiasm for it. Finally, he ensured that each evangelist left with packets of seeds from the farm's yield.[66]

Gifts of seed held symbolic power for missionaries from Alabama. One of the more oppressive guidelines in standard sharecropping contracts of the late nineteenth century was that the shares would be paid in a percentage of the harvest, not in a percentage of seed.[67] Such rules kept the sharecroppers dependent on landowners for the essential equipment to enter the agricultural economy. And dependency made it easier for landowners to set the contract terms, control prices, and limit competition.

Alonzo Edmiston might have had that manipulative practice in mind when he decided to make seed distribution and planting skills training part of the annual conference. By 1923 Belgian authorities had designated chiefs and agricultural monitors to increase cotton production throughout the region using compulsion and force.[68] According to the historian Osumaka Likaka, the need to cope with constant cash crop surveillance contributed to the development of a multiethnic "peasant consciousness" in the colony.[69] In that context, encouragement to grow items for personal consumption was rare.[70] Edmiston heeded the preference of Ibanche farmers who focused on food crops and sustenance.[71] He gathered seed from fruits and vegetables instead, equipping the African evangelists to meet both the spiritual and physical interests of their congregations. He also continued providing agricultural training at the evangelists' annual conferences and encouraging them to practice these techniques in their local villages.[72] His observations helped Alonzo Edmiston gain enough expertise in local agriculture to produce two textbooks on the subject for the short-lived APCM Agricultural College.[73]

A final example of how hospitality factored into the work of Alonzo Edmiston can be seen in the cooking techniques he learned from Luba and Lulua traders and villagers beyond the vicinity of the Ibanche station. During the transition period between the closure of the Agricultural College and the Edmistons' furlough, they visited several Presbyterian evangelists in small villages throughout the Kasai region. While traveling, he took specific notes about the harvesting of white ants for food. He described the height of white ant nests, their size and appearance, and the preferred methods for removing the fattest ants from the nest quickly. When it came to exploring new options for nutrition and marketability, no detail was too small.

Like his experiments with local sugar cane, pineapples, and belebele berries, the notes about white ants represent the missionary's effort to bring African features into his work. As a traveler, he had to rely on the generosity of rural strangers who taught him that the ants were valuable as sources of oil, as fertilizer for mushrooms, and as treats smoked over a fire. Their texture may have reminded Alonzo of pork fatback, chitlins, and other fatty staples of Alabama soul food. He recorded that cooked white ants were "one of the finest kind of food for the people. I have eaten them after they have been smoked and dried, and like them very much."[74]

Storytelling

Such detailed descriptions of and praise for a local food tradition indicate that Alonzo Edmiston did not interpret his agricultural job description only in terms of his ability to translate American techniques to a central African setting. Both Edmistons showed interest in a variety of local resources and skills that seemed to benefit the mission and the community overall. Althea Brown reshaped mission policy by reserving official time for storytelling. The strategy seems to have begun when the couple traveled to Mutoto station for an extended visit in 1920; several Lulua children conversed and played games with Brown during the commute. The children taught her ancestral stories that were repeated to emphasize their meanings. Observing the story time, Alonzo Edmiston wrote: "One thing the natives do know, and that is telling stories. Old, old stories which have been handed down for generations by their forefathers are told and listened to with as much eagerness as if they had never been told before."[75]

When they moved to Mutoto two years later, the Edmistons re-created those storytelling nights with the schoolchildren. Reminiscent of Brown's classical literary club at Fisk University, a storytelling club started in the boys' school by 1930.[76] Male students were encouraged to produce plays for weekly entertainment. They chose topics ranging from comedies to local histories to explaining how colonial governance influenced the regional tribes.[77] With a mix of admiration and condescension, Edmiston called the historical dramas "fine plays of their forefathers and their superstitions."[78] The drama nights typically attracted an audience of more than a thousand villagers to the mission station.[79] Through their weekly affirmation of the boys' creativity, local villagers contributed to the boys' educational experience. Their interest ensured that classroom interactions with teachers or with the boarding school supervisor were not the only meaningful interactions between youths and adults.

Because of this community interest, Alonzo Edmiston advocated expanding the Presbyterians' support for the students' weekly dramas even though they were unusual at other APCM stations.[80] The American missionaries acknowledged the significance of this community participation by inviting foreign visitors to attend these drama nights at the station.[81] Brown helped create costumes and Edmiston encouraged the boys to devote more time to preparation for their plays in order to display excellence to the audience.[82] Bill Worth, the son of an APCM missionary, William Worth, remembered these evenings fondly decades after he left the Belgian Congo. Even at his young age, he valued such events for the cultural insights into the lives of local children, and he associated those pleasant memories with the Edmistons.[83]

Student plays like the ones produced at Mutoto grappled with Belgian colonialism by placing it in conversation with ancestral history and the recent Presbyterian activities. They also had the potential to help students imagine their options in the postcolonial future. For similar reasons, John Mbiti listed "cultural theology" among the main categories of verbal traditions that developed the field of African theology.[84] He traced this theme to a conference titled "Christianity and African Culture" in Accra that was scheduled two years before Ghana gained its independence in 1957. Academics in western and central Africa worked during the following two decades "to show their appreciation of African culture, to see its values, to relate it to the Christian Faith, to make more use of it in the life of the Church, and largely to remove the stigma that has been cast upon African culture by the Western world."[85] Mbiti explained this research process as significant to the successful Africanization of former mission churches on the continent; cultural theology offered a means to ensure that the growing numbers of African pastors and ministers brought non-Western mind-sets as well as ethnic diversity.[86]

At primary and secondary educational levels, access to traditional stories and culture had clear political meaning for postcolonial African scholars. Mercy Amba Oduyoye understood Christian education as part of an

ongoing evaluation by children as they "[come] to faith through the experience of God in history, both personal and communal."[87] And she credited
the first nationalist government in Ghana with funding her education
through a continent-wide political work program that gave young citizens
"a sense of being Africans, Pan-Africans."[88] In reaction to the early years of
decolonization on the African continent, P. Chike Onwuachi faulted European and American missionaries for maintaining education styles that
failed to acknowledge local contexts.[89] This Fisk sociologist recommended
that educational initiatives would best serve the next generation by merging
preparation for Western ideologies with incorporation of "indigenous cultural traditions."[90] By creating a space for the creativity of African youth,
the Edmistons helped schoolchildren practice acting out the changes
brought by Belgian control as just one of several options in their societal
development.

By providing a means to question both African and Western traditions,
storytelling among women also played a formative role in Althea Brown's
work at the Congo Mission. Brown recalled learning the Kuba language in
1902 and 1903 by conversing with the multiple wives of the king, Lukenga,
during visits to the capital city. In addition to correcting her grammar and
syntax, these women probably served as sources for Brown's study of the
political structure and gender roles within the kingdom.[91] One of her essays
on social expectations for Kuba women was included in the biography that
Julia Lake Kellersberger published after her death.

Brown described the bridal dowry system and pregnancy traditions
through the specific roles that family members played as well as through
the way these actions made women feel. She contrasted the "kind" way that
husbands completed additional household chores during a wife's pregnancy
to the way that a man's adultery could "[make] life miserable for his wife."[92]
The descriptions placed emotional weight on the contributions of husbands
and fathers, especially when she identified "laziness on the part of the husband" as the primary reason Kuba women sought divorce.[93] The value
judgments within such statements were probably influenced by Brown's
adherence to the rhetoric of "woman's work for woman"; despite her scholarly interest in Kuba culture, she concluded that the lack of "Christian ideals of womanhood" made these individuals "objects of pity."[94] The historian
Dana Robert found similar assumptions among late nineteenth-century
supporters of the woman's missionary movement "that non-Christian religions led to the degradation of women."[95]

Althea Brown's cultural study also extended beyond religious criticisms, however, to hint at the economic context of rural life in the Congo Free State at the turn of the century. Brown concluded that the Kuba kingdom had an "advanced stage of civilization" that was undercut by certain appetites such as a desire for personal gain.[96] That observation revealed the social critique that may have motivated Kuba women to tell Althea Brown about the dowries and the duties husbands sometimes failed to fulfill. Regional instability caused by mining companies and the cotton industry from the 1920s through the 1950s exacerbated household instability. Contrary to Kuba tradition for those outside the royal family, married men recruited from the Kasai region to work in the mines at Katanga had access to additional wives for "temporary unions."[97] In the men's absence, female villagers faced violence from agricultural supervisors, for which they had little recourse.[98] What Brown offered as a historical account of Kuba society may have originated as an appeal to ensure that threats to women's well-being were recognized as threats to the future of the society.[99]

Awareness of women's social concerns continued in the mission church rituals. In 1923 the APCM adopted a policy that required public confessions from African church members during worship times. Some local Christians (or *balondi* in the Luba language) responded with skepticism about this "extra sacrament," doubting the social benefits of such a revealing ritual. They also suspected that the confessions signaled inequality within the Presbyterian mission; missionaries recorded the publicized sins, but none of the missionaries was required to participate as a confessor.[100] The confession ritual became popular, however, after female believers expanded the definition beyond wrongdoing to include personal stories. Alonzo Edmiston found that local Christians would confess willingly if doing so provided an outlet for their grief.

During an evangelistic trip through the villages near Mutoto, Edmiston encountered a young woman whose baby had died recently. Her pleas to the child's departed spirit were heart-wrenching for him, and the experience might have led him to realize how many other local families needed solace. So he wrote that, during that evening's church service, "we had all the Christians to meet at the church and tell their tales of woe and burdens of heart."[101] Two local women had started the process earlier that week by confessing to overwhelming sadness; their husbands had been drafted into the labor system, and the women feared that they might never return from working somewhere in Kuba country.[102] Such confessions did not induce the type of public shaming that local Christians initially feared. Instead, merging storytelling with denominational requirements helped build public empathy and combat the isolation of grieving people.

There were also occasions when church members used the speaking opportunities inherent in the confession ritual to assert a greater sense of control over church service proceedings. During the special service designed to air church members' emotional burdens, the members announced unanimously that each one was unable to pay the required monthly church dues.[103] And about five months earlier, church members in a different village had collapsed in laughter when a few young men confessed to stealing rats and chickens from their neighbors. Such bold mischievousness struck the congregation as hilarious, and Edmiston could do little but let the disruption settle down on its own.[104]

These episodes showed that the Christians in the region were prepared to combine their personal interests with the standards enforced by the missionaries. When the church dues requirement seemed unattainable, members used another requirement (confession) to prove their commitment and their worthiness to remain in the congregation. And when local people transformed solemn denominational rules into entertainment, Edmiston accepted the coping maneuver for what it was. Whether Christians were laughing or grieving together, they drew the ministers' attention to life changes that were not easily quantified as exclusively a spiritual or a secular issue.

The African women's storytelling at the Congo Mission can be interpreted as a holistic approach to religious activism. Female villagers brought economic and social concerns to the ministers with full expectation that such concerns fell within the purview of the mission church. Similar approaches were advocated by Mercy Amba Oduyoye and the Circle of Concerned African Women Theologians later in the twentieth century. She characterized her own story as a founding female theological student at the University of Ghana by hoping it "opens the eyes of people to see there are no limits."[105] Stories also fit into her theme of the need for Christian women to oppose widespread silence regarding domestic violence and the exploitation of widows.[106] From this theological perspective, Christian gender equality became essential to the future Africanization of the faith. In Oduyoye's words, "No Christianity that ignores the oppression of women should be made at home in Africa as Christ cannot be at home in a domination-riddled Christianity."[107] The adjustments that female church members made to the rite of confession at the Congo Mission suggest that they shared an expectation that social awareness could also become part of the foundation for the African Presbyterian synod.

Redefining *Home* and *Family*

Perhaps the most intimate lesson that some African American missionaries gained from their African neighbors was a broader understanding of *family*. At least two of the Edmistons' black colleagues reported feeling an emotional connection to the people of the Belgian Congo, and Nancy Jacobs, a Fisk student, was described in a newspaper interview as having her African mission experience "deeply fixed in her heart."[108] To help explain their own commitment to the people around Ibanche, the Edmistons depicted their roles within two aspects of African traditional religion: ancestral beliefs and naming rituals.

During his final full year running the Ibanche station, Edmiston recorded a Kuba tradition about ancestral spirits. He summarized the belief that spirits of deceased loved ones were reborn in the babies of relatives, neighbors, or visitors. According to that tradition, he wrote, "Some think my wife carried a few [spirits] with her and the baby when they went home last year. Both of our boys are the souls of some Bakuba who wandered until they found this body to enter and give them health again."[109] Edmiston did not share the belief in spiritual reincarnation, but he did share in its relational benefits. The villagers near Ibanche frequently asked about his sons, Sherman Kueta and Alonzo Leaucourt Bope, after Althea Brown returned to Alabama on furlough in 1916. They remembered that the boys had received their names from Kuba royalty shortly after birth. In her autobiography, Brown recalled that the king "took the little fellow in his arms and named him for himself, Kueta Heshonga. He then sent a girl from the capital to nurse him."[110]

This welcoming gesture represented a "rite of passage" and "the first major religious ceremony" in African tradition, thereby connecting the missionaries' sons to Kuba society.[111] Memory of that event may have helped motivate Edmiston to place his confidence in kinship networks as outlets for church outreach decades later. And recognition of this symbolism continued through the third and fourth generations of the Edmiston family; they still refer to their ancestors Sherman and Alonzo Leaucourt by their African names exclusively.[112]

Figure 4.1   Five of the Edmistons' descendants at the Presbyterian Historical Society archives in Philadelphia. From left to right: Lisa Edmiston, Herbert Edmiston, Althea Edmiston Cousins, Dr. Kimberly Cousins Trent, and Evelyn Edmiston Easton. Photograph by the author.

The Kuba villagers kept expecting the return of the rest of the Edmiston family to Ibanche, even though Brown had received notice that the colonial government delayed permission for the Executive Committee on Foreign Missions to send more African American missionaries to the Belgian Congo.[113] Some days, the uncertainty weighed on Edmiston so heavily that he felt unable to work or preach.[114] The local people shared in his obvious joy when he received a telegram from Brown en route to Kasai. Over five thousand Kuba neighbors showed up to rejoice with him when she returned in December 1917. Her first week back in Ibanche was packed with visits from neighbors stopping by to say *muoyo* (hello) and leaving her welcome-home gifts.[115]

The people's embrace of the Edmiston family went beyond politeness; the Kuba interpreted care of the Edmistons as an obligation similar to their nuclear family responsibilities. The couple reciprocated that deep connection when they were told to leave Ibanche and manage the Agricultural College in Luebo. Edmiston's sadness over uprooting his ministry for the third time, Brown's fear for the future of her Kuba linguistic work, and the added stress of moving to a vermin-infested field near the Luebo station contributed to them both catching serious illnesses within eight months of leaving Ibanche.[116] Their grief over the impending relocation shows in Edmiston's report from the May 1918 mission meeting: "Oh! to leave our work at Ibanche was like leaving a very dear friend. I don't see, don't see how I can stand, and my poor wife how it does break her heart. But we are willing to do the Lord's will and the will of the mission."[117]

The villagers' participation in some of the traditions of their college experiences also helped the Edmistons feel at home while overseas. Brown devoted part of the class time at the rebuilt Ibanche station to training a Jubilee-style choir that could travel to congregations in the surrounding area and in Luebo. The Ibanche choir performed the repertoire of Negro spirituals that Brown and her colleagues had translated years earlier, and they followed the professional, operatic style of the original troupe. Edmiston recorded that the Ibanche Jubilee singers' performances were always well received, and he particularly enjoyed their rendition of "Swing Low, Sweet Chariot."[118] He described the song's effectiveness in advertising the mission in almost ethereal terms: "The Jubilee songs seem to appeal to the very soul of the people. Many of them often express their feeling of gratitude and spiritual uplift after the singing of these songs. At one time, while itinerating, we captured a whole village by the singing of one of these Jubilee Songs. They were running away, but when they heard 'Swing Low Sweet Chariot,' they came back to listen, and made friends with us."

The concerts established a cultural bridge between local people and some of the missionaries, impressing each group with the translations and the quality of the students' performances. Ira Dworkin argued that the melody to "Swing Low Sweet Chariot" suggested origins in precolonial Congo; it may have been updated from a lament for the deceased into a labor protest song during the Congo Free State era.[119] Dworkin contended that Brown's translation augmented the protest sentiment of the melody by referring to suffering and to the sense of being at home in central Africa.[120] The Ibanche Jubilee Singers represented a transfer of the cultural expertise that Althea Brown and Lucy Gantt Sheppard had learned through their historically black colleges, yet the music also brought part of the Edmistons' home to the Belgian Congo in a symbolic sense.

The translated Jubilee songs defied barriers in another sense; Dr. L. J. Coppedge, a white missionary colleague, felt so moved by the choir during a 1917 visit that he "wished they had someone at Luebo to teach the same thing."[121] This apparent compliment to the educational expertise of the Edmistons underscored the fact that segregationist policies had made the hiring of another former Jubilee singer unlikely. Each of the African American missionaries who had previously been based at the Luebo station had been forced into early retirement at least two years earlier. Racial policies within the Congo Mission changed again in the mid-1930s, contributing indirectly to the development of African Presbyterian leadership in the region.

5

On the Perimeter of Two Freedom Struggles, 1930–1936

And to themselves in these the days that try their souls, the chance to soar in the dim blue air above the smoke is to their finer spirits boon and guerdon for what they lose on earth by being black.

W. E. B. Du Bois, *The Souls of Black Folk*, 1903

On 19 October 1934 Althea Brown and Alonzo Edmiston severed one of their long-term connections to the United States; they ended their subscription to the *Chicago Defender* newspaper. This African American publication had built its nationwide reputation on promoting the Great Migration and denouncing white supremacy. To thousands of black Southerners seeking relief, the paper offered the scheduling and job search information they needed to facilitate their relocation. To a missionary couple who had already built their livelihoods beyond the South, the *Chicago Defender* represented their primary way "to keep up with what our people were doing in America."[1] To help "keep the peace of the country," the Edmistons agreed to follow the advice of their white APCM colleague J. Hershey Longenecker that they should no longer have a black periodical delivered to them in the Belgian Congo. This chapter analyzes the historical context that brought the Edmistons' cultural connections under heightened political scrutiny during their final years of ministry.

The manual labor requirements that played an increasing role in Edmiston's boarding school supervision also brought him increasing accolades from European and American agencies interested in colonial development. The APCM expanded Brown's nursing responsibilities at two hospitals, thereby making her integral to one of the key elements of professionalization in central Africa. Meanwhile, the continuing pressures of the Great Depression worldwide heightened concerns about the economic exploitation of people of African descent in various nations. These changes placed the Edmistons under the influence of two rising freedom movements—the Pan-African movement and the U.S. civil rights movement—that would reach a climax after both missionaries had died.

The Edmistons' final years were influenced by the global black free-dom struggle against poverty, political manipulation, and segregation. They maintained connections with American colleagues who gained prom-inence as civil rights activists from the 1930s through the 1950s. Their fam-ily network expanded as the couple's children and siblings joined the Great Migration escaping southern Jim Crow. Meanwhile, Alonzo Edmiston's leadership status grew tenuous because of internal policy changes at the APCM and challenges from rising African ministers in the Congo Presby-terian Church. Though they faced increasing limitations on how they expressed racial consciousness in the Belgian Congo, the Edmistons were not isolated from the social justice arguments that would later promote activism in both of their adopted communities. Their personal interest in social justice through self-determination showed in the ways both mission-aries made extra effort to place themselves within an ongoing tradition of black leadership before their careers ended.

Rebellions and Rumors of Black American Ancestors

The early 1930s brought an increasing frequency of confrontations with missionaries at the Mutoto mission station just as its network of local churches was starting to develop into the foundation for what became the Congo Presbyterian Church. The additional friction was not unusual for the Belgian Congo in this time period; the economic downturn had brought increased tax burdens and industrial layoffs for the colonial subjects. In turn, more groups of people risked resistance to colonial authorities through occasional open rebellions or more common skirting of work productivity requirements. What made conditions at the APCM Mutoto station unique in the 1930s was that local villagers and church members found multiple opportunities to resist successfully through public defiance of someone who represented political and religious authority. A combination of global poli-tics and African traditional religion helped motivate most of the successful protests that were directed against the Edmistons during their final decade of joint ministry. And the increasing application of American Jim Crow segregation to APCM social life helped ensure that Africans' criticisms of the black missionaries would gain an audience.

The historian Martin Thomas explained the multiple uprisings in the Belgian Congo during the early 1930s as consequences of the worldwide Great Depression. Reliance on the Belgian franc in the colonial economy had kept prices high despite the decreasing value of cotton and other man-dated exports. The government compensated by increasing the tax burden on colonial subjects more than 100 percent even while hiring and wage rates for African miners declined.[2] Two of the largest uprisings started in the provinces surrounding Kasai in 1931: the Pende revolt in the Kwango district and the Dengese revolt in Sankuru. Seventy-three arrests and at least 344 casualties were reported that year, and the governor of the Congo-Kasai province declared a state of emergency the following fall.[3] These inci-dents resulted in increased military surveillance of the villages surrounding the Mutoto station as well as additional expectations for Presbyterian par-ticipation in colonial management of the region.

Belgian influence over Alonzo Edmiston's career grew during this decade in the form of professional awards and appointments. First, the colonial government became a source of validation for his career. The king of Belgium authorized three awards for the Edmistons; both received com-mendations for decades of service in 1932, and he received a medal for his agricultural expertise in 1926.[4] The symbolic value of these awards showed in the increasing number of official visitors he received at the Mutoto farm after 1926. The second political influence grew out of his reputation as a farm supervisor. The concluding chapter specifies some of the colonial agri-cultural education and village enhancement plans that might have devel-oped through observation of Edmiston's methods. And the missionary's leadership role in the local native court underlay these changes, placing him at the center of conflicts regarding colonial taxation, abuse of power, and political representation.

Changes in colonial authority had less bearing on the final years of Althea Brown's career except in two respects. Brown was involved in a dis-pute over corporal punishment as the temporary matron of the Mutoto girls' home, and she served as one of the founding nurses at two APCM hospitals. Both circumstances linked Althea Brown to symbolic representa-tions of colonial authority that had stirred concern and suspicion among Africans in other regions of the Belgian Congo. For the villagers near APCM mission stations, the concerns may have been heightened by a rumor that spread through the country by 1933. As in other parts of the continent, myths of African American wealth, status, and technological power were popular in central Africa by the early 1920s.[5] The exodus of Belgian business leaders because of the economic downturn inspired renewed faith in traditional theories of migration and racial empowerment.

As more Europeans left the colony, black Americans were expected to take their places as political and economic innovators. So the scrutiny that Althea Brown and her husband faced from local villagers and Christians during the 1930s could have been rooted in deep-seated optimism in the black missionaries' potential as agents of revolutionary social change.

Wyatt MacGaffey's "The West in Congolese Experience" offers the most extensive scholarly explanation of black Americans' symbolic status in the Belgian Congo. Starting with *America* as a concept in African traditional religion rather than just a geographic location, MacGaffey describes it as a destination for ancestral spirits that could return to the physical world. This theory interpreted skin color as a reflection of spiritual age; Europeans and Americans with pale skin were sometimes considered the embodiment of distant ancestors, while black Americans could be understood as representing more recent relatives.[6] The travel and activities that Europeans and Americans engaged in likewise carried a religious connotation: widespread expectations that their work could involve the transportation of additional spirits away from their families.

The Edmistons' two main occupations—teaching and hospital nursing—were among the two missionary activities believed to require a sacrifice from the local participants. Students and patients would lose their connection to certain ancestral spirits upon entering the missionaries' space in return for receiving educational and medical aid.[7] The rumor of sacrifice became more specific at the Mutoto hospital, where a French-language teacher from the Morrison Bible School died from accidental poisoning. Though Althea Brown was not directly involved, the lawsuit that his family threatened to pursue accused all hospital staff and Presbyterian missionaries of negligence.[8]

Africans who lived near the Mutoto station had rare opportunities to observe whether black American missionaries were bringing the traditional belief to its anticipated conclusion: restoration of ancestral knowledge and self-determination. Writing from personal and academic experience about a decade following the fall of the Belgian Congo, Wyatt MacGaffey traced the symbolic importance of black Americans in the colony directly to African activists' ambitions for an independent Congo in 1959.[9] But, during the Edmistons' lifetimes, traditional belief in black Americans as a preferable replacement for Belgian authority remained just a suspected spark for distant and elusive African nationalism. The more pressing issues were enhanced government surveillance and the reactions of disgruntled colonial subjects.

Government officials worried that the ancestral return "rumor" might inspire rebellions and blamed Protestant missionaries for helping the rumor spread nationally.[10] Indeed, migration of workers from the region around the Congo Mission to the colony's copper mines could have played a role in keeping the black American prophecy popular among Africans from different ethnic groups and colonies. Many men from Kasai villages were employed at the large copper mine in Katanga, which the scholar Luise White links to a northern Rhodesian version of the rumor.[11] Likewise, the Kikongo beliefs featured by MacGaffey may have developed in conversation with stories from the region where the Presbyterian Congo Mission was based.

Whether or not colonial officers blamed the black missionaries at the APCM specifically for suspected antigovernment messaging is unclear, though the historian Bogumil Jewsiewicki suggested the connection.[12] Regardless, the internally imposed limits at the APCM (such as the discontinued *Chicago Defender* subscription) indicate that additional screening of the Edmistons was anticipated by their white colleagues. African traditional prophecies of rapid political and social change led by black Americans set a level of expectation that Althea Brown and Alonzo Edmiston had not expected or intended to meet. The closest approximation of this belief found in Edmiston's journals was his observation that his Kuba neighbors at Ibanche remembered his sons as if they had carried ancestral spirits with them to live in America.[13] Descriptions that fit the anticipated fulfillment of the prophecy—details of how black Americans brought ancestral strength to Africa again—were less specific in the missionaries' records. The cultural literacy approach espoused by Althea Brown offered a clear recognition of history and tradition with the potential to work against the interests of colonial officers. But the missionaries' involvement in state-sponsored institutions also made both Brown and Edmiston vulnerable in the rising trend of complaints against oppressive governance. The following section explains how these problematic political ties motivated challenges against the Edmistons and also boosted the authority of African Christians and students in the APCM.

Resistance against Black Missionary Authority

As mentioned in chapter 2, the Mutoto station missionaries had designated Alonzo Edmiston to participate in the local native court when the program started in the mid-1920s. Created to supplement the work of territorial officers, these tribunals offered a semblance of African leadership dealing with local disputes. But the historic reputation of these native courts was set by the ways they were co-opted to promote the financial interests of the colonial government. In addition to hearing grievances between local Africans, the responsibilities of native court judges had expanded since the 1920s to include supporting the colonial census, monitoring work projects, revenue collection, and authorizing corporal punishment. At Mutoto, the judgments of the native court were based on deliberations between one or two male missionaries and the African pastors or evangelists selected by the APCM. That leadership structure kept the Presbyterian mission engrossed in the political and social grievances that escalated in the first years of the Great Depression. And some of those grievances intersected directly with Alonzo Edmiston's ministerial and agricultural activities.

The colonial census counts were mandated as a strategy to redistribute the labor force as multiple European businesses closed. The Mutoto native court panel assisted colonial officials in 1932 and 1933 by counting and categorizing the African population living in the surrounding villages. Edmiston provided no further details in his journal on how the court used the census information, but he noted that men were counted according to the status of their labor contracts.[14] This information was vital to the future of the regional cotton company as well as the Mutoto station schools. Agricultural production in the Kasai region had been controlled by just one cotton company (Cotonco) since 1928, which had a state-sponsored mandate to profit from the labor of any households within its geographic concession.[15] When Edmiston and the native court committee determined that only a quarter of the four hundred able-bodied African men near the mission station had active labor contracts, the information was reported to a territorial official who decided how to help Cotonco meet or exceed its recommended quota of local men who could be required to work in the cotton fields. The other unemployed men listed in the census were, by virtue of this identification process, likely to be drafted into military service, mining, or public works construction.

Comparisons with other missions activities in the Belgian Congo suggest that census duty involved more than just a cooperative civic exercise for the APCM. Jesuit missions in the colony thrived on the basis of networks of small farms, or *fermes-chapelles*, which operated with the labor of students and converts. Since 1899 these farms had generated significant profit by producing cash crops that were sold to the government and European companies.[16] Jesuits had reached the rare status of operating mission stations with more than subsistence-level resources through the enrollment of hundreds of African children throughout the colony.

Though the Protestant missions organizations, including the APCM, did not match that level of agricultural activity, the Catholic example did keep the issue of access to local youth central to the competition among Christian evangelists. In the midst of their own budget cuts, the Presbyterians worried about losing too many potential students to the Catholic school farms. The monthly records kept by Alonzo Edmiston confirm that student labor had helped fill dietary and construction needs consistently. The census of local households offered a means to estimate how many local children could enroll in mission schools later, and Edmiston's budget records provided a means to calculate how much labor was completed per child. It was no coincidence that the APCM sent two missionaries to appeal for the colonial government's aid in boarding school recruitment efforts three months after the mission helped complete the 1933 census.[17]

Osumaka Likaka concluded in his study of the Belgian Congo cotton economy that "households in cotton concessions were at the mercy of the company; they could not choose to withhold sales, shift to another cash crop, or benefit from competition by other companies."[18] Given the history of plantation farming performed by Catholic students in the colony, this picture of economic subjugation was corroborated by accusations that the colonial official in Mutoto was arresting any chiefs who allowed village outreach by the Presbyterians instead of the Catholic priests. In competition with a mission system that had been accused by African parents of exploiting forced child labor under the guise of education, any similarities or differences in the APCM boarding school programs were amplified.[19] Complaints from local parents and ministers increased, often relating to the question of whether the Presbyterian missionaries would identify and expand the benefits of their programs for the African Christians involved.

The mediator role that Alonzo Edmiston had used in the two previous decades to support villagers' safety was characterized more by rule enforcement in the 1930s. His leadership position with the native court again cast Edmiston as the emissary for a disruptive process when the court started preparations for the Belgian agent's village tours in 1931. Edmiston and another missionary asked each member of the native court to instruct their neighbors to gather their tax payments and help with road construction.[20] The political role started to influence his educational and ministerial choices as well. Suspected theft from the boys' home was confronted with a threat to have the former student fired from his employment by a Belgian officer.[21] He recommended a new location for a village church to influence colonial officials' planning decisions. Edmiston argued that a church building visible from a road would draw enough attention to make its forced removal less likely, and he hoped it would also help the community of churchgoers avoid orders to break up their village and build a road elsewhere.[22]

In addition to these changes there was the constant prospect of colonial surveillance within Edmiston's ministerial jurisdiction; the boys from his foster home and the residents of the mission station village needed written permission from a minister or a government official to leave or reenter the area.[23] The physical risks of this surveillance increased when the Mutoto native court received governmental authority to require flogging as part of the legal sentence for theft. Edmiston was one of two APCM missionaries who opposed that requirement, yet his position meant that he would be involved if corporal punishment was later demanded by the court.[24]

Edmiston's arguments and his presence seem to have carried less weight officially in the 1930s. He contacted one of the local colonial agents on behalf of the Presbyterian evangelists twice in 1933, only to be denied or disregarded. Receiving no stay of the government order to slaughter any livestock in the village that might eat the cotton plants, Edmiston modeled compliance by instructing the mission station employees to kill the pigs near their homes.[25] When the same agent arrested a local chief that month, Edmiston was unable to secure his quick return to the village. But it was more detrimental to his professional reputation that the Belgian officer offered no hospitality or professional recognition when the missionary attended a state court proceeding with some of the chief's subjects two months later. The government official did not allow Edmiston or his group of witnesses to present their evidence. Instead, the time was given to other villagers who testified in ways that contradicted Edmiston's earlier written statement.[26] It was the first time that Alonzo Edmiston had been stripped of professional distinction in his dealings with the Belgian Congo government. The slight left him more sensitive to other changes that might undermine his authority, and the lack of resolution in Edmiston's favor also seems to have diminished his professional standing among local villagers and evangelists.

Female students and church members played a significant role in popularizing challenges to the missionaries' authority during the 1930s, owing partly to the consequences of the increased government surveillance. When the colonial officers deployed the army (Force Publique) to quell major uprisings in the regions around Kasai, reported rates of sexual assault by soldiers increased. Likewise, African workers and villagers reported more cases of Belgian authorities having dalliances with young women at or near the Mutoto mission station around the time a state of emergency was declared in the province. The roles that Alonzo Edmiston and Althea Brown played through evangelism and teaching left them open to criticism from the supporters of female church members and from the students who sought protection.

For example, a village pastor urged Edmiston to intervene in the contested expulsion of a young woman named Luisa from the Presbyterian Church in 1932. She stood accused of adultery; there were claims that she was having an ongoing sexual relationship with a territorial officer called Schilling, who was in charge of the area around Mutoto.[27] The results of Edmiston's interactions with this young woman and her family reveal his failed attempts to negotiate a resolution that protected the church members' interests more than those of the official. Theological analysis of Edmiston's description also indicates how local Christians were adjusting Presbyterian policy to meet their physical and social needs when the mission did not ameliorate their political oppression.

Edmiston's journal records a first mention of Luisa in September 1932, after her membership was revoked for sexual sin. Though the church pastor followed denominational protocol by requiring her to confess before the church session and isolating her for the second infraction, the missionary agreed with Luisa and her brother that these punishments alone were not sufficient to settle the matter.[28] Luisa's demand for additional recognition before the pastor proceeded to "kill her name" from the membership rolls pointed to a way for Presbyterian discipline to take into account broader social networks.

First, it is notable that she negotiated with the pastor from a position of authority as the daughter of the village chief. Luisa cited her influence with Chief Condola and an older brother when she disputed the church fine for adultery, vowing that she could "make plenty of palaver" for the pastor if the entire payment was not returned upon her forced exit from the church.[29] Luisa would abide by the church discipline rules only after the pastor proved he would respect her access to other forms of leadership. The threatened revocation of Luisa's church membership discounted the value of her remaining community alliances.

Second, the family's demands for compensation sought to convince the church to help protect Luisa's autonomy amid a coercive situation. One of the disruptive aspects of colonialism in the Belgian Congo was frequent physical or sexual abuse of African women by some Belgian authorities.[30] The specific official named in the adultery charges against Luisa, Schilling, was the colonial supervisor appointed for the entire Kasai region in the central part of the colony. In that historical context, it was likely that the young woman had little choice in planning the two encounters that caught the attention of her congregation. Still, rather than pleading her innocence, Luisa asked for the punishments to remain equitable and within her means. She and her family complained about the financial penalty only if she would no longer have any claim to support from the church. The controversy escalated when the church pastor decided to use corporal punishment on Luisa instead of offering the requested refund; it was a violent reaction that Luisa's brother vowed he would never forgive.[31]

The emphasis on communal authority and equitability in the case of this former church member stood out for its lack of conformity to gendered expectations of the time. From the 1820s, the early principles for female missionaries emphasized teaching, marriage, and other aspects of domesticity.[32] This emphasis on service assigned sacred value to women's continual sacrifices to try to sustain their families while placing social and political activism beyond the expected female sphere. Luisa's choice to express her own preferences for just treatment defied that missions principle. In the context of African American female leaders, respectability politics presented a rationale for activism that was based on a foundation of personal morality. Historic patterns of sexual violence against African American women during and after slavery were confronted publicly by female leaders who had chaste reputations. The New Woman image of the 1920s and its openness about sexuality posed a perceived threat to black clubwomen who associated promiscuity with reduced civic influence.[33] But the church expulsion case suggests a different framework for female activism that drew on local traditions.

African feminist theologians have credited women with dominating the craft of storytelling, thereby ensuring that their perspectives and emotions were expressed creatively in precolonial societies.[34] Mercy Amba Oduyoye envisioned an empowered future for Christianity in Africa that would acknowledge such stories and end its "deafening silence in the face of indescribable cruelty to the girl-child as she is prepared to please men."[35] Likewise, American feminist theology has explored the implications of justice movements that did not address gender oppression. According to the theologian Kelly Brown Douglas, coordination with African women theologians like Oduyoye in the 1970s became part of that process toward seeking intersectional justice for underrepresented groups.[36] These examples show that late twentieth-century activism by women of African descent did not assume that social changes for non-Western women had to be determined through an external hierarchy. Political and interpersonal tensions escalated at the APCM in the 1930s partly because the options driven by a local woman's initiative were not considered.

Instead, Alonzo Edmiston as the supervising missionary focused on keeping evidence of the affair and possible abuse separate from the church property and from the church members. He concluded in his report that the discipline procedures were inadequate and expressed hope to "heal the rift" between Luisa's family and the pastor by encouraging them to talk peacefully to each other. He recommended that the pastor spend more time greeting congregants and paying home visits. These suggestions fit the African theology paradigm of questioning religious boundaries and placing church work in the local community rather than just inside the building. But the pastor was not reprimanded by the mission for beating Luisa, no refund of her church payment was mandated, and no Presbyterian investigation of the official's role in the controversy took place. The same official was seemingly emboldened by the Presbyterians' focus on punishing only the young woman; Schilling started living with a different young African woman on mission station property in 1934.[37]

The presence of Belgian officials who engaged in sexual impropriety while visiting the mission station bothered Edmiston for both spiritual and social reasons. He and the African workers he supervised had observed male officials either traveling with local female companions or having them brought to their residences since October 1930. The lack of consequences for these presumed sexual affairs broadcast the unstated fact that the Mutoto missionaries either could not or would not stop them. This hint of a political power difference seems to have motivated increasing challenges to the authority of the Presbyterian missionaries.

Increasing "Native Church" Authority

The Kimbanguist movement remains the most publicized independent African church event in the early history of the Belgian Congo for its exponential growth after 1921 and for contemporary suspicions that its popularity threatened Belgian control. Official efforts to thwart later uprisings drew inspiration from two details about its founder, Simon Kimbangu, and his followers' messages following his life-term imprisonment in 1921. Kimbangu's previous employment in the coastal city of Léopoldville prompted concerns that he had gained access to international news, particularly information about the growing Pan-African nationalist movement led by Marcus Garvey. Belgian officials suspected that Kimbangu had embraced the enthusiasm for Garveyism that circulated among urban workers at the time. And when some African leaders who admired Kimbangu argued against providing taxes and labor to the Belgians, officials reacted in fear that the movement could disrupt colonial rule.[38] Kimbanguism was underestimated initially as a fleeting result of fanaticism; it was a political estimation that the historian Martin Thomas attributes to colonial officials' reluctance to recognize Africans' protests as rooted in logical reactions to exploitation.[39] Nevertheless, a common desire to question the omnipresence of white authority continued to motivate resistance in the form of independent Christian groups, uprisings inspired by African traditional religion, and informal work protests.[40]

The leaders of the nascent African Presbyterian synod fit into the context of "native church" pastors and elders who sought recognition and social stability in the wake of well-known African struggles, including the Kimbanguist movement and the Kwango revolt. These ministers' goals included a potentially revolutionary challenge to the social order through their confidence that they deserved increased authority and prestige within mostly white Protestant organizations.[41] Yet the accompanying legal and physical risks required that these appeals be made in ways that avoided direct challenges to colonial authorities and their representatives. Part of what made the rhetorical appeals of African ministers in the APCM successful was that, in the context of the Mutoto mission, their calls for black leadership could sometimes be directed against the authority of an African American. The increasing marginalization of the Edmistons' professional authority helped characterize public challenges against them as African initiatives that did not threaten the social order by American or Belgian standards.

The most poignant example of this political and racial dynamic started with a complaint about the reduced pay rate for local ministers. Near the end of the 1932 annual ministers' conference, the pastors and elders of churches near Mutoto accused the missionaries of diverting funds from their salaries to purchase a fleet of cars. In response to Alonzo Edmiston's defense of the APCM, an evangelist named Tshiekele compared him to a dishonest tax collector. The missionary summarized his reaction to the meeting by writing, "I considered it a strong offense to compare me with the State," yet he had no recourse other than to request an apology from that minister two days later.[42] A direct affront to the morals of a missionary had been issued before all his colleagues without a public retraction, and that complaint was made in the name of denouncing abuse by the colonial government. The fact that this statement could go unpunished in 1932 offered an opening for African Presbyterians in the Belgian Congo to continue using religious venues to make political announcements.

The next power move by leaders of the emerging Presbyterian Church in the Belgian Congo involved its membership criteria. By 1932 the APCM had planted enough village churches in the Kasai region to justify its own religious governing structure. This new African synod provided a forum for coordination between the "sessions" of African evangelists based near each mission station that could be independent of the missionaries' authority. The Mutoto session took the initiative to define the boundaries of the African synod and thereby subordinate the missionaries to its leadership structure. The session chose William Worth Sr. as its emissary to the annual APCM joint meeting that fall, where the proposal to designate the Presbyterian missionaries as members of the "native church" was rejected quickly. In lieu of an official vote, most of the Congo missionaries agreed to leave the proposal off the agenda. And Worth was directed by his colleagues to discourage the Mutoto evangelists from bypassing the missionaries and raising the issue before the African synod another year.[43] Though the conference adjourned with expectations that the missionaries had silenced this self-governance issue and "dropped it for good," the African evangelists' efforts to control APCM decisions proliferated through the rest of the decade.

Criticizing ministerial directives from Alonzo Edmiston or avoiding his input proved to be effective alternatives for the "native church" leaders seeking additional recognition within the APCM. One reason that Edmiston provided a good foil in this endeavor was that his agricultural tithing campaign in area villages had provided several opportunities to question his management efforts publicly. The reduced scope of his authority as a boarding school supervisor and supervisor of evangelists also provided an opening for African ministers to challenge Edmiston without fear of official retribution. But the third reason motivating increased criticisms of Alonzo

Edmiston during his final full decade of ministry had more to do with international political interests.

Though church members in local villages generally responded positively when offered the chance to pay church dues with agricultural goods instead of francs, several evangelists showed less enthusiasm. Some disagreed with the values that Edmiston assigned to each type of produce.[44] One evangelist faced additional demands to share the vegetables from his own garden as well.[45] The entire group of African pastors appointed by the Mutoto missionaries shared the blame when Edmiston called their cash donation at the annual conference "a disgrace" in comparison to those of previous years.[46] They were pressured to raise more cash while accommodating the missionary's goal to make church support less onerous for the members. Overall, the food-for-dues system increased the prestige of Edmiston's evangelism ministry by addressing a budgetary concern for the mission, but it complicated the leadership criteria for African ministers in the process.

As the economic conditions in the Belgian Congo improved slightly between 1933 and 1935, the additional trading options made reliance on the church members' produce less necessary for the subsistence of the Mutoto mission station. Edmiston's boarding school budget was redefined by a committee vote to allow him to purchase manioc only if it was grown by students at the Bible College.[47] The adjustment was significant because it limited his options for using APCM funds to compensate the area pastors, and it signified the boarding school as the only part of the mission station not entrusted with budgetary discretion. Meanwhile, most of his colleagues also started to doubt Edmiston's driving abilities. A disputed committee ruling cost him a spot in the Mutoto mission driving schedule after the car assigned to him rolled over with Althea and the Rochesters inside. The ruling barred him temporarily from organizing evangelistic or recreational trips with any passengers except his wife and African evangelists.[48] The limitations signaled publicly that Alonzo Edmiston's eligibility for financial transactions and interactions with Africans was at risk of further curtailment, and some local church leaders made the most of that vulnerability.

The same time span also brought additional scrutiny of Althea Brown's educational work. As mentioned in chapter 2, several church members in the village closest to Mutoto station disapproved of her committee's decision to require corporal punishment of over two dozen teenage students from the girls' school. The incident spurred immediate protest, which Brown faced personally as the temporary school matron. Instead of waiting in line to be spanked by Alonzo Edmiston and his Caribbean colleague A. A. Rochester, several girls escaped from the room and ran to the village nearby.[49] Their complaints probably had much to do with the sharp decline at the African church service that Edmiston led most often. Also, the father who came to the school to withdraw his child was an African pastor.[50] Since he did not serve in that same village church, his disappointment with the mission school increased the likelihood that complaints against Brown and Edmiston would be broadcast through the rest of the emerging African synod. Though records do not indicate a long-term decline in enrollment at the Mutoto girls' school, a local pastor and church members had led the way in modeling how a decline could start in reaction to the black missionaries' choices.

Reduced financial influence and travel options kept the Edmistons more dependent on the results from the local church and school to prove their continuing success with the APCM. Working closely with African neighbors had proved an asset in the first part of their careers as they found innovative ways to incorporate local interests. Edmiston continued that pattern after he was appointed in 1932 by the new synod to help organize new Presbyterian church sessions, but deferring to the African ministers' decisions required a different skill set.[51] Edmiston had to adjust to the fact that his professional opinion carried less weight in local communities. When he wanted to stop supervising two village evangelists who he thought lacked potential for success in ministry, the session refused to release him from that duty.[52] A pastor in a Luba village refused Edmiston's encouragement to repent of abusive behavior before the congregation.[53] Though Edmiston's advice had been sufficient to help secure the dismissal of an African pastor in 1931, he more often had to continue working with the ministers he deemed inadequate three years later.

On the other hand, the African ministers were getting experience in having their perspectives honored in additional forums. When a local African pastor named Mputu David disapproved of Edmiston's ministry style, Pastor David told him so publicly during a meeting with the synod. The other missionary in attendance argued that the pastor should not be rebuked because, as Edmiston rephrased it, "a person had the privilege of asking whatever question he likes."[54] About three months later, a former pastor named Kabesu bypassed Edmiston entirely by getting his ministerial credentials restored by the chairman of the APCM evangelistic committee. Finding out about this from Kabesu rather than from his colleagues was a shock, particularly since Edmiston had arranged the African pastor's first ministerial position.[55] In these situations, the APCM intervened in defense of an African leader and thereby expanded his public role. Both promotions were achieved in a public forum that minimized Alonzo Edmiston's input or took it out of consideration.

Facing the rising tide of African Christian initiative that often confronted his own authority, Alonzo Edmiston responded with private complaints but public efforts at cooperation.[56] When a discrepancy in the budget sheet for the Mutoto Presbyterian session incited an open accusation that he had taken some of the money without permission, the missionary worked with the pastor who accused him to gather a committee of interested church leaders, adjust the accounting, and make appropriate cuts in expenses.[57] His evangelism plan was revised to offer more solo travel and teaching opportunities for African ministers who specialized in music, fund-raising, and agriculture.[58] Edmiston also encouraged at least one of his colleagues to seek more input from local ministers regarding the requisitioning of resources such as a pastor's livestock for mission station needs.[59] On a personal level, Edmiston accepted the premise that he still had more to learn to improve his own evangelism approach. That included accepting simple corrections—such as an observation from Pastor Ntumba George that it was more polite to greet a woman with the phrase "*Udi ne disanka*" (Are you happy?) instead of "*Udi ne bukola?*" (Are you strong?).[60] These changes represented his preparation for a future Presbyterian Church that included less American and European influence. Given the suspicion with which the Belgian Congo government reacted to African leadership and the Congo Mission's expanded political ties, such changes were risky decisions for an African American missionary to make.

Racial Segregation and Cultural Syncretism

By the mid-1930s, suspicion of African traditional beliefs and practices was one of the common threads in the Belgian government's reactions to colonial uprisings. That logic motivated Belgian provincial and territorial officers to target beliefs, such as the idea that ancestors returned in the form of black Americans, as well as ethnic dances, medicine, and folklore as problems to be contained or eliminated.[61] Meanwhile, according to the historian

Bogumil Jewsiewicki, the colonial government suspected the Protestant missions organizations of promoting seditious messages through their work.[62] Changes in the treatment of African American missionaries after 1932 indicate that the APCM protected its political interests by limiting the amount of social interaction between them and European officials. The process did not lead to the complete exclusion of the Edmistons and the Rochesters, but increased racial segregation at the mission station signaled that their status had declined. The black missionaries faced more social isolation and suspicion, owing partly to political concerns about activism in the United States at the time.

As a cofounder of the New York–based Universal Negro Improvement Association, Marcus Garvey built a professional network of black nationalists, artists, and writers on both sides of the Atlantic Ocean. The appeal of the UNIA among black Southerners made the British colonial governor of Uganda worry that African students visiting historically black colleges could be recruited to Garvey's cause. Garvey also did not hesitate to refer to the international influence of his organization when he defended Harry Thuku, an African nationalist leader, in a protest letter to the Kenyan colonial office.[63] Though Garvey lost some influence after being deported by the U.S. government in 1927, the diasporic ideals of the UNIA found their complement when international protests against the Scottsboro decision brought renewed solidarity to American civil rights activism.[64] The Edmistons were among the international audience who collected updates about this death penalty case against nine African American youths and their Communist defense team.[65] In the context of the 1930s, the previous political argument that African American emigrants offered a solution to racial tension became a push for mission boards to contain the potential radicalism symbolized by these travelers.[66]

Lack of notification proved to be the primary means by which African Americans saw their access to government officials diminish at the Congo Mission after 1931. Plans to host European dignitaries visiting their mission station were often kept from them, or the visitors were encouraged to spend most of their time at other missionaries' homes.[67] For Althea Brown, this was a notable change from the citizen diplomacy she had performed by hosting foreign guests at her Ibanche home. She adjusted by using her flower garden as a way to make an impression on visiting dignitaries; she provided bouquets of roses so often that Belgian officials started to request them by correspondence.[68] The implicit approach to isolating the black missionaries was replaced by a direct route during a wedding reception in 1934. The seating chart for this celebration of their white colleagues Dr. Smith and Miss Minter had all four African Americans assigned to their own table, apart from the European guests and the other missionaries. After discussing her objections with her husband, Brown urged the reception planner not to segregate the group, especially since the event was taking place inside the Rochesters' home. The female missionary who planned the seating adjusted it slightly by placing A. A. Rochester at the head table with the white missionary families, but the slight to the other African Americans remained evident; in a seating chart avowedly designed to honor "rank," all black missionaries except the host were relegated to an end table closest to the door.[69]

Whereas Althea Brown confronted this example of racial segregation at the mission station through direct conversation with one of her white colleagues, Alonzo Edmiston reacted in a way that brought him closer—at least privately—to fulfilling one of the primary fears colonial officials shared regarding African American travelers. He expressed the political and social grievances that he shared with his African neighbors and took a major step toward incorporating aspects of African traditional religion into the structure of the African Presbyterian synod.

The entry from Edmiston's journal that describes the segregated wedding reception also includes an extended explanation for his conviction that the spectacle was "just making a problem between the colored people and the state people out here." He continued with almost a full page of descriptions of how three male officials maintained intimate relations with multiple African women at a time. Edmiston focused most of his recollections on Schilling, the territorial officer who, after engaging in a known affair with a chief's daughter in 1932, had been suspected by villagers of trying to keep a pastor's daughter by force at his local government post. The missionary acknowledged that most of these observations were reported by African workers and church members and that he believed their accounts over the counterarguments of the territorial officer. The frustration evident in his concluding phrase seems to represent the ethical objections of the Africans who exposed this pattern of sexual abuse: "Then you say that they [the Belgian Congo officials] are too good for the colored people to eat with."[70]

Facing new limitations on whom they could associate with and what type of African American news they could receive during 1934, Alonzo Edmiston confessed to feeling that "your color plays a great part [in] our position in Africa nowadays."[71] He and Althea Brown sought respite in two familiar ways. In addition to their respective duties at the mission farm and the hospital, they started new projects to promote respect of other African American and African leaders. The plan to coordinate church outreach through African elders that was described in the previous chapter started in this period, and it represented the pinnacle of Edmiston's acculturation to what became known as the "church as family" principle in African theology.[72]

Two theologians have specialized in presenting a model for Christian congregations that draws from African traditional religion. Mercy Amba Oduyoye envisioned the faith as an extended family with multiple branches linked to a common ancestor. She traced the strength of kinship through the diversity of this large symbolic family rather than through attempted uniformity. Diversity of approaches to spirituality adds to the liveliness and innovation of Christian groups in this metaphor, providing advantages to the entire family in their "mutual commitment" to the goals of their Creator.[73] The Catholic theologian Gerald Tanye broadened the "church-as-family" metaphor to incorporate African traditional recognition of guests, ancestors, and future generations.[74] He argued that effective parishes in Africa would need to display similar hospitality to non-Christians while avoiding any activities that compelled members to "abandon one's social milieu and culture."[75]

Alonzo Edmiston's ministry plan reflected similar attention to African traditions by shifting the Congo Mission's recruitment focus from local youth to the older heads of households. By receiving church information from the elder of their *deku*, or extended family group, potential converts drew closer to the faith without placing social or physical distance between themselves and loved ones. Edmiston had not abandoned the more typical mission strategies of child-care and school programs; he continued managing the boys' boarding school for about five years after this change. Still, the change implied that the Congo Mission would not compete with traditional understandings of the African family group as (in Mercy Oduyoye's words) "a religious community operating in ever-wider units" that passes down group values.[76] By training Presbyterian evangelists to work with family units rather than just individuals, Edmiston proposed a notable development in APCM recruitment strategy that might have helped the African Presbyterian synod persist for years after the American missionaries departed.

Meanwhile, Althea Brown started preparing what became her final publication: a biography of Maria Fearing. The explicit focus on honoring her mentor allowed Brown also to explain the legacy of African American women in the Congo Mission. After describing Fearing's childhood and the educational and religious ambitions that led her to pursue a missions career, the second half of the essay slows the pace to provide details of Fearing's pedagogy. Within this methodical description of how the girls enrolled at the Pantops foster home were instructed to eat, dress, complete chores, and study the Bible was an implied treatise on Brown's own continuing ministry. Brown had incorporated many of these instructions into the plans for the Luebo Agricultural College, which she operated with her husband until 1919.

In particular, the unfulfilled dream of hosting annual conferences of chiefs, parents, and village leaders at the college recalled Brown's memories of Fearing's yard as "a regular rendezvous for native people, young and old." Fearing had welcomed neighbors to gather on the front porch of her house to "talk, sing, play, and tell stories" in a way that was reminiscent of southern folklore tradition.[77] Brown's contribution to the Agricultural College expanded that informal format into a planned cultural celebration with local crafts, regional discourse, and an intended art museum. Likewise, the goal of establishing multiple houses in which Agricultural College students would live cooperatively in small "family" units and share domestic responsibilities originated with the rotating work schedule Brown observed at the foster home. The Luba language study and song translation that kept Fearing's legacy alive in the APCM hymnal set a model for the Kuba language study that Brown continued to promote through her newly published dictionary and grammar.[78]

What made these comparisons in the short biographical essay important for Althea Brown was that the results of the Pantops Home had already been recognized and celebrated by the APCM. Girls sheltered by Maria Fearing became some of the first Presbyterian converts in the Congo Free State and often remained active with the mission as the wives of pastors and evangelists.[79] The success of the program ensured that what started as a self-funded project would be maintained as an official ministry for decades after Fearing was forced into retirement. Brown reviewed her personal connection to African American history for evidence that her career goals remained meaningful. She may have had her own professional flexibility in mind when she described Fearing's willingness to fill several essential roles for the good of her students and colleagues. The timing of the essay project coincided with Brown's temporary appointments as a girls' school matron and nurse for two different Presbyterian hospitals. It had been about thirteen years since her ministries had been based in an area populated primarily by Kuba speakers. Yet Brown did not lose faith that her book would prove valuable to the APCM eventually. The biography of Maria Fearing transcended practical focus on the facts of one life to present an argument for admiration of African American persistence and achievement.

The process of researching the biographical essay contributed an additional way for the Edmistons to celebrate African American leadership in reaction to increased discrimination. Althea Brown based part of her work on information and photographs that she received from Lucius DeYampert during her final furlough in 1935.[80] Returning to Alabama allowed the Edmistons to interact with African American academic, civic, and religious leaders just as some of these leaders were starting their civil rights activism in Selma. The furlough also included valuable time to reconnect with their sons, meet their granddaughter, Althea, and revisit their old campuses. When the Southern Presbyterian Committee on Women's Work published the biographical essay on Maria Fearing just after both Fearing and Brown passed away, it appeared at first that this work and her colleague Robert Bedinger's essay on Brown would represent the final publications highlighting Althea Brown's legacy. But some of the other events during the Edmistons' stay in Selma outlived both of them as antecedents to the civil rights movement.

Citizenship and Freedom Struggles in Selma

Althea Brown and Alonzo Edmiston took their last joint trip to Selma at a time when local black education was in considerable distress. The effects of the Great Depression had left the Selma school board unable to fund continued operations past 1933 without an income tax hike. The financial crisis exacerbated the poor public health conditions that local African American children endured for lack of local investment. Clark School, the one public school designated for black students, had been established in 1894 as a six-room building with the third-lowest funding base in the state.[81] Though the city expanded Clark with three more buildings by 1922, its size and resources remained insufficient for its student body of 1,300 students in 1929.[82] Students found no relief from the cramped classrooms through organized recreation; neither of the city parks or recreation facilities admitted black children before or during the 1930s.[83] A Methodist missionary society provided school meals at Clark temporarily in lieu of provisions from the Selma school board.[84] By 1940 the situation remained distressing enough to prompt local civil rights organizing; the Selma Colored Civic League appealed to the school board for "a high school that will not be a constant hazard to the lives of the children."[85]

The private school alternatives available in the mid-1930s remained inadequate as well. Reductions in charitable giving placed the continuance of two Presbyterian primary and secondary programs—Knox Academy and Ford Industrial—at risk.[86] The school board's plan to borrow three classrooms at Payne University did not eliminate concerns about overcrowding or dangerous conditions; the African Methodist Episcopal Church had already removed part of its own academic program from this campus because the geographic location was considered unhealthy.[87] Considering that most of the black students in Selma were enrolled in religious private schools, the educational plight they faced during the Great Depression was a challenge to Protestant home missions policy.

Both Sherman Kueta and Alonzo Leaucourt Bope Edmiston had advanced to or past university by the time that their parents returned to Selma in 1935. Yet the local school funding issue remained a concern for the family because of its societal implications for the black community. The local cotton profits had been in decline since the World War I era, and there were few newer businesses to compensate for them. Yet the city's funding for black schools remained subpar, thereby reducing residents' career options and implying continued endorsement of the education argument that Senator John Tyler Morgan made in 1888. Morgan had declared that the improvement of black schools would decrease the southern agricultural labor force.[88] As local poverty worsened and relief options for African Americans dwindled, tens of thousands of black Selma residents joined the Great Migration to northern and western cities. The missionaries' sons would follow the northern path after graduation, which made it more difficult for the family to reunite during furloughs.

Kueta Edmiston had attended Clark School before the PCUS Executive Committee on Foreign Mission funded his enrollment in the Fisk University normal program.[89] He carried on his mother's legacy by graduating from the university, starting a family afterward, and sending his daughter, Althea, to the same institution. The fact that Kueta's bride grew up in Selma, however, did not motivate him to settle down there. The older Edmistons devoted part of their furlough time to visiting Kueta, his wife, and the baby at their new home in New York City. Later during their vacation,

Bope took a train from North Carolina to visit his parents in Selma. Althea Brown had enrolled their younger son in the Payne University (AME) private school program before she left him in Selma with family friends in 1917. He experienced severe bouts of influenza and malaria during this period because of the poor public health conditions there.[90] Bope graduated from a public historically black college, North Carolina Agricultural and Technical, after first enrolling in Fisk like his brother. His academic schedule limited his visits, but Bope also had personal reasons to avoid remaining in Selma as an adult. He later told his own son, Herbert, that he had witnessed a lynching there during his childhood—a memory that fit the historical context of rising Ku Klux Klan participation in the region during the 1920s.[91] Despite the reported decline in local lynching rates after 1904, the years in Selma seem to have left the second generation of the Edmiston family disillusioned with southern life.[92] Bope Edmiston settled in Philadelphia and started a family near the historic Wesley AME Zion church that Althea's brother-in-law, the Reverend Fred Douglas, pastored.

With their adult children and grandchildren committing to life in the northeast, Althea Brown and Alonzo Edmiston relied on the spiritual family they had gathered in Selma and Tuscaloosa over the decades. Their participation in a network of black Alabamians during the Great Depression made local segregation issues a regular part of their lives. The residence where they stayed in Selma was located in the relatively small area of the city where black businesses, churches, and homes had been concentrated through the decades. Neither missionary mentioned receiving an invitation to visit the white congregations beyond the invisible borders of the black neighborhood, even though Brown had received a bicycle and other donations from the First Presbyterian Church of Selma in the past. Edmiston purchased Althea's belated birthday gifts in the downtown Selma shopping district where African Americans were not allowed to try on clothes, linger outside, or use a restroom.[93] During previous breaks, the couple had traveled to Nashville for medical treatment from a doctor affiliated with the PCUS. Their options for receiving such extensive treatment for tropical diseases in Selma were limited partly by the fact that the city never had more than two hospitals that admitted black patients during Althea's lifetime. For them, returning to their home base required giving up some freedom of movement and association.

Selma's black community offered several options for coping with the limitations posed by Jim Crow. The Edmistons found housing and a socially conscious environment by staying with local activists. Brown joined a women's club that continued her long-term interest in classical education and community service. Edmiston received additional speaking opportunities through an invitation from the most prosperous black church in the city: Tabernacle Baptist. While involved in these activities, the missionaries interacted with a network of black professionals that became indispensable to the Alabama freedom struggle.

The Edmistons received hospitality and collegiality while spending part of their furlough as the houseguests of Samuel W. and Amelia Pitts Boynton. The house had just been purchased in 1936 by this newlywed pair of Tuskegee alumni. The Boyntons worked for the federal government as extension agents providing rural education in agricultural and domestic skills. Their personal friendship with Dr. George Washington Carver kept them aware of the international visitors and students who contacted the institute to observe southern agricultural practices. Regional reliance on plantation-style farming made the Boyntons' city an ideal destination for such researchers, and the couple continued hosting black dignitaries and community leaders until Samuel Boynton's death in 1963.

The famed history of the Boynton home after 1963 as the local headquarters for the Southern Christian Leadership Conference was a continuation of the activist community begun during those agricultural visits in the 1930s. A young Selma-based lawyer and former office mate remembered Samuel W. Boynton as measuring the results of his farm visitations through success "in bringing black people out of our subhuman status."[94] He had cofounded the second version of the Dallas County Voters League in 1936, the same year that the Edmistons stayed in the Boynton home.[95] Amelia Boynton had registered to vote two years earlier and led secret citizenship classes with her husband so that more rural sharecroppers could do likewise.[96] One of the first guests at the Boynton home was a Tuskegee graduate from Uganda named Daniel Kato. His visit facilitated transnational community building on two levels. Kato impressed Amelia Boynton by holding a conversation with a local sharecropper and first-generation former slave in her ancestral language from Sierra Leone. And the Boyntons' social justice interests likewise impressed Kato; his friendship with Samuel W. Boynton since their years as Tuskegee classmates may have motivated Kato to send letters back to Uganda with information about the National Association for the Advancement of Colored People (NAACP). In turn, that information later inspired the young leader of a Ugandan cultural group to start his own long-term correspondence with African American civil rights groups, starting with Du Bois at the NAACP offices.[97] Though the Edmistons did not mention participating in political activities at the Boynton home, their hosts were well prepared to give the missionaries access to the African American social and cultural news that they no longer received in the Belgian Congo.

The Edmistons also strengthened their social network by participating in neighborhood groups and church services. Brown joined the Progressive Culture Club and Edmiston served as a keynote speaker for one of its events. This black women's group started in 1915 as a "civic, service, and social club," probably modeled on an older club of the same name in Decatur, Alabama.[98] The Decatur chapter has been remembered as a literary society primarily; it had committees dedicated to art, music, and publicity through a World's Fair exhibit. Each committee had designated days to present papers.[99] As an affiliate of the General Federation of Women's Clubs, the Decatur group pledged a focus on "all that tends to elevate the intellectual standard of" its region.[100] The Selma chapter applied that goal but did so within a social context that made their work explicitly political in a way that was not typical for the groups founded by white women.[101] Promoting literature and public speaking in an organization that recruited across generations brought attention to the separate and unequal resources that these young African American women would encounter in the local public school. And if the Selma Progressive Culture Club attempted to start a library, as the Decatur chapter did in 1893, that move would have brought the club in direct confrontation with a notable omission in the city's Jim Crow facilities. Selma barred African Americans from the public library and made no "separate but equal" options available.[102]

The Edmistons attended the local Southern Presbyterian black congregation, Sylvan Street Presbyterian Church, but they often visited the Baptist and African Methodist Episcopal churches that were located just a few blocks from them. Tabernacle Baptist would become legendary in 1965 for hosting controversial civil rights mass meetings that included Dr. Martin Luther King Jr. But the civic reputations of these churches had already started growing by the late 1930s thanks to their programming and the popularity of Pastor D. V. Jemison. As the pastor of Tabernacle Baptist, Jemison had earned a local reputation for promoting gradual social change and accommodation to the Jim Crow racial order. In exchange, he had multiple connections among influential white leaders in Selma. Local jailers sometimes released African American prisoners because of Jemison's intervention, and he was one of the few black leaders to receive approval for a real estate improvement loan.[103] In the 1940s his network of white supporters offered potential advantages to black citizens who hoped to vote under the voucher system.[104] Jemison also campaigned successfully to gain academic accreditation for the local Baptist institution, Selma University, after 1950.[105]

Given his social role, Jemison's decision to invite Alonzo Edmiston to preach was probably part of his plan to avoid the appearance of controversy. Nevertheless, special events such as missions presentations served a civic purpose by associating the church building with notable African American speakers regardless of denominational differences. A similar pattern of cooperation showed in the black Presbyterians' support of Selma University and the collegial rivalry between black Protestant and Catholic club sports teams after World War II.[106] Despite one local teacher's concerns that competition between church leaders sowed division among black residents of Selma, the expansion of programming at Tabernacle Baptist and other African American institutions was a unifying tactic that addressed the injustice of the Alabama sharecropping system.[107]

For families seeking respite from generations of debt peonage to regional white landowners, relocation to the city offered varied job options and "at least a measure of freedom from white control." Thanks to the organizing efforts of a local church member, L. R. Taylor, African American farmers could meet in Selma to discuss New Deal programs and question a federal appointee about increasing their financial benefits.[108] Alonzo Edmiston enjoyed the December 1935 meeting he attended; unlike the Boyntons, he did not need to navigate unpaved rural paths or visit white landowners before requesting permission to meet with black sharecroppers.[109] The resources of congregations and schools helped these rural families remain in Selma for generations, disrupting the pattern of "attitudes of dependency inherent in the tenant farming relationship."[110] Before the mass meetings of the Freedom Riders or the Southern Christian Leadership Conference, Tabernacle Baptist and Selma University were recognized as community centers where neighbors could gather to celebrate black professionals and consider their own futures.

Fisk University as a Freedom Struggle Battleground

The Edmistons' last sabbatical together brought reunions with family and friends but not complete separation from colonial race politics. Visits to their old campuses renewed the collaboration between the first set of black Presbyterian missionaries in ways that had been preempted abroad. And the participation of Thomas Jesse Jones, the Phelps Stokes Fund researcher, on the board of Fisk University amplified any developments at Althea Brown's alma mater as potential influences on African educational policy.

Brown had returned to Fisk University at least three times since her graduation—in 1908 as a visitor to the women's organization she founded, in 1920 to attend a missions-themed dramatic presentation, and in 1921 as a commencement speaker.[111] Between those visits and the enrollment of her younger son, she had multiple opportunities to hear of the shifting power dynamic on campus following student protests in 1924 and 1925. According to his children, Bope Edmiston's progress toward a Fisk bachelor's degree was cut short by his expulsion for violating the student code of conduct.[112] Because of his unexpected need to transfer out of state, the family gained personal perspective on the ramifications of strict enforcement of rules at the campus. Between W. E. B. Du Bois, whose daughter also attended Fisk at the time, and Thomas Jesse Jones, the debate over strict enforcement escalated beyond Nashville to arguments regarding the controllability of African and African American students worldwide.[113]

Fayette A. McKenzie, the Fisk president from 1915 to 1925, became controversial for requiring a code of conduct and dress that many students considered outdated.[114] A 1924 statement of student grievances requested additional peer representation, extracurricular sports programs, and unchaperoned dates as signs that the administration valued input from alumni and students.[115] A speech from Du Bois at his daughter's commencement ceremony placed the campaign against President McKenzie in the broader context of opposing "the widespread idea that influential Southern whites should be induced to help lead Negro college education."[116] Subsequent calls for McKenzie's resignation echoed through the alumni network, particularly after the university president requested support from the Nashville police to quell the protests.

What Du Bois interpreted as "a needed service [to help] save the ideals of a great school" was instead presented to the Fisk Board of Trustees as a direct threat to international race relations.[117] For Thomas Jesse Jones, the board secretary, Fisk University represented both an exemplary learning environment and an experiment in social control.[118] His research on behalf of the Phelps Stokes Fund identified Fisk as one of only three African American institutions that offered academic curriculum befitting a college or university.[119] This status made Fisk an essential model for the teams of African teachers and white colonial officials who received Phelps Stokes funding to visit American historically black campuses during and after 1924.[120] Kenneth King noted that Jones argued that the controversy had significance for "Negro education and for race relationships in America and Africa." Accordingly, he interpreted the resignation of President McKenzie in broad, apocalyptic terms as a portent of destruction for race-based education.[121]

Althea Brown did not join other alumni in expressing support or concern publicly after the campus protests. She had endorsed the university president at the center of the scandal early in his term by devoting part of her speech at the 1921 commencement ceremony to praise "the high standards" he had set for students' coursework, appearance, and behavior. Brown concluded with a proclamation that left no doubt of her continuing sense of solidarity with Fisk University; while sharing the chapel stage with him, she announced, "Dr. McKenzie, we love you for what you have done and what you are doing here, and are going to stand by you in your difficult task."[122] Brown made her preference for the regimented social structure of Fisk clear, but the changes in student life did not seem to dim her enthusiasm for the institution. Brown continued requesting printed copies of her book to be sent to friends in the United States, which probably included those in the Fisk community who had helped raise funds for its initial publication. And one of her last speeches in the United States took place in the Fisk University chapel in 1935. But perhaps the clearest hint of Althea Brown's reactions to the freedom struggle at her alma mater can be seen in the way her family followed the career of her former classmate George Edmund Haynes.

Before a colleague recommended that the Edmistons cancel subscriptions to black newspapers, Alonzo Edmiston saved a clipping from a 1934 *Chicago Defender* article titled "Dr. Haynes Sees 'Teeth' in Auto Industry Code as Bar to Race Discrimination." It features Haynes analyzing New Deal policies in his capacity as the Federal Council of Churches executive secretary for race relations. Since the couple shared the newspaper subscription, this article about the friend who visited the Congo Mission four years earlier probably caught Althea Brown's attention. The fact that it was saved in the journals that functioned as their professional records suggests that the topic of Haynes's civil rights activism also met with the Edmistons' approval. But evidence suggests that Brown and Haynes had chosen opposite sides in racial controversies in past decades. The year before the Fisk student protests started, Brown had praised President McKenzie by comparing him with the university's founding president, Erastus Milo Cravath.[123] But Haynes had instigated the confrontation that led to Cravath's resignation in 1900. While enrolled at Fisk, Haynes wrote to W. E. B. Du Bois and invited him to speak during the 1898 commencement. The request was a challenge to the addition of Booker T. Washington as a member of the Board of Trustees and the subsequent emphasis on industrial education courses at the university. President Cravath left his position when it seemed impossible to reconcile the trustees' demands with those of alumni and students who supported the counterargument from Du Bois.[124] If George E. Haynes continued to support his fellow sociologist and civil rights activist in the campaigns against the university administration, then the disagreement placed Haynes and Brown at odds publicly. Still, she and her husband showed interest in his activism ten years later. The fact that Althea Brown's commitment to her Fisk University community outlasted changes in the administration and the campus code of conduct indicates that she accepted its developing affiliation with the black freedom struggle.

The short article about racial discrimination in the automobile industry was the type of news item that the Edmistons would miss after giving up their subscription to the *Chicago Defender*. Specific content was one of the reasons they regretted that loss. Besides the prospect of losing information about a long-time friend, the Edmistons lost access to information about African Americans with political influence. By 1934 Haynes had already served as the first executive secretary of the National Urban League and as a special assistant to the U.S. secretary of labor. His federally sponsored sociohistorical study of African American labor marked him as an expert whose record of service extended to the White House and to the leaders of the mainline Protestant denominations. The example that Haynes set with his political and religious work echoed the prestige that William Henry Sheppard had earned by contributing to human rights reform in the Congo Free State. But news about progress against race discrimination in the United States stood in contrast to the declining leadership status that the Edmistons perceived for themselves at the mission station.

The last category of social justice activism that the Edmistons observed during their final furlough brought the topic directly to their own profession. They joined a growing trend of interracial ministerial cooperation within the Presbyterian Church in the United States. Specifically, Althea Brown and Alonzo Edmiston joined several of their African American colleagues in bringing more equitability to black leaders' participation in these interracial events.

From 1916 through at least the 1940s, Stillman Institute hosted an annual conference for African American women affiliated with Southern Presbyterian churches. As the first leader of the PCUS Woman's Auxiliary, Hallie Paxson Winsborough co-organized the early meetings featuring activities that included Bible study and domestic training. As the denominational historian Joel L. Alvis noted, these conferences introduced Southern Presbyterian female outreach across the color line but with "implied cultural superiority" through the intent of offering only white speakers and their preferred programs.[125]

Black missionaries disrupted that cultural message by participating from the beginning of the endeavor. Lucy Gantt Sheppard led most of the afternoon vespers service at the 1916 meeting and taught a sewing class at the 1919 meeting. Lucius DeYampert and A. A. Rochester offered speeches about their overseas ministries, and Lilian Thomas DeYampert, Gantt Sheppard, and Maria Fearing closed out day one of the first conference with their own missions presentations.[126] Fearing drew attention again when she reviewed the 1919 conference for the official minutes of the Woman's Auxiliary; she was quoted as saying, "It made me stronger spiritually and more determined to help and encourage others to live near the Lord."[127]

Unlike other African Americans on the attendee list, these speakers were not identified in a Presbyterian newspaper or the denominational meeting minutes with references to their skin color. Instead, the publicized reports respected their titles as "Missionary"; "Mrs." was added in the case of Thomas DeYampert and Gantt Sheppard.[128] Such unusual public recognition from a white southern publication signaled that the black missionaries would continue to receive regard from white church members even though most of them were denied opportunities to return to the Belgian Congo by the time the conferences started.[129]

And since Althea Brown wrote her short biography of Maria Fearing for a book published by the Woman's Auxiliary, she also helped keep African Americans involved in the organization as contributors rather than just recipients of outreach. The addition of Robert Bedinger's essay on Brown and excerpts from her short autobiography cemented the goal of *Glorious Living* to be a tribute to living and recently departed women who exemplified missionary service.[130] The emphasis on teaching styles and ministry strategies in the Maria Fearing biography might have also made an impression on

Glorious Living's compiler, Hallie Paxson Winsborough. Brown's arguments for how specific methods produced effective ministry among African girls fit the analytical style of Winsborough's contemporary work with the Committee on Interracial Cooperation (CIC). In collaboration with a fellow CIC member, Jessie Daniel Ames, Winsborough helped start a Tuscaloosa-based community study that compiled data on black and white manual laborers through the first years of the Great Depression. This church volunteerism also led some Southern Presbyterian women to join Ames in her Association of Southern Women for the Prevention of Lynching, which shows that African American social interests had started to influence how Woman's Auxiliary members interpreted racial justice.[131] Brown dedicated her grammar and dictionary to Winsborough and the Woman's Work Committee for helping make its publication possible.[132]

Meanwhile, Alonzo Edmiston experienced a rare moment of racial equality inspired by a personal loss. He delivered a message in the Southern Presbyterian church that had recommended him to Stillman Institute over thirty years earlier. Like Althea Brown, Edmiston received a ministerial referral from his local PCUS church without having been admitted previously to the congregation.[133] That isolation changed about three months before his return to the Congo Mission because he received word that his foster father, W. C. Edmiston Jr., had passed away. Ann Hines, Alonzo Edmiston's grandmother, had been enslaved as a house servant to the white branch of the Edmiston family since before they relocated to Petersburg, Tennessee, in 1820.[134] Her son, Charlie Edmiston, and her six grandchildren remained on the Edmiston plantation as farmworkers and servants to the second generation of the former slaveholders.[135] Alonzo Edmiston considered W. C. Edmiston Jr. a parental figure, possibly because the loss of both of his parents by 1921 increased his need for additional sources of news about his siblings.[136] The white Edmistons welcomed visits from the missionary couple over the decades, hosting Althea Brown and her baby Kueta in their home rather than in one of the small servants' cabins.[137] So the speech that probably became the first appearance by an African American in the Petersburg First Presbyterian pulpit started as an expression of love for a family friend. William Campbell Edmiston III wrote about twenty years later that the eulogy for his father gained significance over time; a church member reported that it sparked a local Christian revival. The pastor's dismissive choice to introduce Alonzo Edmiston as "a colored boy" did not diminish the symbolic power of that event.[138]

Their final decade of mission work brought Althea Brown and Alonzo Edmiston to the brink of movements that would later reshape American and central African race relations. Their ministry assignments with the native court and the schools required close interaction with the current and future leaders of the new Presbyterian synod in the Belgian Congo. Economic and political oppression sharpened by the global Great Depression motivated some of these African Presbyterians to seek greater control over church affairs and more input on colonial policies. Within the context of increased public segregation at APCM events, the Edmistons became a convenient target for African criticism of imperialism. Like his white colleagues, Alonzo Edmiston sometimes acted as a representative of Belgian state authority in the region, but by the 1930s Edmiston's critics faced less retribution than they would have with other representatives. Likewise, a temporary boycott of the local church showed an African pastor's ability to sway public opinion against Althea Brown's decision to approve corporal punishment of female students. Protestant ministers were among the earliest models of African leadership in contradiction to total white authority, and occasional opposition to Alonzo Edmiston helped African Presbyterian elders and pastors fit that trend.

The Edmistons found more welcome and recognition during their furlough in Selma, but civil rights controversies were also on the horizon there in 1935. Among their hosts and fellow ministers and educators, the couple interacted with at least three of the local activists who would become legendary in the Alabama freedom struggle. By participating in community meetings and offering missionary lectures, they helped popularize the trend of migration of black sharecroppers from rural Dallas County to the relative safety and independence of the black city neighborhood. Brown's writing on behalf of the PCUS Woman's Auxiliary carried on the tradition of interracial cooperation that her black colleagues had begun after being dismissed from mission service. Meanwhile, the couple's benefits from the Southern Presbyterian denomination helped their sons, Kueta and Bope Edmiston, earn college degrees out of state and join the largest African American resistance movement of their time: the Great Migration. As their last years together wound down, Alonzo Edmiston and Althea Brown saw unanticipated threats to their authority in the Belgian Congo but also hints that the work of their friends and families could flourish with the benefit of increasing social opportunities.

Conclusion

Changes in Colonial Politics and School Policies, 1936–1963

By the time the couple returned to the Belgian Congo in 1936, Alonzo Edmiston had cemented two professional connections of significance to his agricultural research. He renewed his connection to Tuskegee in two ways. Upon arrival in New York in 1935, he sent "forty-three specimens of medical herbs and clays" to George Washington Carver for agricultural experimentation.[1] Though the results are not available in Edmiston's records, the samples may have contributed to the soil quality studies that Carver conducted for his 1936 bulletin on restoring prime soil quality.[2] Edmiston also attended the presidential inauguration at Tuskegee Institute that year in the company of other ministers, where he heard distinguished speakers, including Mary McLeod Bethune and Anson Phelps Stokes.[3] The second significant connection during his furlough occurred outside Alabama. His agenda book indicates that he visited the Phelps Stokes Fund office while the Edmistons were in New York with their son Sherman Kueta and their new granddaughter, Althea. Though he left no summary of the meeting, signs suggest that it was positive. He preserved a Christmas card that he received from a member of the Phelps family and received additional international visitors to the Mutoto station farm in the following years. These interactions with well-known persons in the industrial education movement enhanced Edmiston's reputation as an award-winning innovator in the field.

International connections proved advantageous for Alonzo Edmiston during the following year. He had been away on furlough when the Belgian government encouraged Phelps Stokes Fund representatives to visit the APCM in 1921, but Edmiston's work was featured when an American with organizational ties to Thomas Jesse Jones, the fund's spokesman, visited in August 1936.[4] Dr. John Reisner, a representative of Agricultural Missions Inc., toured the Mutoto farm during a multiday visit to the Congo Mission.

He found the produce grown there so impressive that he offered one thousand francs in annual donations for the hiring of an agricultural demonstrator to assist in rural outreach near Mutoto.[5] The financial offer and the expert's defense of the project helped ensure that the station evangelistic committee would approve the plan Edmiston designed, though he doubted that most of his colleagues would have accepted his ministry ideas so well without the incentive.[6]

Partnerships like the one planned in 1936 might have blossomed into a new sphere of influence for the Edmistons except for two tragic circumstances that followed shortly thereafter. Alonzo Edmiston returned to the Belgian Congo prepared to die there if his diabetes proved unmanageable. Instead, Althea Brown died on 9 June 1937 during her second bout with sleeping sickness and malaria. The illness started on 12 July of the previous year, about a week before she hosted a birthday party for him.[7] About a week before her passing, Brown dictated her will and testament to her husband. It left most of her jewelry to their grandchildren and daughters-in-law and her wardrobe to their African friends around the mission station.[8] She singled out an evangelist named Katompa to receive most of these items for his family. In the preceding five years, he had overseen music classes for the boys' school and the evangelist conferences.[9] As thanks, Katompa formed a choir to sing at Brown's funeral before an audience of two thousand mourners. Edmiston wrote to his sons that the tribute choir "sounded like an angelic host from above" as they performed two songs Brown had translated into Luba: "Guide Me, O Thou Great Jehovah" and "Tis Midnight and on Olive's Brow/The Star Is Dimmed That Lately Shone."[10]

Edmiston also published a tribute letter written by an evangelist named Tshisungu Daniel, who had grown up in the Pantops Home under the care of Maria Fearing and her foster daughters. From his childhood at the Luebo mission station to his later reputation as "the Billy Graham of Congo," Daniel maintained personal and professional connections to the African American missionaries for about thirty years.[11] He poured those experiences into his memorial for Althea Brown, which celebrated the idea that her transition from earthly life allowed her to be with Christ and with the deceased members of their spiritual family, such as Fearing, Lilian Thomas, Annie Taylor Rochester, and Bertha Morrison (the wife of former APCM manager William M. Morrison). Likewise, Daniel encouraged Edmiston to take comfort in the company of his friends and "children," who would miss him after his impending retirement.[12]

The second personal misfortune involved Alonzo Edmiston's chronic illness. Upon his returning to Mutoto in 1936, unreliable access to medication shipments made Edmiston's farmwork routine risky. Finding out that neither of the two APCM doctors knew when he would receive supplies to treat his diabetes made Edmiston confide in his journal, "If I was a man of weak disposition I would give up, but I won't say die."[13] He adjusted to the loss of his wife by contributing his journals, letters, and news clippings to help a younger colleague named Julia Lake Kellersberger publish what became *A Life for the Congo: The Story of Althea Brown Edmiston*. And Edmiston continued teaching occasional agriculture classes and overseeing the boys' school until he opted for retirement in 1939.

By then, racial exclusion policies enforced by British colonial officials had multiplied to the extent that the Executive Committee on Foreign Missions did not receive permission for Edmiston to travel on a ship that stopped in South Africa.[14] The delay caused as he waited in vain for permission to travel by the standard route meant that he needed to travel alone during World War II on the alternative route: an overland trip through western Europe. Pain from his long-term illness exacerbated the stress of waiting for an ocean liner to depart Portugal and hoping to avoid a German invasion in the meantime.[15] He arrived safely in Selma in the fall of 1940 and established a new ministry routine of presenting mission talks and Kuba memorabilia at Presbyterian congregations, schools, and other sites throughout the state.[16] He remarried the following year after meeting a fellow African American Presbyterian named Lucille Shelton.

Alonzo Edmiston died at the end of a year that represented the nadir before the height of civil rights activism in Selma. The state's first White Citizen's Council was founded in the city following the 1954 *Brown v. Board of Education* decision, and the Selma chapter used economic intimidation to force most members out of the local NAACP chapter that the Edmistons' onetime host, Sam Boynton, had revitalized the previous year.[17] The voting rights campaigns promoted by that NAACP chapter continued through the Student Nonviolent Coordinating Committee in the early 1960s; Amelia Boynton Robinson became one of the publicized faces of the Bloody Sunday protest on the Edmund Pettus Bridge in 1965.[18]

The death of Althea Brown, the return of Alonzo Edmiston to Selma, and the retirement of A. A. Rochester and his second wife, Edna May Atkinson Rochester, in 1940 left the American Presbyterian Congo Mission without African American staff until 1958.[19] During that interim period, the structure of the APCM schools changed to fit the preferences of the Belgian colonial government. The transformation began in 1932 with a voluntary initiative by the Congo Protestant Council to encourage its affiliated missions to adopt the State Educational Program.[20] The Protestant missions in the colony, having already adapted a standard curriculum across denominations, saw potential for expansion in the government proposal.[21] This program made agricultural training standard practice at each level, and it included the added incentive of land grants offered to each school in compliance.[22] The American Presbyterian Congo Mission was identified as one of the three Protestant organizations that fit the Belgian criteria at the time, but it remained unable to access government subsidies because they were reserved for the Catholic missions until 1946.[23]

Government affiliation entailed more than political prestige. Along with the promise of additional acreage and stipends for missionaries and African teachers, only the sponsored schools could produce graduates eligible to serve as teachers or school "monitors" inspecting campuses throughout an assigned region.[24] The incentive of a future cash salary of one thousand francs available to secondary graduates made conformity to the government standards a valuable recruitment tool, which is why the leader of the Congo Protestant Council sought assurance that voluntary submission to government inspections could make the Protestant mission schools eligible to offer that benefit.[25]

The political context of increased interest in subsidized education after 1932 made any signs of Belgian interest in the APCM educators significant to the future development of missions, particularly the service awards given to the Edmistons and the occasional visits of Belgian dignitaries to their ministry projects.[26] Between 1932 and 1935, Alonzo Edmiston welcomed one Belgian veterinarian who inspected his livestock, supervised a Belgian educator who observed a rural school, and hosted two government officials in the Edmistons' home.[27] In contrast to the Belgian efforts to restrict African American missionaries in 1921, government officials were celebrating their contributions in the 1930s and suggesting ways to improve them.[28] These ministers still received additional colonial monitoring, but they had incentives to perceive that attention as a sign that their academic initiatives had found approval.

Indications that the Edmistons' expertise could help the Congo Mission reach its goal of state education program compliance multiplied from 1932 until over a decade after Alonzo Edmiston's retirement. For example, the Belgian International Colonial Institute specified singing and music as required curriculum at the primary and secondary levels.[29] And all African teachers were expected to maintain a home garden while students practiced a variety of agricultural skills, including fieldwork, gardening, and livestock care.[30] The types of industrial work taught in the subsidized technical schools would be adjusted to the needs of local companies yet standardized for the skills deemed essential "for general progress."[31] Though the Edmistons' Agricultural College had been the only APCM school to offer French instruction in 1918 and 1919, the APCM requested help from the Baptist Missionary Society to strengthen its French curriculum in 1946, "as we are endeavoring to bring our whole system up to government standard."[32] Even hints of Althea Brown's storytelling emphasis appeared in the suggested secondary curriculum of student "talks" or lectures.[33]

Brown and Edmiston were not the only Belgian Congo missionaries to encourage these skills at various points in their careers, but they had shown unique flexibility in their expectations for how students would apply artistic and industrial skills. The couple showed interest in local conditions, especially among the Kuba people, without demanding that students and graduates work only within their villages. That flexibility became more common at the APCM by 1948, when it received authorization to produce graduates who would be expected to serve the government throughout the colony.[34]

The government education program in the Belgian Congo was part of what Martin Thomas summarized as "the renewed focus on agronomics [that] underlined the improvement in social conditions."[35] As Alonzo Edmiston had done for students and African evangelists, the government started distributing seeds for edible crops and clearing additional farmland to make rural life more sustainable.[36] Starting in the 1930s, colonial officials transitioned to incentive-based efforts to extract agricultural labor from the African villagers without reducing social control.[37] The promise of wages for government school graduates who were hired into the system and the partnership with Catholic and Protestant missionaries helped the Belgian Congo develop the largest colonial education program on the continent by the 1950s.[38] These African school monitors were expected to exert authority "beyond the actual school code" to contribute to "the evolution of the techniques and lifestyles of the whole rural society."[39] Beyond the school system, the government also incorporated drama into its regional agricultural fairs as a form of community education.[40] These incentives did not improve the financial or political well-being of most of the population. Rather, they helped create and sustain what Bogumil Jewsiewicki considered "the golden age" of the "paternalistic state" in the Belgian Congo.[41]

This evaluation of the educational legacies of Alonzo Edmiston and Althea Brown does not end with the ways their methods contributed to Southern Presbyterian coordination with Belgian colonialism. It ends in 1963 with a reaffirmation of the couple's original training and goals. By that year, the Presbyterian Church in the United States was participating as a co-sponsor of the Congo Polytechnic Institute, a normal and vocational program launched in 1960. After the evacuation of APCM missionaries from the newly independent Democratic Republic of the Congo, the denomination returned partly through an institute that featured a home economics program designed at a historically black university.[42]

Prime Minister Patrice Lumumba of Congo had extended an invitation during a 1960 campus address for professionals from Howard University to visit his country and help expand its infrastructure.[43] Dr. Flemmie Kittrell of Howard visited the country twice after 1960 to create a program rigorous enough to require a companion pre-university program that would recruit additional female students. Her curriculum included African and world history, a subject that had not been addressed in APCM affiliated schools since the closure of the Edmistons' Agricultural College.[44] Dr. Kittrell's advice inspired the deans and president of Congo Polytechnic Institute to redesign the high school–level program so thoroughly that its graduates would also qualify for admittance to a variety of degree programs at universities in the United States and Europe.[45] The program details were published in September 1963, about a year before the PCUS Board of World Missions endorsed a statement from over two hundred of its missionaries denouncing American segregation.[46]

Althea Brown and Alonzo Edmiston devoted thirty-three years to establishing Presbyterian ministries together that were based on their education at historically black colleges and universities. They treated their combination of classical and industrial training as an asset to help them perceive and address the interests of their African neighbors. In 1963—at the early stage of Congolese independence and increased visibility for the American black freedom struggle—a new coalition of African and African American educators was working with the Southern Presbyterian denomination to continue similar work.

Appendix A

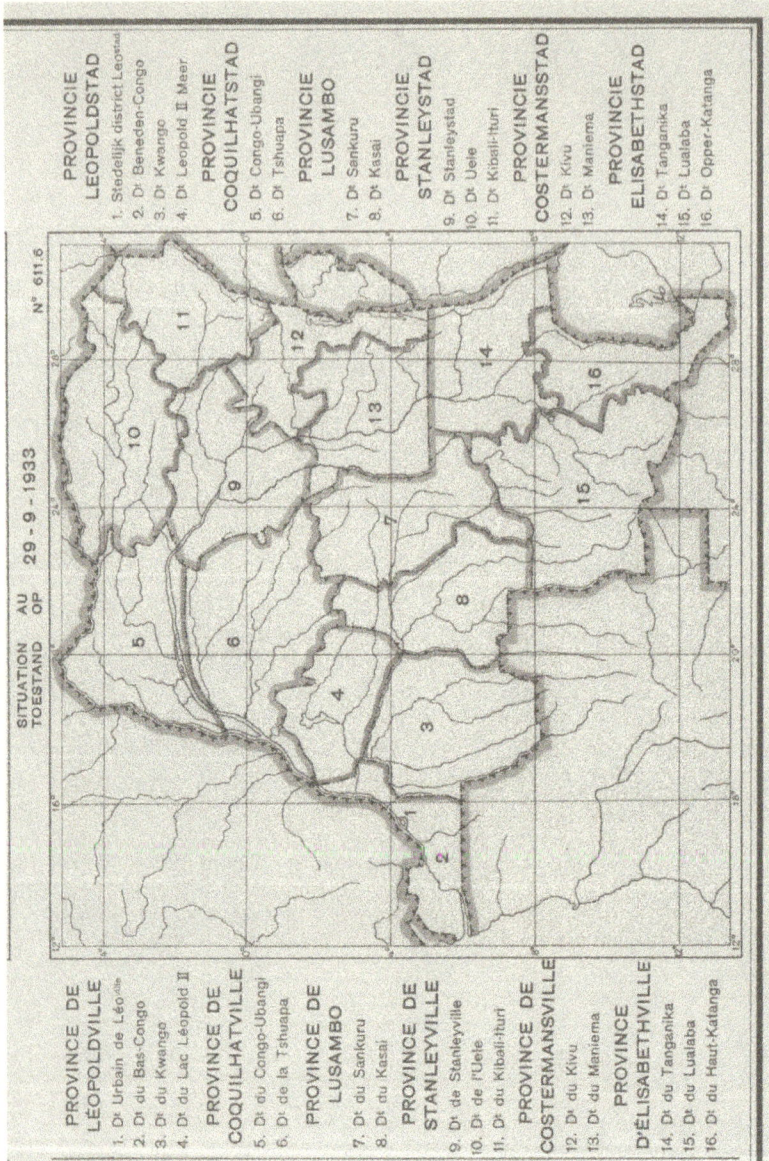

SITUATION AU 29 - 9 - 1933
TOESTAND OP

N° 611.6

PROVINCIE LEOPOLDSTAD
1. Stedelijk district Leopoldstad
2. D' Beneden-Congo
3. D' Kwango
4. D' Leopold II Meer

PROVINCIE COQUILHATSTAD
5. D' Congo-Ubangi
6. D' Tshuapa

PROVINCIE LUSAMBO
7. D' Sankuru
8. D' Kasai

PROVINCIE STANLEYSTAD
9. D' Stanleystad
10. D' Uele
11. D' Kibali-Ituri

PROVINCIE COSTERMANSSTAD
12. D' Kivu
13. D' Maniema

PROVINCIE ELISABETHSTAD
14. D' Tanganika
15. D' Lualaba
16. D' Opper-Katanga

PROVINCE DE LÉOPOLDVILLE
1. D' Urbain de Léo-ville
2. D' du Bas-Congo
3. D' du Kwango
4. D' du Lac Léopold II

PROVINCE DE COQUILHATVILLE
5. D' du Congo-Ubangi
6. D' de la Tshuapa

PROVINCE DE LUSAMBO
7. D' du Sankuru
8. D' du Kasai

PROVINCE DE STANLEYVILLE
9. D' de Stanleyville
10. D' de l'Uele
11. D' du Kibali-Ituri

PROVINCE DE COSTERMANSVILLE
12. D' du Kivu
13. D' du Maniema

PROVINCE D'ÉLISABETHVILLE
14. D' du Tanganika
15. D' du Lualaba
16. D' du Haut-Katanga

Map of the Belgian Congo: Institut Royal Colonial Belge (Brussels), "Carte des Subdivisions Administrative (1933)." From *Atlas général du Congo et du Ruanda-Urundi* (Brussels: Institut Royal Colonial Belge, 1950). The province and district names are listed in French on the left side and Dutch on the right side.

Appendix B

*Letters from Alonzo Edmiston and Althea
Brown Edmiston requesting reappointment
to the American Presbyterian Congo
Mission, 1910*

Tuscaloosa, Ala.
Feb. 16, 1910

The Executive Committee Foreign Missions,
Nashville, Tenn.

Most honored Friends:

Having just received a letter from the Congo and seeing that it is
unfavorable, I wish to make a most humble appeal to you (our most
superior body). I make it especially at this time because I note that you,
our Board, are to be represented very soon on our field in the person of
Dr. [James Overton] Reavis.

Brethren, I have done nothing criminal, nothing wort[h]y of with-
drawal from the work in which my heart is fully and truly consecrated.
My soul is all but perishing within me with longing to return, to be back
to my beloved post. I love the people, and the work which is more precious to me than life itself.

I felt a definite call to Africa at my conversion. I was reared by one of
the most devout white families (Mr. & Mrs. W. C. Edmiston) of Tennessee, by whom I was le[d] to Christ and sent to Stillman Institute
where I spent five years, finishing the theological courses under Dr.
[Clay] Lilly. My plan was to spend three or four more years in special
preparation before making my application to you.

As you already know, I went to Africa on a business trip for the St. Louis Exposition. While there I made a visit to our mission and found it sorely in need of immediate help. The Lapsley [steamship] had just gone down, Messrs. Morrison, Vass, and the Sheppards were in the homeland. [S]o at the urgent request of the brothers I remained, though I was compelled to forfeit every penny of the seven months' salary due to me by the Exposition. Sending in my application to you, I entered the work with great earnestness and tried to do my very best with the training I had already received at Stillman.

During that terrible and bloody revolt, though I suffered the loss of everything I had in the world, I stood by my post in the very face of death and never shrank from a single duty even at the risk of my life. Before the hostilities had fully ceased, having been commanded by the mission, I began alone the rebuilding of Ibanj station and stood at the peril of my life between the hostile tribes until reconciliation was gained.

I did everything I knew how to do to help the natives in their spiritual, moral and temporal uplift. I started the little Industrial School, which, considering the facilities and my small amount of training, was a success.

During the fall of 1907 I watched for three and a half months by the bedside of what I thought to be a dying baby. At the suggestion of the mission, I went to Matadi and put upon an ocean steamer my wife whose condition of health was most critical, and my sick child whom I feared would be buried at sea, and, then feeling lonely and sad, returned to my post on the mission.

Six months later, though severed by ten thousand miles of water and land from my little family, this terrible calamity came which has caused and is still causing both my wife and me exceeding great sorrow. God alone knows how much I have suffered! I made the foregoing statements not that I may hold myself up before you in the light of a hero, God forbid that I would ever seek such, I simply make mention of this in order to say that I am willing to suffer the same and even more a thousand times over again rather than give up the work in Africa.

I admit that I made many mistakes. I have repented of them sorrowingly. However, God is my Judge that I did not make them willfully. They were really and purely misunderstandings which with God's help will never occur again.

Both my wife and I, soon after I came home, wrote most earnest and most pleading letters to the missionaries and, feeling specially sure that all would be reconsidered, I gave my entire time to study, not even taking time to visit my friends. I have not eaten a single meal since my return with my aged father, have not seen my only brother or any of my wife's people.

We had letters last summer that le[d] us to believe that all would end well and that my wife at least would return in the fall or the winter. Our hearts were made extremely happy. But now our sorrow is just as great as at the beginning.

So, now I do most earnestly beseech you that there be no miscarriage of justice in my case. The work is very precious to me. I cannot leave it without continual unhappiness. I am ready to suffer, endure, make any compromise or sacrifice or do any thing else in which there is no disgrace in the sight of God rather than be severed from the African field. I am perfectly willing to go back under condition[s] you may make, fill the neediest place to be filled, and will endeavor with God's help to give as perfect satisfaction that any one of my ability can give. I entered the work for life. I do not want to give it up. There is no one on the African [field] who has endured more or worked harder than I and there is no one on that mission to show the work is more dear than it is to me. My heart is there, I love the people and know I can help them. It is therefore with deepest humility, sincerity, and great earnestness that I make this petition to you and beg you to have me restored while Dr. Reavis is on the field. A letter sent at once will reach him while he is there. I plead not so much for justice but for a reconsideration and an opportunity to continue my work in Africa. I plead all in the name of Christ Whose I am and Whom I serve.

Hopin[g] that you will grant my request,
I beg to be considered,
Faithfully yours,
[Alonzo Edmiston]

Tuscaloosa, Ala.
Feb. 16, 1910

The Executive Committee Foreign Missions,
Nashville, Tenn.
My Dear Friends:

After sixteen long months of anxious, patient, pray[er]ful waiting the long looked for message from Congo has come and unfavorable!!

I felt so sure that all would be reconsidered. I had so many bright reassuring letters from various members of the mission. Why this sudden change I am not able to understand! The whole thing comes like a dreadful nightmare! Or a death knell!! My heart is now very, very sad! Is aching, bleeding, bleeding, breaking!

I am not willing to give up and never will give Africa up as long as I am on this side of the grave. I have been for nearly sixteen years Christ's appointed missionary to Africa and for nearly nine years your appointed missionary to Africa. I have tried so hard to be faithful to you and to Him. I have stood at my post through thick and thin; through cloud and sunshine; through darkness and through light. There was no task too hard for me to undertake; no place too hard for me to fill. I tried to give my best self to the work and also [keep] any friends of the homeland in touch with and interested in the work by letters and articles. For nearly three years I was the only foreign woman at Ibanj Station and for nearly a year I was the only woman missionary on the entire mission. Though [I] was often sick and lonely, and though I lost everything I had in the world during that awful uprising of the Bakuba, I never for a moment lost heart, became discouraged or complained.

In coming to you I gave myself unreservedly. I set my heart like flint against all desires in this land. I gave myself to you, God, and the Southern Presbyterian Church for life. I started out to live and die in your Christ and the Church's service in Africa. You expected this of me and now I beg, I plead that you do not permit me to be severed from the work without a sufficient and just cause. If you do, though I shall listen amid the earthquake, the lightning, and the thunder, for the Still Small Voice, I shall never, never, no never be altogether happy again in this life and I shall go to my grave in great, great sorrow with a crushed and broken heart.

This work and the people are very dear to me, and, now that I am able to speak both languages in which the work is carried on, I know that I can do much good.

We have done nothing worthy of being taken from the field and the charge brought against us can be altogether corrected. We have repented of it a thousand times over. We have promised and do again most solemnly promise you, the mission and God, that we will endeavor, with divine help [to] avoid like mistakes or making any others. Like my husband I am willing to go back to the field under any condition, make any sacrifice or compromise.

When two of your missionaries were to go on trial at Leopoldville, all the Christians of America and England lifted up their voices to you in their [counsel], praying that there might not be [a] miscarriage of justice. Everything was done by the Church and the Executive Committee in their behalf.

We are also two of your missionaries and, as it were, on trial. So I do earnestly beg that you do not permit a miscarriage of justice in our behalf. It is with great earnestness that I make this petition and I plead as one pleads for his life both temporal and eternal. I plead in the name of the ever living, gentle, loving Christ by Whom I feel commissioned to and Whose work in Africa I beg to continue.

Earnestly praying that you will readdress the mission through
Mr. Reavis, and with very best wishes,
I am yours in His service,
[Althea Brown Edmiston]

Alonzo Edmiston to the Executive Committee on Foreign Missions, 16 February 1910, and Althea Brown Edmiston to the Executive Committee on Foreign Missions, 16 February 1910, both AEP, RG 495, box 6, folder 1, PHS.

Appendix C

Tribute Letter about Althea Edmiston from Tshisungu Daniel to Alonzo Edmiston, Luebo, 20 June 1937

Father/Mr. Luongoso,

My wife and I were at Bulape. We stayed there three days to help with God's work and God was with us in His work.

Thus while I was in the midst of joy, I heard news that tore my heart into two pieces, about the death of Mama Tshitolo.[1] I remembered all her teaching/lessons and her hard work that she did for Jesus and how she loved the Bena Kasai [people of the Kasai] like her own children whom she had actually borne. I knew in my heart that Mama is with her Lord Jesus to receive the reward of her work that she had done for Him on earth.

I remember Jesus' word to His disciples that, Do not let your hearts be troubled. Believe in God, and believe in me also; in my Father's house there are many places [dwellings]. If that were not true I would tell you; I am going to prepare a place for you and I will come back again to get you for you to be where I am [with Me]. Truly, Mama is with Jesus, she is united now with her friend Mama Thomas and Mama Fearing and Mama Mutoto and Mama Tela and the wife of the long ago doctor and with Kuonyi Nshila. You know the day of your rest [retirement] to go to America: [tell] your children and your friends so that they may come to the mooring place [where boats arrive and depart] to greet [clasp hands with] you because of the great many years that they will not see you again with their eyes. In the same way all the friends of Mama have welcomed her with joy. She has gone before us, and she will welcome us another day or some year, that is God the Father's business.

When Mama was sick, in the gathering at my house we remembered her greatly in our prayers in all our worship places.[2] Mama has friends everywhere in the world who are grieving for her. I believe that you are near to the Great Gatherer, indeed the Holy Spirit, and to our Lord Jesus Christ; our gathering together as people will end, but [the gathering together of those] in Jesus will last forever.

I am your child,
Daniel Tshisungu

Acknowledgments

This book began fifteen years ago when Dr. Sylvia Jacobs of North Carolina Central University encouraged me to research a Presbyterian missionary, Maria Fearing. It was an honor to receive mentorship from a scholar whose works helped establish the field of African American missionary history. I dedicate this work to her memory and to the memory of Dr. Lamin Sanneh of Yale Divinity School. As a cofounder of the Yale Edinburgh Group on World Christianity and the History of Mission, he modeled scholarship and academic collaborations that represented the past well while speaking to future social justice concerns.

The School of Arts and Humanities at the University of Texas at Dallas and the Presbyterian Heritage Center in Montreat, North Carolina, provided generous funding for my research trips. I am grateful for the hospitality and feedback that I received from colleagues, archivists, church members, and missionary families while traveling. The Edmiston family provided valuable access to historic images and to the ways that they continue their grandparents' legacy. I thank Althea Edmiston Cousins, Evelyn Edmiston Easton, Herbert Edmiston, Dr. Kimberly Cousins Trent, and Lisa Edmiston for meeting me at the Presbyterian Historical Society and for welcoming me like a newfound relative. Members of the Congo Mission Network shared documents and memories generously and made the first presentation of this book research possible. I thank Helga Stixrud Rose and Bill Worth Jr. for providing interviews about their years at the APCM. I also thank Dr. Elsie Anne McKee of Princeton Theological Seminary, Winifred Vass Rutenbar, and Katherine McKee for making it possible to feature Tshisungu Daniel in the conclusion. Sue and John Fricks provided a copy of a church history manuscript that provided useful insight into this African evangelist's connections to the African American missionaries.

My advisers and mentors during my years at the University of North Carolina at Chapel Hill and Duke University would not let me give up on this project. Special thanks go to Dr. William Fitzhugh Brundage, Dr. Sylvia

Hoffert, Dr. Genna Rae McNeil, Dr. Theda Perdue, Dr. Grant Wacker, and Dr. Heather Williams. My colleagues at Del Mar College and the Feminist Research Collective and the junior faculty writing group at the University of Texas at Dallas provided a productive environment in which to explore research ideas. I thank them for giving me additional motivation to complete this book. Robert Benedetto offered generous advice over the years. Dr. Jill Kelly of Southern Methodist University shared writing sessions and advice that helped me plan the transnational aspects of this project in the earliest stages; I am grateful for her feedback and for her accountability as I analyzed the colonial history of the Belgian Congo. I also thank Ann Twombly and the anonymous readers whose advice maximized the potential of earlier drafts of this manuscript.

The archivists at Fisk University, the Presbyterian Historical Society (PHS), Stillman College, and Tuskegee University provided workspace during my extended visits and suggested sources I had not considered previously. I thank Lisa Jacobson, Fred Tangeman, and the other PHS staff members for processing the Edmiston Papers, for recording parts of the Edmistons' visit on social media, and for permitting early access to the unprocessed Congo records from the 1950s and 1960s. I am indebted to Jessie Carney Smith of Fisk and Robert Heath of Stillman for providing uncatalogued documents that helped me trace the college experiences of Althea Brown and Alonzo Edmiston. Stephen Posey of the Selma Public Library also provided information about local civil rights activism and black churches in the 1930s and 1940s. These later discoveries were possible because Director John P. Whitted and the former archivist of the Savery Library at Talladega College suggested that I borrow and digitize the microfilmed copy of Alonzo Edmiston's journals in 2007 and 2015.

In addition to academic conferences, I presented parts of this book in the following venues: the Congo Mission Network annual meeting in Montreat, North Carolina; Alabama State University in Montgomery; Rosebank Methodist Church in Cape Town, South Africa; and Grace Hope Presbyterian Church in Louisville, Kentucky (the congregation founded by William H. and Lucy Gantt Sheppard). I thank Dr. Harrison Taylor and his colleagues in the ASU History Department for the invitation, and I thank Elisabeth Cameron, the Reverend Angela Johnson, Sue Kuyper, and Johnny Young for their hospitality. For sparking my lifelong interest in black internationalism, I thank my parents, Louisa and Nathaniel Hill.

Notes

Introduction

1. Julia Lake Kellersberger, *A Life for the Congo: The Story of Althea Brown Edmiston* (New York: Fleming H. Revell, 1947), 121.

2. Ira Dworkin, *Congo Love Song: African American Culture and the Crisis of the Colonial State* (Chapel Hill: University of North Carolina Press, 2017); Jan Vansina, *Being Colonized: The Kuba Experience in Rural Congo, 1880–1960* (Madison: University of Wisconsin Press, 2010); Katherine Harris, *Pan-African Language Systems: Ebonics & African Oral Heritage* (London: Karnak House, 2003).

3. Kimberly Hill, "Anti-Slavery Work of the American Women of the Presbyterian Congo Mission," in *Faith and Slavery in the Presbyterian Diaspora,* ed. Peter C. Messer and William Harrison Taylor (Bethlehem, Pa.: Lehigh University Press, 2016), 205–11; Dworkin, *Congo Love Song.*

4. Vansina, *Being Colonized,* 300.

5. Examples include Sylvia M. Jacobs, "Their 'Special Mission': Afro-American Women as Missionaries to the Congo, 1894–1937," in *Black Americans and the Missionary Movement in Africa,* ed. Sylvia M. Jacobs (Westport, Conn.: Greenwood Press, 1982), 155–76; Sylvia M. Jacobs, "Nineteenth Century Black Methodist Missionary Bishops in Liberia," *Negro History Bulletin* 44, no. 4 (1981): 83–93; and Mark Ellingsen, "Changes in African American Mission: Rediscovering African Roots," *International Bulletin of Missionary Research* 36, no. 3 (2012): 136–42.

6. Gregory Mixon's intellectual history of Bishop Henry McNeal Turner combines social history of black educators in Alabama and news coverage of lynchings. The approach is effective for placing Turner's African Methodist Episcopal Church mission travels in South Africa in the historical context of denouncing white supremacy and Booker T. Washington's business focus. Gregory Mixon, "Henry McNeal Turner versus the Tuskegee Machine: Black Leadership in the Nineteenth Century," *Journal of Negro History* 79, no. 4 (1994): 363–80.

7. Jeannine DeLombard, "Sisters, Servants, or Saviors? National Baptist Women Missionaries in Liberia in the 1920s," *International Journal of African Historical Studies* 24, no. 2 (1991): 323–47; James A. Quirin, "'Her Sons and Daughters Are Ever on the Altar': Fisk University and Missionaries to Africa, 1866–1937," *Tennessee Historical Quarterly* 60, no. 1 (2011): 16–37.

8. Andrew Zimmerman, *Alabama in Africa: Booker T. Washington, the German Empire, and the Globalization of the New South* (Princeton: Princeton University Press, 2010).

9. Sylvia Jacobs, "Three African American Women Missionaries in the Congo, 1887–1899: The Confluence of Race, Culture, Identity, and Nationality," in *Competing Kingdoms: Women, Mission, Nation, and the American Protestant Empire, 1812–1960,* ed. Barbara Reeves-Ellington, Kathryn Kish Sklar, and Connie A. Shemo (Durham, N.C.: Duke University Press, 2010), 318–41.

10. John Hope Franklin and Evelyn Brooks Higginbotham, *From Slavery to Freedom: A History of African Americans,* 9th ed. (New York: McGraw-Hill, 2011), 295–303.

11. Reginald Ellis, *Between Washington and Du Bois: The Racial Politics of James Edward Shepard* (Gainesville: University Press of Florida, 2017); Joe M. Richardson, *A History of Fisk University, 1865–1946* (University: University of Alabama Press, 1980), 57–59.

12. Richardson, *A History of Fisk University,* 57–59.

13. Robert M. Park, "Tuskegee International Conference on the Negro," *Journal of Race Development* 3, no. 1 (1912): 118.

14. Brian Stanley, "From 'the Poor Heathen' to 'the Glory and Honour of All Nations': Vocabularies of Race and Custom in Protestant Missions, 1844–1928," *International Bulletin of Missionary Research* 34, no. 1 (2010): 6–7.

15. Zimmerman, *Alabama in Africa,* 17–18.

16. David A. Hollinger, *Protestants Abroad: How Missionaries Tried to Change the World but Changed America* (Princeton: Princeton University Press, 2017), 12, 104.

17. Caroline Phelps Stokes quoted in L. J. Lewis, introduction to *Phelps-Stokes Reports on Education in Africa* (London: Oxford University Press, 1962), 2.

18. Kenneth King, *Pan-Africanism and Education: A Study of Race, Philanthropy and Education in the Southern States of America and East Africa* (1971; repr., Brooklyn: Diasporic Africa Press, 2016), 31–33.

19. Ibid., 41–43.

20. Ibid., 222–24.

21. For an example, see Harris, *Pan-African Language Systems.*

22. Vansina, *Being Colonized,* 15.

23. Ibid., 24–31; Stanley Shaloff, *Reform in Leopold's Congo* (Richmond, Va.: John Knox Press, 1970), 42–44.

24. Vansina, *Being Colonized,* 24–26.

25. Adam Hochschild, *King Leopold's Ghost* (Boston: Houghton Mifflin, 1999), 26–28.

26. Vansina, *Being Colonized,* 18–19; Hochschild, *King Leopold's Ghost,* 82–87.

27. Vansina, *Being Colonized,* 66–67; Hochschild, *King Leopold's Ghost,* 117–18, 170–72.

28. Hochschild, *King Leopold's Ghost,* 109–11.

29. See Joseph Conrad, *Heart of Darkness* (1899; repr. New York: Dover, 1990).

30. Shaloff, *Reform in Leopold's Congo,* 20–21.

31. Barbara Ann Yates, "The Missions and Educational Development in Belgian Africa, 1876–1908" (Ph.D. diss., Teachers College, Columbia University, 1967), 19–47.

32. Ibid., 339, 397–98.

33. Ibid., 8, 157.

34. James Campbell, *Middle Passages: African American Journeys to Africa* (New York: Penguin Press, 2006), 167.

35. See Shaloff, *Reform in Leopold's Congo;* Robert Benedetto, ed., *Presbyterian Reformers in Central Africa,* trans. Winifred K. Vass (New York: E. J. Brill, 1996); Hochschild, *King Leopold's Ghost.*

36. Shaloff, *Reform in King Leopold's Congo,* 75–76.

37. Ibid., 75–99, 110–20; William M. Morrison, "Statement to His Majesty's Government on Conditions in the Congo," 4 May 1903, in Benedetto, *Presbyterian Reformers in Central Africa,* 153.

38. William E. Phipps, *William Sheppard: Congo's African American Livingstone* (Louisville: Geneva Press, 2002), 155; Pagan Kennedy, *Black Livingstone: A True Tale of Adventure in the Nineteenth-Century Congo* (2002; repr., Santa Fe: Santa Fe Writers Project, 2013), 105.

39. Benedetto, ed., *Presbyterian Reformers in Central Africa,* 11.

40. Shaloff, *Reform in King Leopold's Congo,* 108–27; Benedetto, *Presbyterian Reformers in Central Africa,* 8–26.

41. Hochschild, *King Leopold's Ghost,* 256–57.

42. Vansina, *Being Colonized,* 103–4.

43. Ibid., 158–59.

44. Ibid., 151–54.

45. A. L. Edmiston, entry for 14 August 1916, A. L. Edmiston Diaries, African Missions Collection, Talladega College Library.

46. Osumaka Likaka, *Rural Society and Cotton in Colonial Zaire* (Madison: University of Wisconsin Press, 1997), 4, 32–33.

47. Spelling of this mission station name in publications varies: Ibanche, Ibaanche, Ibaanj, Ibanj, and Ibanc. This book uses the spelling most often included in Alonzo Edmiston's records.

1. Industrial Education and Symbolic Home Building in the Congo Free State, 1898–1907

1. S. P. Verner, "Edmiston Did Not Return to Savagery," unnamed publication, undated (1905–1908), Alonzo Edmiston Papers (hereafter cited as AEP), RG 495, box 6, folder 26, Presbyterian Historical Society, Philadelphia (hereafter cited as PHS).

2. William E. Phipps, *William Henry Sheppard: Congo's African American Livingstone* (Louisville, Ky.: Geneva Press, 2002), 179; Campbell, *Middle Passages,* 163–64, 179.

3. David H. Jackson Jr., *Booker T. Washington and the Struggle against White Supremacy: The Southern Educational Tours, 1908–1912* (New York: Palgrave Macmillan, 2002), 2–5.

4. Donald F. Roth, "The 'Black Man's Burden': The Racial Background of Afro-American Missionaries and Africa," in *Black Americans and the Missionary Movement in Africa,* ed. Sylvia M. Jacobs (Westport, Conn.: Greenwood Press, 1982), 36.

5. Yekutiel Gershoni, *Africans on African-Americans: The Creation and Uses of an African-American Myth* (New York: New York University Press, 1997), 4.

6. Campbell, *Middle Passages,* 147, 167.

7. Walter E. Fluker, *The Ground Has Shifted: The Future of the Black Church in Post-Racial America* (New York: New York University Press, 2016), 76.

8. Jacobs, "Their 'Special Mission,'" 169.

9. Yates, "The Missions and Educational Development in Belgian Africa," 116–17.

10. Ogbu U. Kalu, *Clio in a Sacred Garb: Essays on Christian Presence and African Responses, 1900–2000* (Trenton, N.J.: Africa World Press, 2008), 92.

11. Walter L. Williams, *Black Americans and the Evangelization of Africa* (Madison: University of Wisconsin Press, 1982), 89–91.

12. Ibid., 167.

13. Ibid., 19–20, 171.

14. Ibid., 22–23; Hochschild, *King Leopold's Ghost,* 79–80, 152–53.

15. Morgan quoted in Hochschild, *King Leopold's Ghost,* 79.

16. Kalu, *Clio in a Sacred Garb,* 92.

17. Kevin Gaines, *Uplifting the Race: Black Leadership, Politics, and Culture in the Twentieth Century* (Chapel Hill: University of North Carolina Press, 1996), 211–14.

18. For an example, see Williams, *Black Americans and the Evangelization of Africa,* 92–103.

19. Daniel Alexander Payne, *History of the African Methodist Episcopal Church,* ed. Charles Spencer Smith (Nashville: A. M. E. Sunday School Union, 1891), 477–79, "Documenting the American South," https://docsouth.unc.edu/church /payne/payne.html, accessed 6 September 2019.

20. Ibid., 479.

21. Ibid., 485–89.

22. Roderick J. MacDonald, "Reverend Hanock Msokera Phiri and the Establishment in Nyasaland of the African Methodist Episcopal Church," *African Historical Studies* 3, no. 1 (1970): 76.

23. Isaac C. Lamba, "Cape Dutch Reformed Church Mission in Malawi: A Preliminary Historical Examination of Its Educational Philosophy and Application, 1889–1931," *Transafrican Journal of History* 12 (1983): 56; MacDonald, "Reverend Hanock Msokera Phiri," 76.

24. Mixon, "Henry McNeal Turner versus the Tuskegee Machine," 365, 372.

25. Jacobs, "Nineteenth Century Black Methodist Missionary Bishops in Liberia," 92.

26. Ibid., 93.

27. Payne, *History of the African Methodist Episcopal Church,* 402–3.

28. Evelyn Brooks Higginbotham, *Righteous Discontent: The Women's Movement in the Black Baptist Church, 1880–1920* (Cambridge: Harvard University Press, 1994), 49–50.

29. DeLombard, "Sisters, Servants, or Saviors?" 330, 333.

30. Ibid., 339.

31. Ibid., 337.

32. Rudolf C. Heredia, "Education and Mission: School as Agent of Evangelisation," *Economic and Political Weekly* 30, no. 37 (1995): 2337.

33. A Missionary, "Our Future Industrial Hope," *Missionary* (November 1906): 507–8.

34. Kenneth W. Goings and Eugene M. O'Connor, "Lessons Learned: The Role of the Classics at Black Colleges and Universities," *Journal of Negro Education* 79, no. 4 (2010): 523.

35. Ibid.

36. Jacobs, "Their 'Special Mission,'" 162.

37. Kimberly D. Hill, "Maria Fearing: Domestic Adventurer," in *Alabama Women: Their Lives and Times,* ed. Susan Youngblood Ashmore and Lisa Lindquist Dorr (Athens: University of Georgia Press, 2017), 93–94.

38. Quirin, "'Her Sons and Daughters Are Ever on the Altar,'" 25–27.

39. Richardson, *A History of Fisk University,* 35.

40. Dworkin, *Congo Love Song,* 137.

41. Hilary Green, *Educational Reconstruction: African American Schools in the Urban South, 1865–1900* (New York: Fordham University Press, 2016), 135, 205.

42. Robert Benedetto, "The Presbyterian Mission Press in Central Africa, 1890–1922," *American Presbyterians* 68, no. 1 (1990): 65–67.

43. Ibid., 63.

44. Dworkin, *Congo Love Song,* 145. Tshiluba, a Bantu language, is one of the national languages of the Democratic Republic of the Congo.

45. Ibid., 141–43.

46. Althea Brown Edmiston, *Grammar and Dictionary of the Bushonga or Bukuba Language as Spoken by the Bushonga or Bukuba Tribe Who Dwell in the Upper Kasai District, Belgian Congo, Central Africa* (Luebo: J. Leighton Wilson Press, 1932), v.

47. Benedetto, "The Presbyterian Mission Press in Central Africa," 59–60.

48. Mrs. Althea Brown Edmiston, "From Ibanj, Congo Free State," *Missionary* (October 1907): 482.

49. Brown Edmiston, "Six Months at Ibanj," *Missionary* (June 1906): 256–57.

50. Brown Edmiston, "From Ibanj, Congo Free State," 483.

51. Pagan Kennedy, *Black Livingstone: A True Tale of Adventure in the Nineteenth-Century Congo* (New York: Viking, 2002), 132–43.

52. David H. Sick, "Alabamian Argonautica: Myth and Classical Education in *The Quest of the Silver Fleece,*" *Classical World* 110, no. 3 (2017): 381.

53. W. E. B. Du Bois, *The Souls of Black Folk* (1903; repr., New York: Dover, 1994), 41–42.

54. Althea Brown Edmiston, "Missions in Congo Free State, Africa," *American Missionary* 62, no. 10 (1908): 308.

55. Ibid., 309.

56. Ibid. François Delsarte was a French instructor of music and performance who developed a unique expressive style. See George Taylor, "François Delsarte: A Codification of Nineteenth-Century Acting," *Theatre Research International* 24, no. 1 (1999): 71–82.

57. Carter Godwin Woodson, *The Mis-Education of the Negro* (1933; repr., n.p.: Tribeca Books, 2014), 7.

58. Ibid., 3–4.

59. Brown Edmiston, *Grammar and Dictionary of the Bushonga or Bukuba Language,* v.

60. Amy R. Slagell, "The Rhetorical Structure of Frances Willard's Campaign for Woman Suffrage, 1876–1896," *Rhetoric & Public Affairs* 4, no. 1 (2001): 13–14.

61. King, *Pan-Africanism and Education,* 36.

62. Reginald Ellis argued against this dichotomy in his book about James Edward Shepard, the founder of what became North Carolina Central University. And Andrew Barnes found enthusiasm for industrial education in his study of Christian newspapers in western and southern Africa, partly because many of the authors associated it with the types of cultural development that Du Bois associated with classical studies. Ellis, *Between Washington and Du Bois;* Andrew Barnes, *Global Christianity and the Black Atlantic* (Waco, Tex.: Baylor University Press, 2017), xi.

63. Paula Giddings, *When and Where I Enter* (New York: William Morrow, 1984), 101–5.

64. Ibid., 101.

65. Barnes, *Global Christianity and the Black Atlantic;* Zimmerman, *Alabama in Africa.*

66. Yates, "The Missions and Educational Development in Belgian Africa," 116–17.

67. Rev. A. L. Edmiston, "Industrial School in the Congo," *Missionary* (September 1907): 438–39.

68. J. McClung Sieg, "Schools in Congo: Work in the Day and Sunday Schools," *Missionary* (June 1906): 253; Edmiston, "Industrial School in the Congo."

69. Edmiston, "Industrial School in the Congo," 438.

70. Ibid., 439.

71. Jack E. Nelson, "Class Formation and the Professionalization of an African Clergy," *Journal of Religion in Africa* 22, no. 2 (1992): 137.

72. Dworkin, *Congo Love Song,* 148–50, 154–55.

73. William Campbell Edmiston, *The Fat of the Land* (St. Augustine, Fla.: Record Press, 1958), 6–7, 40–41.

74. Althea Brown Edmiston, "Autobiography," December 1923, 2, Althea Brown Edmiston Biographical File, PHS; Kellersberger, *A Life for the Congo,* 34.

75. Kellersberger, *A Life for the Congo,* 34–35.

76. J. McClung Sieg, "Some Observations in the Kassai," *Missionary* (May 1906): 209; Kennedy, *Black Livingstone,* 100–101.

77. Kennedy, *Black Livingstone,* 100–101, 78–80.

78. Campbell, *Middle Passages,* 165; Rev. S. P. Verner, "Bringing the Pygmies to America," *Independent* 57, no. 2909 (1904): 485–89.

79. S. P. Verner, "The Adventures of an Explorer in Africa," *Harper's Weekly,* October 22, 1904, 1618.

80. Dworkin, *Congo Love Song,* 133.

81. Hill, "Anti-Slavery Work of the American Women of the Presbyterian Congo Mission," 205–11.

82. Kellersberger, *A Life for the Congo,* 74–75.

83. Dworkin, *Congo Love Song,* 347–48n28.

84. W. Edmiston, *The Fat of the Land* (St. Augustine, Fla.: Record Press, 1958), 6–7.

85. Alonzo Edmiston, "First Experiences of Congo Life," *Kassai Herald,* n.d. (ca. 1904–5), 29–30, AEP, RG 495, box 6, folder 26, PHS.

86. Kellersberger, *A Life for the Congo,* 74–75.

87. Ibid.

88. Quoted ibid., 73–75.

89. Phipps, *William Sheppard,* 116–20.

90. Benedetto, "The Presbyterian Mission Press in Central Africa," 60; Dworkin, *Congo Love Song,* 347–48nn21, 22.

91. Alonzo Edmiston to the Executive Committee on Foreign Missions, 16 February 1910, AEP, RG 495, box 6, folder 1, PHS, Philadelphia, reproduced in Appendix B of this book.

92. Brown Edmiston quoted in Kellersberger, *A Life for the Congo,* 69.

93. Alonzo Edmiston, "Fall of Ibanj," in Benedetto, *Presbyterian Reformers in Central Africa,* 226.

94. Brown Edmiston quoted in Kellersberger, *A Life for the Congo,* 69–70.

95. Edmiston, "Fall of Ibanj," 227.

96. Benedetto, *Presbyterian Reformers in Central Africa,* 229n9.

97. Alonzo Edmiston to the Executive Committee on Foreign Missions, 16 February 1910.

98. Moses Edward James, "A History of the Snedecor Memorial Synod of the Presbyterian Church in the United States" (senior thesis, Johnson C. Smith University, 1952), 1, 12–14.

99. "Education of the Negro," *Duluth Evening Herald,* 24 February 1906, 16.

100. Ibid.; "Colored Missionary to Africa Is Honored by King of Belgium," *Selma Times-Journal,* n.d. (1926), AEP, RG 495, box 6, folder 26, PHS.

101. Kellersberger, *A Life for the Congo,* 33.

102. Robert Dabney Bedinger, "Althea Brown Edmiston: A Congo Crusader," in *Glorious Living: Informal Sketches of Seven Women Missionaries of the Presbyterian Church, U.S.,* comp. Hallie Paxson Winsborough, ed. Sarah Lee Vinson Timmons (Atlanta: Committee on Woman's Work, Presbyterian Church, U.S., 1937), 271.

103. Records of the Executive Committee on Foreign Missions indicate that Alonzo Edmiston proposed to Althea Brown early in the fall of 1904. The committee approved the engagement on October 11, 1904. Dworkin, *Congo Love Song,* 133–34.

104. Quoted in Kellersberger, *A Life for the Congo,* 76.

105. Ibid., 70.

106. Ibid., 76.

107. Ibid., 76–77.

108. Brown Edmiston quoted ibid.

109. Edmiston, "Fall of Ibanj," 225–26.

110. Ibid., 225–27.

111. Phipps, *William Sheppard,* 110–17.

112. Brown Edmiston quoted in Kellersberger, *A Life for the Congo,* 73.

113. Brown Edmiston, "Six Months at Ibanj," 256.

114. Brown Edmiston, "Missions in Congo Free State, Africa," 310.

115. Ibid., 306–9.

116. Edmiston, "Industrial School in the Congo," 439.

117. William L. Sachs, "'Self-Support': The Episcopal Mission and Nationalism in Japan," *Church History* 58, no. 4 (1989): 492; David W. Scott, "The Value of Money: Funding Sources and Philanthropic Priorities in Twentieth-Century American Mission," *Religions* 9, no. 4 (2018): 122.

118. Edmiston, "Industrial School in the Congo," 439.

119. Sachs, "'Self-Support,'" 492.

120. Scott, "The Value of Money," 122.

121. Brown Edmiston quoted in Kellersberger, *A Life for the Congo,* 77.

122. Dworkin, *Congo Love Song,* 136.

2. Congo Missionaries and the Perpetuation of Manual Labor, 1908–1936

1. A. L. Edmiston, entry for 29 September 1936, A. L. Edmiston Diaries, African Collection, Talladega College Library, Talladega, Ala.

2. Edmiston, entry for 3 December 1929, A. L. Edmiston Diaries.

3. William Marion Sikes, "The Historical Development of Stillman Institute" (master's thesis, University of Alabama, 1930), 6, 47–49.

4. Ernest Trice Thompson, *Presbyterians in the South,* vol. 3, *1890–1972* (Richmond, Va.: John Knox Press, 1973), 88–89, 144–45.

5. James, "A History of the Snedecor Memorial Synod," 16–22.

6. Phipps, *William Sheppard,* 13.

7. Joseph O. Baylen and John Hammond Moore, "Senator John Tyler Morgan and Negro Colonization in the Philippines, 1901 to 1902," *Phylon* 29, no. 1 (1968): 65–75.

8. Ernest Trice Thompson, "Black Presbyterians, Education, and Evangelism after the Civil War," *Journal of Presbyterian History* 76, no. 1 (1998): 57–58, 66.

9. Thompson, *Presbyterians in the South,* 3:87.

10. Thompson, "Black Presbyterians, Education, and Evangelism after the Civil War," 63, 66–67.

11. For an example of a Committee on Colored Evangelization report, see *Minutes of the General Assembly of the Presbyterian Church in the United States* (Richmond, Va.: Presbyterian Committee of Publication, 1907), 88–91.

12. James, "A History of the Snedecor Memorial Synod," 14.

13. The annual meeting minutes of the Executive Committee on Home Missions no longer reprinted the annual reports on Stillman Institute, instead referencing parts of the report in various sections. For an example, see *Minutes of the Executive Committee on Home Missions, 1921–1933,* 7, 395–96, 399, RT 716, box 2, PHS.

14. Alonzo Edmiston to the Executive Committee on Foreign Missions, 16 February 1910, 3. See Appendix B for the full text of the letters from Alonzo and Althea Brown Edmiston requesting reinstatement.

15. Althea Brown Edmiston to the Executive Committee on Foreign Missions, 16 February 1910, AEP, RG 495, box 6, folder 1, PHS.

16. Phipps, *William Sheppard,* 177–83.

17. Samuel Chester to the Rev. J. McC. Sieg, 16 August 1910, American Presbyterian Congo Mission (hereafter cited as APCM) Records, RG 432, box 78, folder 5, PHS; Samuel Chester to the Rev. A. L. Edmiston, 20 August 1910, APCM Records, RG 432, box 78, folder 5, PHS.

18. Samuel Chester to the Rev. J. McC. Sieg, 16 August 1910.

19. "A Charming Woman," unnamed publication, 1909, AEP, RG 495, box 6, folder 26, PHS.

20. S. H. Chester to the Rev. W. M. Morrison, 22 October 1908, 1, PCM Records, RG 432, box 78, folder 3, PHS.

21. Samuel Chester to the Rev. J. McC. Sieg, 16 August 1910, 2.

22. American Presbyterian Congo Mission to the Executive Committee, 1 July 1910, APCM Records, RG 432, box 78, folder 5, PHS.

23. E. W. Smith to the Rev. W. M. Morrison, 10 July 1915, Luebo, Africa, APCM Records, RG 432, box 78, folder 15, PHS.

24. Ibid.

25. Ibid.

26. Stanley, "From 'the Poor Heathen' to 'the Glory and Honour of All Nations,'" 4–5.

27. Brian Stanley identified the African delegate as Mark Christian Hayford from the Gold Coast. The African American delegates representing the National Baptist Convention were W. W. Brown and J. G. Jordan. Brian Stanley, "The World Missionary Conference, Edinburgh 1910: Sifting History from Myth," *Expository Times* 121, no. 7 (2010): 326; Brian Stanley, "Edinburgh and World Christianity," *Studies in World Christianity* 17, no. 1 (2011): 78; World Missionary Conference, *The History and Records of the Conference* (Edinburgh: Oliphant, Anderson, and Ferrier, 1910), 52.

28. Francis Anekwe Oborji, "Edinburgh 1910 and Christian Identity Today: An African Perspective," *Missiology: An International Review* 41, no. 3 (2013): 302–4.

29. King, *Pan-Africanism and Education,* 88–89.

30. Ibid., 91, 132.

31. David Henry Anthony, *Max Yergan: Race Man, Internationalist, Cold Warrior* (New York: New York University Press, 2006); Daniel Perlman, "Stirring the White Conscience: The Life of George Edmund Haynes" (Ph.D. diss., New York University, 1972).

32. Edmiston, entry for 4 May 1934, A. L. Edmiston Diaries.

33. Ibid.

34. Dworkin, *Congo Love Song,* 132–34.

35. S. H. Chester to the Rev. W. M. Morrison, 5 March 1908, 2–3, APCM Records, RG 432, box 78, folder 3, PHS.

36. S. H. Chester to the Rev. W. M. Morrison, 22 October 1908, 1, APCM Records, RG 432, box 78, folder 3, PHS.

37. S. H. Chester to the Rev. W. M. Morrison, 5 March 1908, 2–3.

38. S. H. Chester to the Rev. W. M. Morrison, 15 December 1915, Luebo, Africa, APCM Records, RG 432, box 78, folder 8, PHS.

39. S. H. Chester to the Rev. W. M. Morrison, 23 August 1910, APCM Records, RG 432, box 78, folder 5, PHS.

40. W. M. Morrison to S. H. Chester, 23 September 1915, Nashville, Tenn., APCM Records, RG 432, box 78, folder 8, PHS; S. H. Chester to the Rev. W. M. Morrison, 15 December 1915.

41. Mission secretary to Dr. Egbert W. Smith, 21 October 1923, Nashville, Tenn., APCM Records, RG 432, box 78, folder 18, PHS.

42. American Presbyterian Congo Mission to the Executive Committee, 1 July 1910, APCM Records, RG 432, box 78, folder 5, PHS.

43. Tera W. Hunter, *To 'Joy My Freedom: Southern Black Women's Lives and Labors after the Civil War* (Cambridge: Harvard University Press, 1997), 94–97.

44. Ibid., 232–34.

45. William M. Morrison to Booker T. Washington, 15 November 1904, quoted in in Benedetto, *Presbyterian Reformers in Central Africa,* 223.

46. Booker T. Washington, *On Mother Earth* (1902; repr., Carlisle, Mass.: Applewood Books, 2018).

47. Hill, "Maria Fearing: Domestic Adventurer," 100–102; Phipps, *William Sheppard,* 13.

48. [W. M. Morrison] to Dr. E. W. Smith, 5 January 1918, Nashville, Tenn., APCM Records, RG 432, box 78, folder 16, PHS.

49. Zimmerman, *Alabama in Africa,* 180–81.

50. Ibid., 64–65.

51. Ibid., 173–74.

52. E. D. Morel, *The Black Man's Burden* (1903; repr., New York: Monthly Review Press, 1969), 22–23.

53. Zimmerman, *Alabama in Africa,* 199, 204.

54. W. L. Hillhouse, "Report of the Hillhouse Plantation for 1916," 13 March 1917, APCM Records, RG 432, box 21, folder 18, PHS; acting representative for W. L. Hillhouse to Monsieur la Commissaire de District, 19 December 1917, APCM Records, RG 432, box 21, folder 18, PHS.

55. Luebo Ad Interim Committee to W. L. Hillhouse, 6 June 1917, APCM Records, RG 432, box 21, folder 18, PHS.

56. Robert Dabney Bedinger, *Triumphs of the Gospel in the Belgian Congo* (Richmond, Va.: Presbyterian Board of Publications, 1920), 75–76.

57. Benedetto, "The Presbyterian Mission Press in Central Africa," 61.

58. John A. Tully, *The Devil's Milk: A Social History of Rubber* (New York: Monthly Review Press, 2011), 119–20.

59. Likaka, *Rural Society and Cotton in Colonial Zaire,* 13–16.

60. Luebo Ad Interim Committee to W. L. Hillhouse, 6 June 1917.

61. Laurens Hillhouse, "Report of Hillhouse Plantation for 1916," 13 March 1917, 4.

62. Ibid., 3.

63. Likaka, *Rural Society and Cotton in Colonial Zaire,* 13.

64. Roy Cleveland to the People at Home, 8 June 1914, Roy F. Cleveland and LeNoir Ramsey Cleveland Correspondence, RG 462, box 1, folder 1, PHS.

65. LeNoir Cleveland to the Homefolk, 21 June 1914, 4–5, Roy F. Cleveland and LeNoir Ramsey Cleveland Correspondence, RG 462, box 1, folder 1, PHS.

66. LeNoir Cleveland to her mother, 9 July 1914, Roy F. Cleveland and LeNoir Ramsey Cleveland Correspondence, RG 462, box 1, folder 1, PHS.

67. Ibid.; R. F. Cleveland to Friends of the Homeland, 1 January 1922, Roy F. Cleveland and LeNoir Ramsey Cleveland Correspondence, RG 462, box 1, folder 16, PHS.

68. LeNoir Cleveland to her mother, 20 May 1914, Roy F. Cleveland and LeNoir Ramsey Cleveland Correspondence, RG 462, box 1, folder 1, PHS.

69. Alonzo Edmiston, "Statements Concerning Experimental Farm, December 1915," 1–2, APCM Records, RG 432, box 21, folder 1, PHS.

70. Ibid.

71. Ibid., 2.

72. Ibid.; emphasis added.

73. Ibid.

74. Osumaka Likaka provided a table of cotton output from Belgian Congo cotton growers that shows consistent increases in the harvest tonnage and acres of land developed after 1920. Likaka, *Rural Society and Cotton in Colonial Zaire,* 42.

75. Ibid., 27, 50–53.

76. The entries in Alonzo Edmiston's journals from February 1916 through September 1918 mention the amount and timing of rainfall at Ibanche on about a biweekly basis. For example, he described "a big rain today about noon" in the same entry in which he announced that the chiefs near the Ibanche station traveled to Luebo to request the reopening of their local mission station. Edmiston, entry for 22 February 1916, A. L. Edmiston Diaries. And his 1917 report from the Ibanche station commented on strategies that would improve local soil cultivation. Alonzo Edmiston, "Ibanche Report" (1917), 6, included in A. L. Edmiston Diaries.

77. Edmiston, entries for 7–11 January and 1 February 1918, A. L. Edmiston Diaries.

78. The spreadsheet of Ibanche station credits submitted to the American Presbyterian Congo Mission attributed a value of 2,747 francs to the items sent from Ibanche to Luebo in 1918, an increase of 778 francs from the previous year. Alonzo Edmiston, "A. P. C. M. Ibanche Station Statement of Accounts, 1916–1918," 27–31, AEP, RG 495, box 6, folder 34, PHS.

79. Edmiston, "Ibanche Report," 6.

80. Ibid., 1–2.

81. Edmiston, entry for 15 December 1917, A. L. Edmiston Diaries.

82. Edmiston, entry for 25 May 1918, A. L. Edmiston Diaries.

83. Likaka, *Rural Society and Cotton in Colonial Zaire,* 24–25.

84. Ibid.

85. Ibid., 25, 32–34.

86. Ibid., 16–18.

87. Ibid., 47.

88. *Minutes of the General Assembly of the Presbyterian Church in the United States* (Richmond, Va.: Presbyterian Committee of Publication, 1921), 86–87.

89. Edmiston, entries for 6 August 1930 and 2 January 1933, A. L. Edmiston Diaries.

90. Edmiston, entries for 6 August 1930, 25 July 1931, and 25 June 1934, A. L. Edmiston Diaries.

91. Edmiston, entry for 25 July 1931, A. L. Edmiston Diaries.

92. Edmiston, entry for 14 February 1933, A. L. Edmiston Diaries.

93. Likaka, *Rural Society and Cotton in Colonial Zaire,* 53.

94. Ibid., 49–51.

95. Martin Thomas, *Violence and Colonial Order: Police, Workers and Protest in the European Colonial Empires, 1918–1940* (New York: Cambridge University Press, 2012), 318.

96. Likaka, *Rural Society and Cotton in Colonial Zaire,* 53.

97. Edmiston made lists to document the condition of outstation churches that included the number of disciples, students, books, and women's study groups. He also observed the evangelists' homes and their construction of latrines. For example, see Edmiston, entry for 12 April 1931, A. L. Edmiston Diaries.

98. Edmiston, entries for 11–18 December 1919, A. L. Edmiston Diaries.

99. Dworkin, *Congo Love Song,* 156–57.

100. Likaka, *Rural Society and Cotton in Colonial Zaire,* 57.

101. Althea Brown Edmiston, "Maria Fearing: A Mother to African Girls," in Winsborough, *Glorious Living,* 307.

102. Likaka, *Rural Society and Cotton in Colonial Zaire,* 35.

103. Edmiston, entries for 14 August 1932 and 4 July 1934, A. L. Edmiston Diaries.

104. Edmiston, entry for 23 July 1934, A. L. Edmiston Diaries.

105. Edmiston, entry for 27 July 1934, A. L. Edmiston Diaries.

106. Edmiston, entry for 29 July 1934, A. L. Edmiston Diaries.

107. Thomas, *Violence and Colonial Order,* 312.

108. Likaka, *Rural Society and Cotton in Colonial Zaire,* 55.

109. S. H. Chester to the Rev. W. M. Morrison, 12 September 1910, APCM Records, RG 432, box 78, folder 5, PHS.

110. Edmiston, entries for 9–24 January 1919, A. L. Edmiston Diaries.

111. Edmiston, entry for 23 June 1933, A. L. Edmiston Diaries.

112. Edmiston, entries for 1 April 1933 and 1 November 1932, A. L. Edmiston Diaries.

113. Edmiston, entry for 2 May 1933, A. L. Edmiston Diaries.

114. Edmiston, entries for 27–28 December 1931, A. L. Edmiston Diaries.

115. Likaka, *Rural Society and Cotton in Colonial Zaire,* 35.

116. Benedetto, "The Presbyterian Mission Press in Central Africa," 61; Dworkin, *Congo Love Song,* 150–51.

117. Edmiston, entry for 31 May 1932, A. L. Edmiston Diaries.

118. Edmiston, entries for 3 September 1932, 6 November 1932, and 7 January 1933, A. L. Edmiston Diaries.

119. Edmiston, entries for 7–10 November 1932, A. L. Edmiston Diaries.

120. Edmiston, entry for 8 November 1932, A. L. Edmiston Diaries.

121. Edmiston, entry for 10 November 1934, A. L. Edmiston Diaries.

122. Edmiston, entry for 22 October 1933, A. L. Edmiston Diaries.

123. Edmiston, entry for 14 February 1934, A. L. Edmiston Diaries.

124. Edmiston, entry for 5 July 1933, A. L. Edmiston Diaries.

125. Edmiston, entry for 2 March 1934, A. L. Edmiston Diaries.

126. Charles Crane to the Rev. John Morrison, 16 January 1939, APCM Records, RG 432, box 26, folder 16, PHS.

127. Ibid.; William C. Worth, "Results of Agricultural Work in M.B.S.," 17 November 1932, APCM Records, RG 432, box 26, folder 16, PHS.

128. Likaka, *Rural Society and Cotton in Colonial Zaire,* 61–62, 67.

129. Edmiston, entry for 5 June 1934, A. L. Edmiston Diaries.

130. A. L. Edmiston, "Untitled Memo: In Our Agricultural Work at Mutoto," undated, APCM Records, RG 432, box 26, folder 16, PHS. Susan Pearson dates the introduction of baby beauty contests to county and state fairs in the 1850s; separate competitions for African American babies were introduced in 1855. Pearson analyzes this trend as a celebration of gendered labor and as a "racial spectacle" reminiscent of slavery. Linda Gordon argues that the African American reformers who continued the practice in the twentieth century embraced the contests as one of several domestic or sports-related activities that raised support for their private organizations, such as the Gate City Free Kindergarten Association of Atlanta. Susan J. Pearson, " 'Infantile Specimens': Showing Babies in Nineteenth-Century America," *Journal of Social History* 42, no. 2 (2008): 345, 350–52; Linda Gordon, "Black and White Visions of Welfare: Women's Welfare Activism, 1890–1945," *Journal of American History* 78, no. 2 (1991): 560–61.

131. Alonzo Edmiston devoted one scrapbook to photographs of the fields, experiments, and exhibitions at Mutoto. AEP, RG 495, box 8, PHS.

132. Likaka, *Rural Society and Cotton in Colonial Zaire,* 57.

3. Implementing Historically Black Education Strategies at the Presbyterian Congo Mission, 1918–1919

1. Alonzo Edmiston, "Aims and Policies of the Agricultural School to Be Started at Lucbo for the A.P.C.M.," June 1918, 4, APCM Records, RG 432, box 21, folder 1, PHS.

2. Edmiston, entry for 18 June 1918, A. L. Edmiston Diaries.

3. Edmiston, "Aims and Policies of the Agricultural School," 1–4.

4. King, *Pan-Africanism and Education,* 93.

5. Ibid., 225–26.

6. Ibid., 9.

7. Kevern Verney, *The Art of the Possible: Booker T. Washington and Black Leadership in the United States, 1881–1925* (New York: Routledge, 2001), 30, 34.

8. Zimmerman, *Alabama in Africa,* 180.

9. King, *Pan-Africanism and Education,* 222–24.

10. Richardson, *A History of Fisk University,* 59–61.

11. Ibid., 57–58.

12. The phrase *Fisk program* is shortened from a 1932 W. E. B. Du Bois quote reprinted in King, *Pan-Africanism and Education,* 182–83. The full sentence reads: "We firmly believe that the contrary is true and that with all that Hampton and Tuskegee have done, and they have done much, nevertheless their peculiar program of industrial education has not been successful and has been given up, while the essential soundness of the Atlanta, Fisk and Howard program of general and higher education and teacher training has with all its omissions proved the salvation of the Negro race."

13. Zimmerman, *Alabama in Africa,* 112–76.

14. Verney, *The Art of the Possible,* 122.

15. Cliff Stratton, *Education for Empire: American Schools, Race, and the Paths of Good Citizenship* (Oakland: University of California Press, 2017), 152–54; Green, *Educational Reconstruction,* 133–39.

16. Stratton, *Education for Empire,* 147–51.

17. Barnes, *Global Christianity and the Black Atlantic,* 97, 110–11.

18. Ibid., 111.

19. Richardson, *A History of Fisk University,* 57.

20. King, *Pan-Africanism and Education,* 56.

21. Richardson, *A History of Fisk University,* 6–7, 18.

22. Ibid., 17, 54, 57.

23. Ibid., 67.

24. Brown Edmiston, "Autobiography," 2.

25. Richardson, *A History of Fisk University,* 59.

26. King, *Pan-Africanism and Education,* 50–56, 96–98.

27. Alonzo Edmiston, "A. P. C. M. Report of the Agricultural School, Nov. 1919," 3, APCM Records, RG 432, box 21, folder 1, PHS.

28. Mary Kirkland to the Rev. Egbert W. Smith, 30 August 1918, Nashville, Tenn., 3, APCM Records, RG 432, box 78, folder 15, PHS.

29. Edmiston, entry for 22 June 1918, A. L. Edmiston Diaries.

30. Edmiston, "A. P. C. M. Report of the Agricultural School, Nov. 1919," 3.

31. Ibid., 2–3.

32. Ibid., 3.

33. Carroll Stegall started the Carson Industrial School after arriving at the Congo Mission in 1915, and J. Hershey Longenecker took the management role temporarily after his arrival in 1917. Stegall returned to manage the industrial school program until his retirement in 1951. Dworkin, *Congo Love Song,* 155; Edmiston, "Aims and Policies of the Agricultural School," 2; J. Hershey Longenecker, *Memories of Congo: Tales of Adventure and Work in the Heart of Africa* (Johnson City, Tenn.: Royal Publishers, 1964), 21–22; Benedetto, introduction to *Presbyterian Reformers in Central Africa,* 29.

34. Edmiston, "A. P. C. M. Report of the Agricultural College, Nov. 1919," 2.

35. Dworkin, *Congo Love Song,* 155.

36. W. A. Hunton, "The Providential Preparation of the American Negro for Mission Work in Africa," in *World-wide Evangelization the Urgent Business of the Church: Addresses Delivered before the Fourth International Convention of the Student Volunteer Movement for Foreign Missions, Toronto, Canada, February 26–March 2, 1902* (New York: Student Volunteer Movement for Foreign Missions, 1902), 297.

37. Hill, "Anti-Slavery Work by the American Women of the Presbyterian Congo Mission," 207–13.

38. Hunton, "The Providential Preparation of the American Negro," 297.

39. Edmiston, "Aims and Policies of the Agricultural School," 2.

40. Ibid.

41. Edmiston, "A. P. C. M. Report of the Agricultural College, Nov. 1919," 1.

42. Edmiston, "Aims and Policies of the Agricultural School," 1.

43. Alonzo Edmiston documented each time he met a former Pantops Home resident or mission student promoting Presbyterian ministry in a rural village. He seems to have kept this part of his records to highlight the work of African Presbyterians and to share memories of his African American colleagues who had returned to the United States. For descriptions of three Pantops alumnae, see Edmiston, entry for 1 January 1920, A. L. Edmiston Diaries.

44. Richardson, *A History of Fisk University*, 16.

45. Alonzo Edmiston, "Report of the Agricultural School of the A.P.C.M., Luebo, Oct. 30, 1918," 1, APCM Records, RG 432, box 21, folder 1, PHS.

46. Ibid.

47. Edmiston, "A. P. C. M. Report of the Agricultural College, Nov. 1919," 1.

48. Ibid.

49. Paul W. Terry and L. Tennent Lee, *A Study of Stillman Institute, a Junior College for Negroes* (Tuscaloosa: University of Alabama Press, 1947), 238; Sikes, "The Historical Development of Stillman Institute," 80.

50. Terry and Lee, *A Study of Stillman Institute*, 235.

51. Sikes, "The Historical Development of Stillman Institute," 55; Terry and Lee, *A Study of Stillman Institute*, 236–37.

52. Sikes, "The Historical Development of Stillman Institute," 56.

53. Terry and Lee, *A Study of Stillman Institute*, 238–39; Sikes, "The Historical Development of Stillman Institute," 4.

54. Terry and Lee, *A Study of Stillman Institute*, 239, 243.

55. Sikes, "The Historical Development of Stillman Institute," 89.

56. Ibid., 4; Terry and Lee, *A Study of Stillman Institute*, 238.

57. Terry and Lee, *A Study of Stillman Institute*, 242.

58. Ibid., 240.

59. Ibid.

60. Ibid., 237–38.

61. Ibid., 246–48.

62. W. Edmiston, *The Fat of the Land,* 42–43.

63. *Twenty-second Annual Catalogue of the Tuskegee Normal and Industrial Institute, 1902–1903* (Tuskegee, Ala.: Tuskegee Institute Steam Press, 1903), 39, Special Collections and Archives, Tuskegee University.

64. Ibid., 36–37.

65. "Missionary Sees New Hope for Congoland," unnamed publication, undated, AEP, RG 495, box 6, folder 26, PHS.

66. Zimmerman, *Alabama in Africa,* 180–81.

67. George Washington Carver, *Bulletin No. 1: Feeding Acorns* (Tuskegee, Ala.: Normal School Steam Press, 1898), 5, https://archive.org/details/CAT31355440/page/n2, accessed 10 September 2019.

68. *Twenty-first Annual Catalogue of the Tuskegee Normal and Industrial Institute, 1901–1902* (Tuskegee, Ala.: Tuskegee Institute Steam Press, 1902), 81, Special Collections and Archives, Tuskegee University.

69. Zimmerman, *Alabama in Africa,* 56–57.

70. Carver, *Bulletin No. 1: Feeding Acorns,* 4–5.

71. Ibid., 4.

72. Ibid., 8–9.

73. Edmiston, entries for 30 July–4 August 1917, A. L. Edmiston Diaries.

74. Ibid.; Edmiston, entries for 31 August–5 September 1917, A. L. Edmiston Diaries.

75. Edmiston, entry for 9 September 1918, A. L. Edmiston Diaries.

76. Edmiston, "A. P. C. M. Report of the Agricultural College, Nov. 1919," 4.

77. George Washington Carver, *Bulletin No. 3: Fertilizer Experiments on Cotton* (Tuskegee, Ala.: Normal School Steam Press, 1899), 11, https://archive.org/details/CAT31355448/page/n2, accessed 10 September 2019.

78. Zimmerman, *Alabama in Africa,* 180.

79. Maud Seghers, "Phelps-Stokes in Congo: Transferring Educational Policy Discourse to Govern Metropole and Colony," *Pedagogica Historica* 40, no. 4 (2004): 476–77.

80. Alonzo Edmiston, "A. P. C. M. Report of the Agricultural College, Nov. 1919," 4.

81. Bedinger, *Triumphs of the Gospel in the Belgian Congo,* 65.

82. Henry F. Williams, *In South America: the Brazil Missions of the Presbyterian Church in the United States* (Richmond, Va.: Presbyterian Board of Publications, 1910), 25.

83. Carver, *Bulletin No. 1: Feeding Acorns,* 5.

84. For examples of such charts and photographs from the Tuskegee Experiment Station, see Carver, *Bulletin No. 3: Fertilizer Experiments on Cotton,* 5–12.

85. Edmiston, entry for 7 December 1919, A. L. Edmiston Diaries.

86. Edmiston, "Aims and Policies of the Agricultural School," 3.

87. Ibid.

88. *Catalogue of Fisk University, 1899–1900* (Nashville, Tenn.: Marshall & Bruce, 1900), 77, Spence Family Collection, 1812–1961, box 81, folder 2, Special Collections and Archives, Fisk University, Nashville.

89. Richardson, *A History of Fisk University,* 148.

90. Rodney T. Cohen, *Fisk University* (Charlestown, S.C.: Arcadia Publishing, 2001), 28. The DLV club was the first campus organization at Fisk University for women pursuing the bachelor of arts degree. "Literary Notes: D. L. V. Club Anniversary," *Fisk Herald,* May 1908, 22.

91. Susan C. Jarratt, "Classics and Counterpublics in Nineteenth-Century Historically Black Colleges," *College English* 72, no. 2 (2009): 138.

92. *Catalogue of the Officers and Students of Fisk University, 1900–1901* (Nashville, Tenn.: Marshall and Bruce, 1901), 23, Spence Family Collection, 1812–1961, box 81, folder 3, Special Collections and Archives, Fisk University, Nashville.

93. King, *Pan-Africanism and Education,* 215.

94. Jarratt, "Classics and Counterpublics in Nineteenth-Century Historically Black Colleges," 138–40.

95. Brown Edmiston, "Autobiography," 2.

96. Richardson, *A History of Fisk University,* 34–39.

97. Edmiston, "A. P. C. M. Report of the Agricultural College, Nov. 1919," 1.

98. Edmiston, entry for 13 March 1919, A. L. Edmiston Diaries.

99. Edmiston, "A. P. C. M. Report of the Agricultural College, Nov. 1919," 3.

100. Edmiston, entry for 14 March 1919, A. L. Edmiston Diaries.

101. Edmiston, entry for 10 November 1919, A. L. Edmiston Diaries.

102. Ibid.

103. Unknown correspondent to the Rev. E. W. Smith, 10 October 1917, Nashville, Tenn., APCM Records, RG 432, box 78, folder 16, PHS.

104. Longenecker, *Memories of Congo,* 21–23.

105. Ibid., 22, 49–51.

106. Edmiston, entry for 11 November 1919, A. L. Edmiston Diaries.

107. Edmiston, entry for 14 March 1919, A. L. Edmiston Diaries.

108. Edmiston, "Aims and Policies of the Agricultural College," 3.

109. The final Agricultural College report promoted the student bank program with this argument: "We try to teach them that economy is the only thing that will rid the Country of that great and awful curse which they call mabanza (debts)." Edmiston, "A. P. C. M. Report of the Agricultural College, Nov. 1919," 2.

110. Yates, "The Missions and Educational Development in Belgian Africa," 403.

111. Edmiston, "Report of the Agricultural School of the A.P.C.M., Luebo, Oct. 30, 1918," 1; Edmiston, "A. P. C. M. Report of the Agricultural College, Nov. 1919," 2.

112. Edmiston, "Report of the Agricultural School of the A.P.C.M., Luebo, Oct. 30, 1918," 1; Edmiston, "A. P. C. M. Report of the Agricultural College, Nov. 1919," 2.

113. Edmiston, entry for 15 February 1919, A. L. Edmiston Diaries.

114. Likaka, *Rural Society and Cotton in Colonial Zaire,* 13.

115. Yates, "The Missions and Educational Development in Belgian Africa," 113–16.

116. Vansina, *Being Colonized,* 87–91.

117. Edmiston, "Aims and Policies of the Agricultural College," 3; Edmiston, "A. P. C. M. Report of the Agricultural College, Nov. 1919," 3–4.

118. Likaka, *Rural Society and Cotton in Colonial Zaire,* 5–6.

119. Ibid., 4.

4. Neighbors Recognizing and Redefining Identities in the Belgian Congo, 1916–1935

1. Edmiston, entry for 17 November 1934, A. L. Edmiston Diaries.

2. Brown Edmiston, "Six Months at Ibanj," 255.

3. Verney, *The Art of the Possible,* 30, 34; Zimmerman, *Alabama in Africa,* 56–57; Longenecker, *Memories of Congo,* 21–23.

4. Longenecker, *Memories of Congo;* A Missionary, "Our Future Industrial Hope"; Rev. A. L. Edmiston, "Industrial School in the Congo," *Missionary* (September 1907): 438–39.

5. Mercy Amba Oduyoye traced the first African theology scholarship to 1958, the year after British colonialism fell in Ghana. Oluwatomisin Oredein, "Interview with Mercy Amba Oduyoye: Mercy Amba Oduyoye in Her Own Words," *Journal of Feminist Studies in Religion* 32, no. 2 (2016): 157–60.

6. Mercy Amba Oduyoye, "Christianity and African Culture," *International Review of Mission* 84, no. 332–33 (1995): 80.

7. Phipps, *William Sheppard,* 71–74.

8. Ibid., 111–16.

9. Vansina, *Being Colonized,* 119–20.

10. Gwinyai Henry Muzorewa, "African Theology: Its Origin and Development" (Ph.D. diss., Union Theological Seminary, 1982), 46–47, 137.

11. Yates, "The Missions and Educational Development in Belgian Africa," 209–10.

12. Ibid., 207.

13. William Henry Sheppard, *Presbyterian Pioneers in Congo* (Richmond, Va.: Presbyterian Committee of Publication, 1917), 128–39.

14. Jan Vansina, *Paths in the Rainforests: Toward a History of Political Tradition in Equatorial Africa* (Madison: University of Wisconsin Press, 1990), 242–45.

15. Ibid., 246.

16. Vansina, *Being Colonized,* 63–81.

17. Edmiston, entry for 10 May 1918, A. L. Edmiston Diaries.

18. Edmiston, entry for 10 August 1916, A. L. Edmiston Diaries.

19. Edmiston, entry for 13 November 1919, A. L. Edmiston Diaries.

20. Ibid.

21. An undated report from Mushenge was inserted between Alonzo Edmiston's journal entries for the month of October 1923. A. L. Edmiston Diaries.

22. Kellersberger, *A Life for the Congo,* 94–102.

23. Ibid., 127.

24. Edmiston, entry for 27 December 1916, A. L. Edmiston Diaries.

25. Edmiston, entry for 15 July 1917, A. L. Edmiston Diaries.

26. Edmiston, entries for 14 September 1916, 31 December 1916, and 2 March 1917, A. L. Edmiston Diaries.

27. Alonzo Edmiston, Report from Ibanche, 6 March 1916, APCM Records, RG 432, box 27, folder 2, PHS.

28. Edmiston, entry for 4 March 1917, A. L. Edmiston Diaries.

29. Edmiston, entry for 2 April 1916, A. L. Edmiston Diaries.

30. Edmiston, entry for 1 March 1916, A. L. Edmiston Diaries.

31. Edmiston, entry for 20 February 1916, A. L. Edmiston Diaries.

32. Muzorewa, "African Theology," 26, quoting Harry Sawyerr, "What Is African Theology?" *African Theological Journal* 4 (1971): 24.

33. Muzorewa, "African Theology," 43; Gwinyai Henry Muzorewa, *An African Theology of Mission* (Lewiston, N.Y.: Edwin Mellen Press, 1990), 92.

34. Muzorewa, "African Theology," 43–44.

35. Edmiston, entries for 27 February 1916 and 17 August 1917, A. L. Edmiston Diaries.

36. W. M. Morrison to Monsieur le Commandant Knauer, 12 April 1916, Luebo, APCM Records, RG 432, box 27, folder 2, PHS.

37. Edmiston, entry for 15 July 1917, A. L. Edmiston Diaries.

38. Edmiston, entry for 8 February 1916, A. L. Edmiston Diaries.

39. Edmiston, entries for 12–14 March 1916, A. L. Edmiston Diaries.

40. Edmiston, entry for 21 October 1917, A. L. Edmiston Diaries.

41. Edmiston, entry for 4 February 1918, A. L. Edmiston Diaries.

42. Alonzo Edmiston to Dr. Morrison, 21 December 1917, Ibanche, APCM Records, RG 432, box 37, folder 20, PHS.

43. Edmiston, entry for 22 August 1917, A. L. Edmiston Diaries.

44. Edmiston, entries for 22 August, 30 August, 6 October, and 3 December 1917, A. L. Edmiston Diaries.

45. Edmiston, entries for 30 July–4 August 1917, A. L. Edmiston Diaries.

46. Edmiston, entry for 9 September 1918, A. L. Edmiston Diaries.

47. Edmiston, entry for 15 December 1917, A. L. Edmiston Diaries.

48. Edmiston, entries for 31 August–5 September 1917 and 24 January 1920, A. L. Edmiston Diaries.

49. Edmiston, entries for 19–26 January 1917, A. L. Edmiston Diaries.

50. Vansina, *Being Colonized,* 89–90.

51. A. L. Edmiston, 1917 Ibanche Report, A. L. Edmiston Diaries; Vansina, *Being Colonized,* 88–89.

52. Muzorewa, "African Theology," 47.

53. John Mbiti, "The Future of Christianity in Africa," *CrossCurrents* 28, no. 4 (1978–79): 392–93.

54. Muzorewa, "African Theology," 43, quoted originally in Kofi Appiah-Kubi and Sergio Torres, *African Theology en Route* (Maryknoll, N.Y.: Orbis Books, 1979), 110–11.

55. Edmiston, entry for 30 January 1917, A. L. Edmiston Diaries.

56. Edmiston, entry for 30 January 1918, A. L. Edmiston Diaries.

57. *The Westminster Larger Catechism* (1648), Center for Reformed Theology and Apologetics, Question 168, http://www.apuritansmind.com/westminster -standards/larger-catechism/, accessed 25 June 2018.

58. Gerald K. Tanye, *The Church-as-Family and Ethnocentrism in Sub-Saharan Africa* (Berlin: Lit Verlag, 2010), 30.

59. Edmiston, entry for 27 May 1918, A. L. Edmiston Diaries.

60. Edmiston, 1917 Ibanche Report, 6.

61. C. Peter Williams, *The Ideal of the Self-Governing Church: A Study in Victorian Missionary Strategy* (New York: E. J. Brill, 1990); Andrew T. Roy, "Overseas Missions Policies—An Historical Overview," *Journal of Presbyterian History* 57, no. 3 (1979): 196–203.

62. Edmiston, entries for 20–26 July 1918, A. L. Edmiston Diaries.

63. Edmiston, entries for 19 August 1924 and 6 January 1927, A. L. Edmiston Diaries.

64. Edmiston, entries for 9 December 1924 and 22 January 1927, A. L. Edmiston Diaries.

65. Alonzo Edmiston's photographs from Bulape and other mission stations are available in the AEP, RG 495, box 8, PHS.

66. Edmiston, entry for 30 March 1923, A. L. Edmiston Diaries.

67. For an example, see "A Sharecrop Contract" (1882), Roy Rosenzweig Center for History and New Media, https://chnm.gmu.edu/courses/122/recon /contract.htm, accessed 24 August 2017.

68. Likaka, *Rural Society and Cotton in Colonial Zaire,* 13–15, 27, 32–33.

69. Ibid., 10.

70. Ibid., 4.

71. Edmiston, entries for 16–17 February 1916, A. L. Edmiston Diaries.

72. Edmiston, entry for 12 April 1928, A. L. Edmiston Diaries.

73. Edmiston, entries for 19 December 1918 and 4–5 March, 1919, A. L. Edmiston Diaries; "Reverend A. L. Edmiston Missionary to Africa," typed career abstract, undated, Althea B. Edmiston Collection, MSS 883, box 1, folder 1, Manuscript, Archives, and Rare Book Library, Emory University, Atlanta.

74. Edmiston, entry for 12 January 1920, A. L. Edmiston Diaries.

75. Edmiston, entry for 1 January 1920, A. L. Edmiston Diaries.

76. Edmiston, entry for 28 November 1930, A. L. Edmiston Diaries.

77. Edmiston, entries for 3 July 1931, 17 February 1933, 14 April 1934, and 28 December 1934, A. L. Edmiston Diaries.

78. Edmiston, entry for 3 July 1931, A. L. Edmiston Diaries.

79. Edmiston, entries for 7 and 28 July 1933, A. L. Edmiston Diaries.

80. Edmiston, entry for 6 June 1934, A. L. Edmiston Diaries.

81. Edmiston, entry for 7 July 1933, A. L. Edmiston Diaries.

82. Edmiston, entries for 23 December 1927 and 19 January 1935, A. L. Edmiston Diaries.

83. Bill Worth Jr., conversation with the author, Congo Mission Network Conference, Presbyterian Heritage Center, Montreat, N.C., 9 September 2016.

84. John Mbiti, "Theology of the New World: Some Current Concerns of African Theology," *Expository Times* 87, no. 6 (1976): 164.

85. Ibid., 166.

86. Ibid., 167.

87. Mercy Amba Oduyoye, "Youth in God's World: A Response after Twenty-four Years," *Ecumenical Review* 44, no. 2 (1992): 237.

88. Oredein, "Interview with Mercy Amba Oduyoye," 157.

89. P. Chike Onwuachi, "African Traditional Culture and Western Education," *Journal of Negro Education* 35, no. 3 (1966): 290.

90. Ibid., 292.

91. Brown Edmiston, *Grammar and Dictionary of the Bushonga or Bukuba Language,* vii.

92. Kellersberger, *A Life for the Congo,* 112.

93. Ibid., 111–12.

94. Ibid., 113.

95. Dana Robert, *American Women in Mission: A Social History of Their Thought and Practice* (Macon, Ga.: Mercer University Press, 1996), 130.

96. Kellersberger, *A Life for the Congo,* 113.

97. Luise White, *Speaking with Vampires: Rumor and History in Colonial Africa* (Berkeley: University of California Press, 2000), 276; Kellersberger, *A Life for the Congo,* 111.

98. Likaka, *Rural Society and Cotton in Colonial Zaire,* 55–56.

99. Martha Frederiks, "Miss Jairus Speaks: Developments in African Feminist Theology," *Exchange* 32, no. 1 (2003): 68–69.

100. Edmiston, entries for 13–15 August 1923, A. L. Edmiston Diaries.

101. Edmiston, entry for 15 August 1923, A. L. Edmiston Diaries.

102. Edmiston, entry for 13 August 1923, A. L. Edmiston Diaries.

103. Edmiston, entry for 15 August 1923, A. L. Edmiston Diaries.

104. Edmiston, entry for 11 March 1923, A. L. Edmiston Diaries.

105. Oredein, "Interview with Mercy Amba Oduyoye," 162.

106. Oduyoye, "Christianity and African Culture," 80, 87.

107. Ibid., 87.

108. L. A. DeYampert to Dr. Chester, 7 December 1915, Selma, Ala., APCM Records, RG 432, box 78, folder 8, PHS; Brown Edmiston, "Maria Fearing," 315; Quirin, "'Her Sons and Daughters Are Ever on the Altar,'" 25, 31.

109. Edmiston, entry for 2 August 1917, A. L. Edmiston Diaries.

110. Brown Edmiston, "Autobiography," 6.

111. Tanye, *The Church-as-Family and Ethnocentrism in Sub-Saharan Africa*, 31.

112. Althea Edmiston Cousins, Evelyn Edmiston Easton, Herbert Edmiston, Dr. Kimberly Cousins Trent, and Lisa Edmiston, conversation with the author, 20 April 2018, PHS.

113. Ira Dworkin noted that the Belgian minister of colonies, Louis Franck, sought to monitor African American travelers to the Belgian Congo from the early 1920s. He explained it as a means to make the Belgian standards for missionary oversight similar to American segregated education and British colonial policy. Dworkin, *Congo Love Song*, 154–55; Edmiston, entries for 29 September and 11 October 1917, A. L. Edmiston Diaries.

114. Edmiston, entry for 25 November 1917, A. L. Edmiston Diaries.

115. Edmiston, entries for 2–6 January 1918, A. L. Edmiston Diaries.

116. Edmiston, entries for 22–23 June 1918, 14 October 1918, and 9 February 1919, A. L. Edmiston Diaries.

117. Edmiston, entry for 16 May 1918, A. L. Edmiston Diaries.

118. Edmiston, 1917 Ibanche Report, 5; Edmiston, entry for 7 June 1918, A. L. Edmiston Diaries.

119. Dworkin, *Congo Love Song*, 143–46.

120. Ibid.

121. Edmiston, entry for 3 June 1917, A. L. Edmiston Diaries.

5. On the Perimeter of Two Freedom Struggles, 1930–1936

1. Edmiston, entry for 19 October 1934, A. L. Edmiston Diaries; Dworkin, *Congo Love Song*, 153–54.

2. Thomas, *Violence and Colonial Order*, 322.

3. Ibid., 301–2, 312–14.

4. Edmiston, entries for 6 February 1926 and 10 September 1932, A. L. Edmiston Diaries.

5. Gershoni, *Africans on African-Americans*, 9–15.

6. Wyatt MacGaffey, "The West in Congolese Experience," in *Africa & the West: Intellectual Responses to European Culture*, ed. Philip D. Curtin (Madison: University of Wisconsin Press, 1972), 54–56.

7. Ibid., 56–58; B. [Bogumil] Jewsiewicki, "Political Consciousness among African Peasants in the Belgian Congo," *Review of African Political Economy* 19 (September–December 1980): 28.

8. Edmiston, entry for 1 January 1935, A. L. Edmiston Diaries.

9. MacGaffey, "The West in Congolese Experience," 58–59.

10. Jewsiewicki, "Political Consciousness among African Peasants in the Belgian Congo," 28.

11. White, *Speaking with Vampires,* 276, 288–89.

12. Jewsiewicki, "Political Consciousness among African Peasants in the Belgian Congo," 28.

13. Edmiston, entry for 2 August 1917, A. L. Edmiston Diaries.

14. Edmiston, entry for 14 February 1933, A. L. Edmiston Diaries.

15. Likaka, *Rural Society and Cotton in Colonial Zaire,* 16–18, 24.

16. Yates, "Missions Education in the Belgian Congo," 195–96.

17. Edmiston, entry for 13 March 1933, A. L. Edmiston Diaries.

18. Likaka, *Rural Society and Cotton in Colonial Zaire,* 18.

19. Ibid., 35.

20. Edmiston, entry for 18 June 1931, A. L. Edmiston Diaries.

21. Edmiston, entry for 27 February 1933, A. L. Edmiston Diaries.

22. Edmiston, entry for 17 November 1934, A. L. Edmiston Diaries.

23. Edmiston, entry for 28 November 1933, A. L. Edmiston Diaries.

24. Edmiston, entry for 5 March 1934, A. L. Edmiston Diaries.

25. Edmiston, entries for 4–12 March 1933, A. L. Edmiston Diaries.

26. Edmiston, entries for 13 March and 23 May 1933, A. L. Edmiston Diaries.

27. Jan Vansina described a Charles Schillings who served as the senior territorial agent in the Kuba territory by 1939. Vansina, *Being Colonized,* 199.

28. Edmiston, entries for 2–3 September 1932, A. L. Edmiston Diaries.

29. Ibid.

30. Likaka, *Rural Society and Cotton in Colonial Zaire,* 55.

31. Edmiston, entries for 2–3 September 1932, A. L. Edmiston Diaries.

32. Ann White, "Counting the Cost of Faith: America's Early Female Missionaries," *Church History* 57, no. 1 (1988): 20–26.

33. Deborah Gray White, *Too Heavy a Load: Black Women in Defense of Themselves, 1894–1994* (New York: W. W. Norton, 1999), 53, 130–31.

34. Frederiks, "Miss Jairus Speaks," 72–73.

35. Mercy Amba Oduyoye, "The Church of the Future, Its Mission and Theology: A View from Africa," *Theology Today* 52, no. 4 (1996): 500.

36. Kelly Brown Douglas, *The Black Christ* (1994; repr., Maryknoll, N.Y.: Orbis Books, 2019), 119–20.

37. Edmiston, entry for 19 October 1934, A. L. Edmiston Diaries.

38. Stefano Picciaredda, "Il movimento kimbanguista nell'inchiesta Voisin: La figura del profeta, le missioni inglesi e la pioggia di fuoco," *Africa: Rivista Trimestrale di Studi e Documentazione dell'Istituto Italiano per l'Africa e l'Oriente* 51, no. 1 (1996): 28–31.

39. Thomas, *Violence and Colonial Order,* 308–9, 324.

40. Jewsiewicki, "Political Consciousness among African Peasants in the Belgian Congo," 26–27.

41. Nelson, "Class Formation and the Professionalization of an African Clergy," 135.

42. Edmiston, entries for 13–15 April 1932, A. L. Edmiston Diaries.

43. Edmiston, entry for 26 October 1932, A. L. Edmiston Diaries.

44. Edmiston, entry for 14 February 1934, A. L. Edmiston Diaries.

45. Edmiston, entry for 2 September 1932, A. L. Edmiston Diaries.

46. Edmiston, entry for 5 July 1933, A. L. Edmiston Diaries.

47. Edmiston, entry for 4 April 1934, A. L. Edmiston Diaries.

48. Edmiston, entry for 31 May 1932, A. L. Edmiston Diaries.

49. Edmiston, entry for 23 July 1934, A. L. Edmiston Diaries.

50. Edmiston, entry for 27 July 1934, A. L. Edmiston Diaries.

51. Edmiston, entry for 4 April 1934, A. L. Edmiston Diaries.

52. Edmiston, entry for 5 October 1933, A. L. Edmiston Diaries.

53. Edmiston, entry for 12 November 1934, A. L. Edmiston Diaries.

54. Edmiston, entry for 4 April 1934, A. L. Edmiston Diaries.

55. Edmiston, entry for 25 June 1934, A. L. Edmiston Diaries.

56. Edmiston, entry for 28 February 1935, A. L. Edmiston Diaries.

57. Edmiston, entries for 9–10 January 1935, A. L. Edmiston Diaries.

58. Edmiston, entries for 23 November 1932, 13 April 1934, 10 March 1934, and 10 November 1934, A. L. Edmiston Diaries.

59. Edmiston, entries for 13–16 January 1934, A. L. Edmiston Diaries.

60. Edmiston, entry for 17 November 1934, A. L. Edmiston Diaries.

61. Thomas, *Violence and Colonial Order*, 308.

62. Jewsiewicki, "Political Consciousness among African Peasants in the Belgian Congo," 28.

63. King, *Pan-Africanism and Education*, 71, 79.

64. Gerald Horne, *Black Revolutionary: William Patterson and the Globalization of the African American Freedom Struggle* (Urbana: University of Illinois Press, 2013), 5–6.

65. Dworkin, *Congo Love Song*, 152–53.

66. King, *Pan-Africanism and Education*, 91, 132.

67. Edmiston, entries for 19 June 1934 and 19 March 1935, A. L. Edmiston Diaries.

68. Edmiston, entries for 19 December 1933 and 25 October 1934, A. L. Edmiston Diaries.

69. Edmiston, entry for 19 October 1934, A. L. Edmiston Diaries.

70. Ibid.

71. Edmiston, entry for 19 June 1934, A. L. Edmiston Diaries.

72. Edmiston, entry for 17 November 1934, A. L. Edmiston Diaries.

73. Mercy Amba Oduyoye, "The African Family as a Symbol of Ecumenism," *Ecumenical Review* 43, no. 4 (1991): 466–67, 470.

74. Tanye, *The Church-as-Family and Ethnocentrism in Sub-Saharan Africa*, 24, 30.

75. Ibid., 78.

76. Oduyoye, "The African Family as a Symbol of Ecumenism," 469.

77. Brown Edmiston, "Maria Fearing," 301.

78. Ibid., 301, 305–6.

79. Ibid., 308, 316; Edmiston, entry for 1 January 1920, A. L. Edmiston Diaries.

80. Edmiston, entry for 19 October 1935, A. L. Edmiston Diaries.

81. Alston Fitts, *Selma: A Bicentennial History* (Tuscaloosa: University of Alabama Press, 2017), 145–47.

82. Ibid., 191.

83. Ibid., 212; J. Mills Thornton, *Dividing Lines: Municipal Politics and the Struggle for Civil Rights in Montgomery, Birmingham, and Selma* (Tuscaloosa: University of Alabama Press, 2002), 419.

84. Fitts, *Selma: A Bicentennial History,* 194.

85. Ibid., 198.

86. Ibid., 195.

87. Ibid., 190.

88. Ibid., 126.

89. Edwin Willis to the Rev. A. L. Edmiston, 16 August 1921, Selma, Ala., AEP, RG 495, box 6, folder 2, PHS.

90. [Alonzo and Althea Brown Edmiston] to Dr. S. H. Chester, 13 July 1920, Nashville, Tenn., AEP, RG 495, box 6, folder 1, PHS.

91. Herbert Edmiston, conversation with the author, Philadelphia, 20 April 2018.

92. Fitts, *Selma: A Bicentennial History,* 158.

93. J. L. Chestnut Jr. and Julia Cass, *Black in Selma: The Uncommon Life of J. L. Chestnut, Jr.* (New York: Farrar, Straus and Giroux, 1990), 21, 93.

94. Ibid., 134.

95. Thornton, *Dividing Lines,* 439.

96. Amelia Boynton Robinson, *Bridge across Jordan,* rev. ed. (Washington, D.C.: Schiller Institute, 1991), 110; Amelia Robinson, "The History of the Black Civil Rights Movement and Its Lessons for Today," in *Saint Augustine, Father of European and African Civilization,* ed. Helga Zepp-LaRouche and Lyndon LaRouche (New York: New Benjamin Franklin House, 1985), Kindle edition, location 2028.

97. Gershoni, *Africans on African-Americans,* 8.

98. Sharon J. Jackson, *Selma* (Charleston, S.C.: Arcadia Publishing, 2014), 112.

99. Jane Cunningham Croly, *History of the Women's Club Movement in America* (New York: H. G. Allen, 1898), 233–34.

100. Mary La Fayette Robbins, *Alabama Women in Literature* (Selma: Selma Printing Co., 1895), 39–40.

101. Anne Ruggles Gere, *Writing Groups: History, Theory, and Implications* (Carbondale: Southern Illinois University Press, 1987), 41.

102. Fitts, *Selma: A Bicentennial History,* 210–13.

103. Chestnut and Cass, *Black in Selma,* 39–41, 44–45.

104. Thornton, *Dividing Lines*, 436–37. The Alabama voucher system was a voter suppression tactic designed to supplement poll taxes and literacy tests. A potential African American voter needed recommendations from one or two white citizens to validate his or her voter registration. Additional requirements that these recommenders needed to appear in person made registration in rural areas a tedious endeavor.

105. Fitts, *Selma: A Bicentennial History*, 211.

106. Chestnut and Cass, *Black in Selma*, 156; Fitts, *Selma: A Bicentennial History*, 212.

107. Chestnut and Cass, *Black in Selma*, 43.

108. Quote from Thornton, *Dividing Lines*, 415; Edmiston, entry for 9 December 1935, A. L. Edmiston Diaries.

109. Robinson, *Bridge across Jordan*, 53.

110. Thornton, *Dividing Lines*, 415.

111. "Literary Notes: D. L. V. Club Anniversary," *Fisk Herald* (May 1908): 22; "Pilgrims of Three Centuries," *Fisk University News* 11, no. 3 (1920): 28; "The Anniversary and Commencement Season at Fisk: A Message from Africa," *Fisk University News* 11, no. 9 (1921): 16–17.

112. Evelyn Easton and Herbert Edmiston, conversation with the author, Philadelphia, 20 April 2018.

113. King, *Pan-Africanism and Education*, 140–42.

114. Richardson, *A History of Fisk University*, 85–87.

115. Ibid., 96.

116. W. E. B. Du Bois, *The Autobiography of W. E. B. Du Bois: A Soliloquy on Viewing My Life from the Last Decade of Its First Century* (New York: International Publishers, 1968), 130.

117. Ibid., 131; King, *Pan-Africanism and Education*, 141.

118. William H. Watkins, *The White Architects of Black Education: Ideology and Power in America, 1865–1954* (New York: Teachers College Press, 2001), 114.

119. King, *Pan-Africanism and Education*, 39.

120. Ibid., 178–80.

121. Ibid., 141.

122. Isaac Fisher, ed., "Fortieth Anniversary of the Alumni Association," *Fisk University News* 11 no. 9 (1921): 20.

123. Ibid.

124. Du Bois, *The Autobiography of W. E. B. Du Bois*, 130.

125. Joel L. Alvis, *Religion and Race: Southern Presbyterians, 1946–1983* (Tuscaloosa: University of Alabama Press, 1994), 78–79.

126. "The Conference of Negro Women at Stillman Institute, Tuscaloosa, Ala., September 16–23, 1916," *Presbyterian of the South* (Atlanta), 11 October 1916, 9; "Conference for Colored Women," *Presbyterian of the South*, 3 October 1919, 10. Both available in "Stillman College and the Jim Crow Era News Coverage," http://hgreen.people.ua.edu/stillman-jim-crow—documents.html, documents 6 and 9, accessed 16 February 2019.

127. "The Seventh Annual Report of the Superintendent, Woman's Auxiliary, 1918–1919," in *Minutes of the Fifty-ninth General Assembly of the Presbyterian Church in the United States* (Richmond, Va.: Presbyterian Committee of Publication, 1919), 7.

128. "The Conference of Negro Women at Stillman Institute, 9; "Conference for Colored Women," 10.

129. Marie Foster, a civil rights activist with the Dallas County Voters League in the early 1960s, noted that she could not recall a reference to a black woman as "Mrs." in a local newspaper. Chestnut and Cass, *Black in Selma,* 135.

130. Winsborough, introduction to *Glorious Living,* 8.

131. Alvis, *Religion and Race,* 80.

132. Brown Edmiston, *Grammar and Dictionary of the Bushonga or Bukuba Language,* iii.

133. "Education of the Negro," *Duluth Evening Herald,* 24 February 1906, 16.

134. W. Edmiston, *The Fat of the Land,* 33.

135. Ibid., 40–41; Kellersberger, *A Life for the Congo,* 74.

136. Edmiston, entries for 6–8 January 1936, A. L. Edmiston Diaries.

137. W. Edmiston, *The Fat of the Land,* 44–45; Kellersberger, *A Life for the Congo,* 74.

138. W. Edmiston, *The Fat of the Land,* 181–82.

Conclusion

1. "Missionary Sees New Hope for Congoland," unnamed publication, undated, AEP, RG 495, box 6, folder 26, PHS.

2. George Washington Carver, *Bulletin No. 42: How to Build and Maintain the Virgin Fertility of Our Soils,* George Washington Carver Bulletins, box 3, folder 42, Tuskegee University Archives, Tuskegee, Ala.

3. Edmiston, entry for 28 October 1935, A. L. Edmiston Diaries.

4. Dworkin, *Congo Love Song,* 154; Thomas Jesse Jones, *The Rural Billion and the Agricultural Missions Foundation* (New York: Agricultural Missions Foundation, 1935).

5. Edmiston, entries for 20–30 August 1936, A. L. Edmiston Diaries.

6. Edmiston, entry for 1 September 1936, A. L. Edmiston Diaries.

7. Edmiston, entries for 12–18 July 1936, A. L. Edmiston Diaries.

8. Edmiston, entry for 3 June 1937, A. L. Edmiston Diaries.

9. Edmiston, entries for 23 November 1932 and 13 April 1934, A. L. Edmiston Diaries.

10. Kellersberger, *A Life for the Congo,* 168–69.

11. See appendix C for the full text of the tribute letter. Tshisungu Daniel to Tatu Luongoso, 1 July 1937, Bakwa Mamba, reprinted in "Mama Tshitolo: Madame A. L. Edmiston," *News of the Kasai People/L.L.B.K.,* August 1937, 14–15, Vass Family Papers, RG 476, box 2, folder 6, PHS; Brown Edmiston, "Maria Fearing," 316.

12. Tshisungu Daniel to Tatu Luongoso, 1 July 1937.

13. Edmiston, entry for 22 April 1936, A. L. Edmiston Diaries.

14. Edmiston, entry for 28 October 1939, A. L. Edmiston Diaries.

15. Edmiston, entries for 29 April–19 August 1940, A. L. Edmiston Diaries.

16. "Order of Service: Good Hope Presbyterian Church, Bessemer, Alabama," 19 October 1947, Althea Brown Edmiston Papers, MSS 883, box 1, folder 1, Manuscript, Archives, and Rare Book Library, Emory University, Atlanta; "Reverend A. L. Edmiston Missionary to Africa," undated, Althea Brown Edmiston Papers, MSS 883, box 1, folder 1, Manuscript, Archives, and Rare Book Library, Emory University, Atlanta.

17. Fitts, *Selma: A Bicentennial History,* 200; Chestnut and Cass, *Black in Selma,* 74, 78, 85.

18. Chestnut and Cass, *Black in Selma,* 205–6.

19. Benedetto, *Presbyterian Reformers in Central Africa,* 33.

20. Emory Ross to Educationist Friends, 11 June 1932, Leopoldville, APCM Records, RG 432, box 44, folder 14, PHS.

21. Vansina, *Being Colonized,* 288.

22. "International Missionary Council: Education Memorandum on Situation in Congo," London, January 1932, 1–4, APCM Records, RG 432, box 44, folder 14, PHS; Robert Harms, *Africa in Global History: With Sources* (New York: W. W. Norton, 2018), 474.

23. R. Godding to Monsieur le Secrétaire Général, 23 February 1946, Brussels, APCM Records, RG 432, box 44, folder 14, PHS; Vansina, *Being Colonized,* 292.

24. Emory Ross, "State Educational Program," 8 June 1932, Leopoldville, 1, APCM Records, RG 432, box 44, folder 14, PHS.

25. Emory Ross to the Rev. E. F. Guyton, 7 June 1932, Thysville, APCM Records, RG 432, box 44, folder 14, PHS; "International Missionary Council: Education Memorandum on Situation in Congo," London, January 1932, 3–5, APCM Records, RG 432, box 44, folder 14, PHS.

26. Edmiston, entry for 10 November 1932, A. L. Edmiston Diaries.

27. Edmiston, entries for 21 July 1932, 10 November 1933, 19 December 1933, and 19 March 1935, A. L. Edmiston Diaries.

28. Dworkin, *Congo Love Song,* 154–55.

29. King, *Pan-Africanism and Education,* 163; "International Missionary Council: Education Memorandum on Situation in Congo."

30. "International Missionary Council: Education Memorandum on Situation in Congo."

31. Ibid.

32. John Morrison to the Rev. Edgar H. Morrish, 3 December 1946, Léopoldville, APCM Records, RG 432, box 44, folder 14, PHS.

33. "International Missionary Council: Education Memorandum on Situation in Congo," 2–4.

34. Vansina, *Being Colonized,* 292.

35. Thomas, *Violence and Colonial Order,* 323.

36. Ibid.

37. Likaka, *Rural Society and Cotton in Colonial Zaire,* 57–60.

38. Harms, *Africa in Global History,* 521.

39. "Note Relative aux Attributions de l'Inspecteur de l'Enseignement Agricole," 1957, 2, APCM Records, RG 432, box 44, folder 14, PHS; translated from French by the author.

40. Likaka, *Rural Society and Cotton in Colonial Zaire,* 67.

41. Jewsiewicki, "Political Consciousness among African Peasants in the Belgian Congo," 25.

42. Melanie McAlister, *The Kingdom of God Has No Borders: A Global History of American Evangelicals* (New York: Oxford University Press, 2018), 40–42; Agricultural and Technical Assistance Foundation, "Report to: The Woman's Division of Christian Service, Re: The Home Economic and Home and Family Life Program of the Congo Polytechnic Institute," Presbyterian Church in the U. S. General Executive Board, Division of International Mission, Area Secretary for Africa, Europe, and the Near East Records, RG 506, box 3, folders 19 and 20, PHS.

43. Dworkin, *Congo Love Song,* 257–58.

44. Agricultural and Technical Assistance Foundation, "Report to: The Woman's Division of Christian Service," 15; Vansina, *Being Colonized,* 291.

45. Agricultural and Technical Assistance Foundation, "Report to: The Woman's Division of Christian Service," 1.

46. G. Thompson Brown, "Overseas Mission Program and Policies of the Presbyterian Church in the U.S., 1861–1983," *American Presbyterians* 65, no. 2 (1987): 166–67.

Appendix C

Tshisungu Daniel to Tatu Luongoso, 20 June 1937, Luebo, reprinted in "Mama Tshitolo: Madame A. L. Edmiston," *News of the Kasai People/L.L.B.K.,* August 1937, 14–15, Vass Family Papers, RG 476, box 2, folder 6, PHS. Translated by Dr. Elsie Anne McKee, Princeton Theological Seminary.

1. *Tshitolo* means "careful plucking" and refers to "her meticulous nature and attention to details." The nicknames *Luongoso* and *Lungonzo* for Alonzo Edmiston mean "banana plant blossom," an allusion to his farming. Robert Benedetto, *Presbyterian Reformers in Central Africa,* 228.

2. "Worship places" is translated from *tshitanda,* which usually means an open-sided structure, sticks holding up a palm-branch roof.

Bibliography

Archival Sources

Alonzo Edmiston Papers. RG 495. Presbyterian Historical Society, Philadelphia.

Althea Brown Edmiston Papers. MSS 883. Manuscript, Archives, and Rare Book Library, Emory University, Atlanta.

American Presbyterian Congo Mission Records. RG 432. Presbyterian Historical Society, Philadelphia.

Brown Edmiston, Althea. "Autobiography." December 1923. Althea Brown Edmiston Biographical File. Presbyterian Historical Society, Philadelphia.

Carver, George Washington. *Bulletin No. 1: Feeding Acorns.* Tuskegee, Ala.: Normal School Steam Press, 1898. https://archive.org/details/CAT31355440/page/n2, accessed 10 September 2019.

———. *Bulletin No. 3: Fertilizer Experiments on Cotton.* Tuskegee, Ala.: Normal School Steam Press, 1899. https://archive.org/details/CAT31355448/page/n2, accessed 10 September 2019.

———. *Bulletin No. 42: How to Build and Maintain the Virgin Fertility of Our Soils.* George Washington Carver Bulletins, box 3, folder 42. Tuskegee University Archives, Tuskegee, Ala.

Catalogue of Fisk University, 1899–1900. Nashville, Tenn.: Marshall & Bruce, 1900. Spence Family Collection, 1812–1961, box 81, folder 2. Special Collections and Archives, Fisk University, Nashville.

Catalogue of the Officers and Students of Fisk University, 1900–1901. Nashville, Tenn.: Marshall and Bruce, 1901. Spence Family Collection, 1812–1961, box 81, folder 3. Special Collections and Archives, Fisk University, Nashville.

"Conference for Colored Women," *Presbyterian of the South* (Atlanta), 3 October 1919, 10. Reprinted in "Stillman College and the Jim Crow Era News Coverage." http://hgreen.people.ua.edu/stillman-jim-crow---documents.html, accessed 16 February 2019.

"The Conference of Negro Women at Stillman Institute, Tuscaloosa, Ala., September 16–23, 1916." *Presbyterian of the South* (Atlanta), 11 October 1916, 9. Reprinted in "Stillman College and the Jim Crow Era News Coverage." http://hgreen.people.ua.edu/stillman-jim-crow---documents.html, accessed 16 February 2019.

Edmiston, A. L. A. L. Edmiston Diaries. African Missions Collection, Talladega College Library, Talladega, Ala.

Minutes of the Executive Committee on Home Missions, 1921–1933. RT 716, box 2. Presbyterian Historical Society, Philadelphia.

Presbyterian Church in the U.S. General Executive Board. Division of International Mission. Area Secretary for Africa, Europe, and the Near East Records. RG 506, box 3, folders 19 and 20. Presbyterian Historical Society, Philadelphia.

Roy F. Cleveland and LeNoir Ramsey Cleveland Correspondence. RG 462. Presbyterian Historical Society, Philadelphia.

"A Sharecrop Contract" (1882). Roy Rosenzweig Center for History and New Media. https://chnm.gmu.edu/courses/122/recon/contract.htm, accessed 24 August 2017.

Twenty-first Annual Catalogue of the Tuskegee Normal and Industrial Institute, 1901–1902. Tuskegee, Ala.: Tuskegee Institute Steam Press, 1902. Special Collections and Archives, Tuskegee University.

Twenty-second Annual Catalogue of the Tuskegee Normal and Industrial Institute, 1902–1903. Tuskegee, Ala.: Tuskegee Institute Steam Press, 1903. Special Collections and Archives, Tuskegee University.

Vass Family Papers. RG 476. Presbyterian Historical Society, Philadelphia.

The Westminster Larger Catechism (1648). Center for Reformed Theology and Apologetics. http://www.apuritansmind.com/westminster-standards/larger-catechism/, accessed 25 June 2018.

Published Sources

Alvis, Joel L. *Religion and Race: Southern Presbyterians, 1946–1983.* Tuscaloosa: University of Alabama Press, 1994.

"The Anniversary and Commencement Season at Fisk: A Message from Africa," *Fisk University News* 11, no. 9 (1921): 16–17.

Anthony, David Henry. *Max Yergan: Race Man, Internationalist, Cold Warrior.* New York: New York University Press, 2006.

Barnes, Andrew. *Global Christianity and the Black Atlantic.* Waco, Tex.: Baylor University Press, 2017.

Baylen, Joseph O., and John Hammond Moore. "Senator John Tyler Morgan and Negro Colonization in the Philippines, 1901 to 1902." *Phylon* 29, no. 1 (1968): 65–75.

Bedinger, Robert Dabney. "Althea Brown Edmiston: A Congo Crusader." In *Glorious Living: Informal Sketches of Seven Women Missionaries of the Presbyterian Church, U.S.*, compiled by Hallie Paxson Winsborough, edited by Sarah Lee Vinson Timmons, 263–86. Atlanta: Committee on Woman's Work, Presbyterian Church, U.S., 1937.

————. *Triumphs of the Gospel in the Belgian Congo.* Richmond, Va.: Presbyterian Board of Publications, 1920.

Benedetto, Robert. "The Presbyterian Mission Press in Central Africa, 1890–1922." *American Presbyterians* 68, no. 1 (1990): 55–69.

————, ed. *Presbyterian Reformers in Central Africa.* Translated by Winifred K. Vass. New York: E. J. Brill, 1996.

Brown, G. Thompson. "Overseas Mission Program and Policies of the Presbyterian Church in the U.S., 1861–1983." *American Presbyterians* 65, no. 2 (1987): 157–70.

Brown Edmiston, Mrs. Althea. "From Ibanj, Congo Free State." *Missionary* (October 1907): 482–83.

————. *Grammar and Dictionary of the Bushonga or Bukuba Language as Spoken by the Bushonga or Bukuba Tribe Who Dwell in the Upper Kasai District, Belgian Congo, Central Africa.* Luebo: J. Leighton Wilson Press, 1932.

————. "Maria Fearing: A Mother to African Girls." In *Glorious Living: Informal Sketches of Seven Women Missionaries of the Presbyterian Church, U.S.*, compiled by Hallie Paxson Winsborough, edited by Sarah Lee Vinson Timmons, 289–318. Atlanta: Committee on Women's Work, Presbyterian Church, U.S., 1937.

————. "Missions in Congo Free State, Africa." *American Missionary* 62, no. 10 (1908): 306–10.

————. "Six Months at Ibanj." *Missionary* (June 1906): 255–57.

Campbell, James. *Middle Passages: African American Journeys to Africa.* New York: Penguin Press, 2006.

Chestnut, J. L., Jr., and Julia Cass. *Black in Selma: The Uncommon Life of J. L. Chestnut, Jr.* New York: Farrar, Straus and Giroux, 1990.

Cohen, Rodney T. *Fisk University.* Charleston, S.C.: Arcadia Publishing, 2001.

Conrad, Joseph. *Heart of Darkness.* 1899. Reprint, New York: Dover, 1990.

Croly, Jane Cunningham. *History of the Women's Club Movement in America.* New York: H. G. Allen, 1898.

DeLombard, Jeannine. "Sisters, Servants, or Saviors? National Baptist Women Missionaries in Liberia in the 1920s." *International Journal of African Historical Studies* 24, no. 2 (1991): 323–47.

Douglas, Kelly Brown. *The Black Christ.* 1994. Reprint, Maryknoll, N.Y.: Orbis Books, 2019.

Du Bois, W. E. B. *The Autobiography of W. E. B. Du Bois: A Soliloquy on Viewing My Life from the Last Decade of Its First Century.* New York: International Publishers, 1968.

————. *The Souls of Black Folk.* 1903. Reprint, New York: Dover, 1994.

Dworkin, Ira. *Congo Love Song: African American Culture and the Crisis of the Colonial State.* Chapel Hill: University of North Carolina Press, 2017.

Edmiston, Rev. A. L. "Industrial School in the Congo," *Missionary* (September 1907): 438–39.

Edmiston, William Campbell. *The Fat of the Land*. St. Augustine, Fla.: Record Press, 1958.

"Education of the Negro." *Duluth Evening Herald*, 24 February 1906, 16.

Ellingsen, Mark. "Changes in African American Mission: Rediscovering African Roots." *International Bulletin of Missionary Research* 36, no. 3 (2012): 136–42.

Ellis, Reginald. *Between Washington and Du Bois: The Racial Politics of James Edward Shepard*. Gainesville: University Press of Florida, 2017.

Fisher, Isaac, ed. "Fortieth Anniversary of the Alumni Association." *Fisk University News* 11, no. 9 (1921): 20.

Fitts, Alston. *Selma: A Bicentennial History*. Tuscaloosa: University of Alabama Press, 2017.

Fluker, Walter E. *The Ground Has Shifted: The Future of the Black Church in Post-Racial America*. New York: New York University Press, 2016.

Franklin, John Hope, and Evelyn Brooks Higginbotham. *From Slavery to Freedom: A History of African Americans*. 9th edition. New York: McGraw-Hill, 2011.

Frederiks, Martha. "Miss Jairus Speaks: Developments in African Feminist Theology." *Exchange* 32, no. 1 (2003): 66–82.

Gaines, Kevin. *Uplifting the Race: Black Leadership, Politics, and Culture in the Twentieth Century*. Chapel Hill: University of North Carolina Press, 1996.

Gere, Anne Ruggles. *Writing Groups: History, Theory, and Implications*. Carbondale: Southern Illinois University Press, 1987.

Gershoni, Yekutiel. *Africans on African-Americans: The Creation and Uses of an African-American Myth*. New York: New York University Press, 1997.

Giddings, Paula. *When and Where I Enter*. New York: William Morrow, 1984.

Goings, Kenneth W., and Eugene M. O'Connor. "Lessons Learned: The Role of the Classics at Black Colleges and Universities." *Journal of Negro Education* 79, no. 4 (2010): 521–31.

Gordon, Linda. "Black and White Visions of Welfare: Women's Welfare Activism, 1890–1945." *Journal of American History* 78, no. 2 (1991): 559–90.

Green, Hilary. *Educational Reconstruction: African American Schools in the Urban South, 1865–1900*. New York: Fordham University Press, 2016.

Harms, Robert. *Africa in Global History: With Sources*. New York: W. W. Norton, 2018.

Harris, Katherine. *Pan-African Language Systems: Ebonics & African Oral Heritage*. London: Karnak House, 2003.

Heredia, Rudolf C. "Education and Mission: School as Agent of Evangelisation." *Economic and Political Weekly* 30, no. 37 (1995): 2332–40.

Higginbotham, Evelyn Brooks. *Righteous Discontent: The Women's Movement in the Black Baptist Church, 1880–1920*. Cambridge: Harvard University Press, 1994.

Hill, Kimberly. "Anti-Slavery Work of the American Women of the Presbyterian Congo Mission." In *Faith and Slavery in the Presbyterian Diaspora*, edited by

Peter C. Messer and William Harrison Taylor, 205–30. Bethlehem, Pa.: Lehigh University Press, 2016.

———. "Maria Fearing: Domestic Adventurer." In *Alabama Women: Their Lives and Times*, edited by Susan Youngblood Ashmore and Lisa Lindquist Dorr, 90–107. Athens: University of Georgia Press, 2017.

Hochschild, Adam. *King Leopold's Ghost*. Boston: Houghton Mifflin, 1999.

Hollinger, David A. *Protestants Abroad: How Missionaries Tried to Change the World but Changed America*. Princeton: Princeton University Press, 2017.

Horne, Gerald. *Black Revolutionary: William Patterson and the Globalization of the African American Freedom Struggle*. Urbana: University of Illinois Press, 2013.

Hunter, Tera W. *To 'Joy My Freedom: Southern Black Women's Lives and Labors after the Civil War*. Cambridge: Harvard University Press, 1997.

Hunton, W. A. "The Providential Preparation of the American Negro for Mission Work in Africa." In *World-wide Evangelization the Urgent Business of the Church: Addresses Delivered before the Fourth International Convention of the Student Volunteer Movement for Foreign Missions, Toronto, Canada, February 26–March 2, 1902*. New York: Student Volunteer Movement for Foreign Missions, 1902.

Jackson, David H., Jr. *Booker T. Washington and the Struggle against White Supremacy: The Southern Educational Tours, 1908–1912*. New York: Palgrave Macmillan, 2002.

Jackson, Sharon J. *Selma*. Charleston, S.C.: Arcadia Publishing, 2014.

Jacobs, Sylvia M. "Nineteenth Century Black Methodist Missionary Bishops in Liberia." *Negro History Bulletin* 44, no. 4 (1981): 83–93.

———. "Their 'Special Mission': Afro-American Women as Missionaries to the Congo, 1894–1937." In *Black Americans and the Missionary Movement in Africa*, edited by Sylvia M. Jacobs, 155–76. Westport, Conn.: Greenwood Press, 1982.

———. "Three African American Women Missionaries in the Congo, 1887–1899: The Confluence of Race, Culture, Identity, and Nationality." In *Competing Kingdoms: Women, Mission, Nation, and the American Protestant Empire, 1812–1960*, edited by Barbara Reeves-Ellington, Kathryn Kish Sklar, and Connie A. Shemo, 318–41. Durham, N.C.: Duke University Press, 2010.

James, Moses Edward. "A History of the Snedecor Memorial Synod of the Presbyterian Church in the United States." Senior thesis, Johnson C. Smith University, 1952.

Jarratt, Susan C. "Classics and Counterpublics in Nineteenth-Century Historically Black Colleges." *College English* 72, no. 2 (2009): 134–59.

Jewsiewicki, B. [Bogumil]. "Political Consciousness among African Peasants in the Belgian Congo." *Review of African Political Economy* 19 (September–December 1980): 23–32.

Jones, Thomas Jesse. *The Rural Billion and the Agricultural Missions Foundation*. New York: Agricultural Missions Foundation, 1935.

Kalu, Ogbu U. *Clio in a Sacred Garb: Essays on Christian Presence and African Responses, 1900–2000.* Trenton, N.J.: Africa World Press, 2008.

Kellersberger, Julia Lake. *A Life for the Congo: The Story of Althea Brown Edmiston.* New York: Fleming H. Revell, 1947.

Kennedy, Pagan. *Black Livingstone: A True Tale of Adventure in the Nineteenth-Century Congo.* 2002. Reprint, Santa Fe: Santa Fe Writers Project, 2013.

King, Kenneth. *Pan-Africanism and Education: A Study of Race, Philanthropy and Education in the Southern States of America and East Africa.* 1971. Reprint, Brooklyn: Diasporic Africa Press, 2016.

Lamba, Isaac C. "Cape Dutch Reformed Church Mission in Malawi: A Preliminary Historical Examination of Its Educational Philosophy and Application, 1889–1931." *Transafrican Journal of History* 12 (1983): 51–74.

Lewis, L. J. *Phelps-Stokes Reports on Education in Africa.* London: Oxford University Press, 1962.

Likaka, Osumaka. *Rural Society and Cotton in Colonial Zaire.* Madison: University of Wisconsin Press, 1997.

"Literary Notes: D.L.V. Club Anniversary." *Fisk Herald* (May 1908): 22–23.

Longenecker, J. Hershey. *Memories of Congo: Tales of Adventure and Work in the Heart of Africa.* Johnson City, Tenn.: Royal Publishers, 1964.

MacDonald, Roderick J. "Reverend Hanock Msokera Phiri and the Establishment in Nyasaland of the African Methodist Episcopal Church." *African Historical Studies* 3, no. 1 (1970): 75–87.

MacGaffey, Wyatt. "The West in Congolese Experience." In *Africa & the West: Intellectual Responses to European Culture,* edited by Philip D. Curtin, 49–74. Madison: University of Wisconsin Press, 1972).

Mbiti, John. "The Future of Christianity in Africa." *CrossCurrents* 28, no. 4 (1978–79): 387–94.

———. "Theology of the New World: Some Current Concerns of African Theology." *Expository Times* 87, no. 6 (1976): 164–68.

McAlister, Melanie. *The Kingdom of God Has No Borders: A Global History of American Evangelicals.* New York: Oxford University Press, 2018.

Minutes of the Fifty-ninth General Assembly of the Presbyterian Church in the United States. Richmond, Va.: Presbyterian Committee of Publication, 1919.

Minutes of the General Assembly of the Presbyterian Church in the United States. Richmond, Va.: Presbyterian Committee of Publication, 1907.

Minutes of the General Assembly of the Presbyterian Church in the United States. Richmond, Va.: Presbyterian Committee of Publication, 1921.

A Missionary. "Our Future Industrial Hope." *Missionary* (November 1906): 507–8.

Mixon, Gregory. "Henry McNeal Turner versus the Tuskegee Machine: Black Leadership in the Nineteenth Century." *Journal of Negro History* 79, no. 4 (1994): 363–80.

Morel, E. D. *The Black Man's Burden*. 1903. Reprint, New York: Monthly Review Press, 1969.

Muzorewa, Gwinyai Henry. "African Theology: Its Origin and Development." Ph.D. diss., Union Theological Seminary, 1982.

———. *An African Theology of Mission*. Lewiston, N.Y.: Edwin Mellen Press, 1990.

Nelson, Jack E. "Class Formation and the Professionalization of an African Clergy." *Journal of Religion in Africa* 22, no. 2 (1992): 133–51.

Oborji, Francis Anekwe. "Edinburgh 1910 and Christian Identity Today: An African Perspective." *Missiology: An International Review* 41, no. 3 (2013): 300–314.

Oduyoye, Mercy Amba. "The African Family as a Symbol of Ecumenism." *Ecumenical Review* 43, no. 4 (1991): 465–78.

———. "Christianity and African Culture." *International Review of Mission* 84, no. 332–23 (1995): 77–90.

———. "The Church of the Future, Its Mission and Theology: A View from Africa." *Theology Today* 52, no. 4 (1996): 494–505.

———. "Youth in God's World: A Response after Twenty-four Years." *Ecumenical Review* 44, no. 2 (1992): 234–39.

Onwuachi, P. Chike. "African Traditional Culture and Western Education." *Journal of Negro Education* 35, no. 3 (1966): 289–92.

Oredein, Oluwatomisin. "Interview with Mercy Amba Oduyoye: Mercy Amba Oduyoye in Her Own Words." *Journal of Feminist Studies in Religion* 32, no. 2 (2016): 153–64.

Park, Robert M. "Tuskegee International Conference on the Negro." *Journal of Race Development* 3, no. 1 (1912): 117–20.

Payne, Daniel Alexander. *History of the African Methodist Episcopal Church*. Edited by Charles Spencer Smith. Nashville, Tenn.: A.M.E. Sunday School Union, 1891. "Documenting the American South." https://docsouth.unc.edu/church/payne/payne.html, accessed 6 September 2019.

Pearson, Susan J. "'Infantile Specimens': Showing Babies in Nineteenth-Century America." *Journal of Social History* 42, no. 2 (2008): 341–70.

Perlman, Daniel. "Stirring the White Conscience: The Life of George Edmund Haynes." Ph.D. diss., New York University, 1972.

Phipps, William E. *William Henry Sheppard: Congo's African American Livingstone*. Louisville, Ky.: Geneva Press, 2002.

Picciaredda, Stefano. "Il movimento kimbanguista nell'inchiesta Voisin: La figura del profeta, le missioni inglesi e la pioggia di fuoco." *Africa: Rivista Trimestrale di Studi e Documentazione dell'Istituto Italiano per l'Africa e l'Oriente* 51, no. 1 (1996): 27–49.

"Pilgrims of Three Centuries." *Fisk University News* 11, no. 3 (1920): 26–28.

Quirin, James A. "'Her Sons and Daughters Are Ever on the Altar': Fisk University and Missionaries to Africa, 1866–1937." *Tennessee Historical Quarterly* 60, no. 1 (2011): 16–37.

Richardson, Joe M. *A History of Fisk University, 1865–1946.* University, Ala.: University of Alabama Press, 1980.

Robbins, Mary La Fayette. *Alabama Women in Literature.* Selma: Selma Printing Co., 1895.

Robert, Dana. *American Women in Mission: A Social History of Their Thought and Practice.* Macon, Ga.: Mercer University Press, 1996.

Robinson, Amelia Boynton. *Bridge across Jordan.* Revised edition. Washington, D.C.: Schiller Institute, 1991.

———. "The History of the Black Civil Rights Movement and Its Lessons for Today." In *Saint Augustine, Father of European and African Civilization*, edited by Helga Zepp-LaRouche and Lyndon LaRouche, location 2028–2128. New York: New Benjamin Franklin House, 1985. Kindle edition.

Roth, Donald F. "The 'Black Man's Burden': The Racial Background of Afro-American Missionaries and Africa." In *Black Americans and the Missionary Movement in Africa*, edited by Sylvia M. Jacobs, 31–40. Westport, Conn.: Greenwood Press, 1982.

Roy, Andrew T. "Overseas Missions Policies—An Historical Overview." *Journal of Presbyterian History* 57, no. 3 (1979): 186–228.

Sachs, William L. "'Self-Support': The Episcopal Mission and Nationalism in Japan." *Church History* 58, no. 4 (1989): 489–501.

Scott, David W. "The Value of Money: Funding Sources and Philanthropic Priorities in Twentieth-Century American Mission." *Religions* 9, no. 4 (2018): 122–29. https://doi.org/10.3390/rel9040122.

Seghers, Maud. "Phelps-Stokes in Congo: Transferring Educational Policy Discourse to Govern Metropole and Colony." *Pedagogica Historica* 40, no. 4 (2004): 455–77.

Shaloff, Stanley. *Reform in Leopold's Congo.* Richmond, Va.: John Knox Press, 1970.

Sheppard, William Henry. *Presbyterian Pioneers in Congo.* Richmond, Va.: Presbyterian Committee of Publication, 1917.

Sick, David H. "Alabamian Argonautica: Myth and Classical Education in *The Quest of the Silver Fleece*." *Classical World* 110, no. 3 (2017): 373–97.

Sieg, Rev. J. McClung. "Schools in Congo: Work in the Day and Sunday Schools." *Missionary* (June 1906): 253–55.

———. "Some Observations in the Kassai." *Missionary* (May 1906): 209–10.

Sikes, William Marion. "The Historical Development of Stillman Institute." Master's thesis, University of Alabama, 1930.

Slagell, Amy R. "The Rhetorical Structure of Frances Willard's Campaign for Woman Suffrage, 1876–1896." *Rhetoric & Public Affairs* 4, no. 1 (2001): 1–23.

Stanley, Brian. "Edinburgh and World Christianity." *Studies in World Christianity* 17, no. 1 (2011): 72–91.

———. "From 'the Poor Heathen' to 'the Glory and Honour of All Nations': Vocabularies of Race and Custom in Protestant Missions, 1844–1928." *International Bulletin of Missionary Research* 34, no. 1 (2010): 3–10.

————. "The World Missionary Conference, Edinburgh 1910: Sifting History from Myth." *Expository Times* 121, no. 7 (2010): 325–31.

Stratton, Cliff. *Education for Empire: American Schools, Race, and the Paths of Good Citizenship.* Oakland: University of California Press, 2017.

Tanye, Gerald K. *The Church-as-Family and Ethnocentrism in Sub-Saharan Africa.* Berlin: Lit Verlag, 2010.

Terry, Paul W., and L. Tennent Lee. *A Study of Stillman Institute, a Junior College for Negroes.* Tuscaloosa: University of Alabama Press, 1947.

Thomas, Martin. *Violence and Colonial Order: Police, Workers and Protest in the European Colonial Empires, 1918–1940.* New York: Cambridge University Press, 2012.

Thompson, Ernest Trice. "Black Presbyterians, Education, and Evangelism after the Civil War." *Journal of Presbyterian History* 76, no. 1 (1998): 55–70.

————. *Presbyterians in the South*, vol. 3, *1890–1972*. Richmond, Va.: John Knox Press, 1973.

Thornton, J. Mills. *Dividing Lines: Municipal Politics and the Struggle for Civil Rights in Montgomery, Birmingham, and Selma.* Tuscaloosa: University of Alabama Press, 2002.

Tully, John A. *The Devil's Milk: A Social History of Rubber.* New York: Monthly Review Press, 2011.

Vansina, Jan. *Being Colonized: The Kuba Experience in Rural Congo, 1880–1960.* Madison: University of Wisconsin Press, 2010.

————. *Paths in the Rainforests: Toward a History of Political Tradition in Equatorial Africa.* Madison: University of Wisconsin Press, 1990.

Verney, Kevern. *The Art of the Possible: Booker T. Washington and Black Leadership in the United States, 1881–1925.* New York: Routledge, 2001.

Verner, S. P. "The Adventures of an Explorer in Africa." *Harper's Weekly*, October 22, 1904, 1618–20.

————. "Bringing the Pygmies to America." *Independent* 57, no. 2909 (1904): 485–89.

Washington, Booker T. *On Mother Earth.* 1902. Reprint, Carlisle, Mass.: Applewood Books, 2018.

Watkins, William H. *The White Architects of Black Education: Ideology and Power in America, 1865–1954.* New York: Teachers College Press, 2001.

White, Ann. "Counting the Cost of Faith: America's Early Female Missionaries." *Church History* 57, no. 1 (1988): 19–30.

White, Deborah Gray. *Too Heavy a Load: Black Women in Defense of Themselves, 1894–1994.* New York: W. W. Norton, 1999.

White, Luise. *Speaking with Vampires: Rumor and History in Colonial Africa.* Berkeley: University of California Press, 2000.

Williams, C. Peter. *The Ideal of the Self-Governing Church: A Study in Victorian Missionary Strategy.* New York: E. J. Brill, 1990.

Williams, Henry F. *In South America: The Brazil Missions of the Presbyterian Church in the United States.* Richmond, Va.: Presbyterian Board of Publications, 1910.

Williams, Walter L. *Black Americans and the Evangelization of Africa*. Madison: University of Wisconsin Press, 1982.

Winsborough, Hallie Paxson, comp. *Glorious Living: Informal Sketches of Seven Women Missionaries of the Presbyterian Church, U.S.* Edited by Sarah Lee Vinson Timmons. Atlanta: Committee on Woman's Work, Presbyterian Church, U.S., 1937.

Woodson, Carter Godwin. *The Mis-Education of the Negro*. 1933. Reprint, n.p.: Tribeca Books, 2014.

World Missionary Conference. *The History and Records of the Conference*. Edinburgh: Oliphant, Anderson, and Ferrier, 1910.

Yates, Barbara Ann. "The Missions and Educational Development in Belgian Africa, 1876–1908." Ph.D. diss., Teachers College, Columbia University, 1967.

Zimmerman, Andrew. *Alabama in Africa: Booker T. Washington, the German Empire, and the Globalization of the New South*. Princeton: Princeton University Press, 2010.

Index

New Directions in Southern History

Series editors

Michele Gillespie, Wake Forest University
William A. Link, University of Florida

The Lost State of Franklin: America's First Secession
Kevin T. Barksdale

The Civil War Guerrilla: Unfolding the Black Flag in History, Memory, and Myth
edited by Joseph M. Beilein Jr. and Matthew C. Hulbert

Bluecoats and Tar Heels: Soldiers and Civilians in Reconstruction North Carolina
Mark L. Bradley

Becoming Bourgeois: Merchant Culture in the South, 1820–1865
Frank J. Byrne

Willis Duke Weatherford: Race, Religion, and Reform in the American South
Andrew McNeill Canady

Cowboy Conservatism: Texas and the Rise of the Modern Right
Sean P. Cunningham

A Tour of Reconstruction: Travel Letters of 1875
Anna Dickinson (J. Matthew Gallman, ed.)

Raising Racists: The Socialization of White Children in the Jim Crow South
Kristina DuRocher

Rethinking the Civil War Era: Directions for Research
Paul D. Escott

Lum and Abner: Rural America and the Golden Age of Radio
Randal L. Hall

Mountains on the Market: Industry, the Environment, and the South
Randal L. Hall